The Anglo-saxon Review, Volume 10

THE
ANGLO-SAXON
REVIEW
A QUARTERLY MISCELLANY

EDITED **BY**

LADY RANDOLPH SPENCER CHURCHILL
(MRS. GEORGE CORNWALLIS-WEST)

Vol. **X.** September 1901

NEW YORK: G. P. PUTNAM'S SONS
LONDON: MRS. GEORGE CORNWALLIS-WEST
49 RUPERT STREET, W.

1901

Printed by BALLANTYNE, HANSON & CO.
At the Ballantyne Press
London & Edinburgh

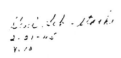

CONTENTS

Lady Blessington.

From the picture by Sir Thomas Lawrence in the Wallace Collection

Swan Electric Engraving Co

ILLUSTRATIONS

NOTE ON THE BINDING OF THIS VOLUME. BY CYRIL DAVENPORT, F.S.A.

EVERAL beautiful bindings were made in France about the middle of the sixteenth century which bear upon them the Royal coat-of-arms of Henri II., King of France, and several badges and cyphers.

Of these badges and cyphers some are undoubtedly Royal; but others are not decidedly so. Several of the bindings came from the Château d'Anet, and they are in many cases supposed to have belonged to the chatelaine of that house, Diane de Poictiers, Duchesse de Valentinois.

It is probable that an entirely satisfactory explanation of the cyphers used equally upon the contemporary French Royal bindings, and on those which certainly belonged to Diane herself, will never be forthcoming; but it appears to me that the whole difficulty centres round the use of the letter 'D' by Henri, both before he came to the throne and afterwards.

It is natural enough to explain the existence of the 'D' by considering it as the initial of the Duchesse; but it occurs at what may well be an earlier date than that at which her influence reached its zenith at the French Court, and, moreover, in a position which is not consonant with this interpretation.

On some of the beautiful portraits of Henri's Queen, Catherine de' Medici, enamelled by Leonard Limousin, she is shown wearing a jewelled necklace, the alternate links of which are in the form of a cypher composed of the letters H, D, and C. The same cypher can be seen on the embroidered border of the bodice of the Queen's dress and also on the sleeves.

Another enamel by the same artist, done about the same time, shows Henri on horseback, and on the front part of the saddle-cloth the same cypher appears. It is not at all likely that Catherine wore a necklace or embroidered borders on which the initial of Diane de Poictiers appeared, and it seems to me that a possible explanation of the cypher may be 'H(enri) le D(auphin) et C(atherine).' If this be true, it will explain the D wherever it occurs on Royal books in conjunction with the H; but it is not likely ever to have stood alone; there-

ON THE BINDING OF THIS VOLUME

fore, it seems likely that whenever two interlaced D's adossés are found on a book, even if it bears Royal marks, it did at one time form part of Diane's library. It would not, however, be necessary for her to add marks to those already existing on many of Henri's books; for on them she found bows, crescents, and cyphers, which would all do for her as well.

Henri the Dauphin used a crescent as his badge, with the motto 'Donec totum impleat orbem,' with reference, of course, to his approaching greatness, and Catherine also used a crescent or crescents, which show as one of her badges on the painted glass of a window of the Sainte Chapelle in company with quivers and arrows.

Besides the 'D H C' cypher, there is, however, another in which the letter C. is supplanted by another D. This monogram shows on the binding herewith, and was undoubtedly used by Diane; but still I think originally it only meant Henri le Dauphin. It certainly occurs on several of the books bound for Henri when he was King, and often in company with the simple crowned H. It seems from this that it was an undoubtedly Royal badge, and it is very unlikely that as such it would have been used if it had then been considered to belong to any subject.

There appears to be no doubt that many of the Royal books bearing the coat-of-arms of France were sent to the library of Anet by Henri's order; and in consequence of the existence of the letter D in several of the cyphers, and the bows, quivers, and arrows, which, as we have seen, were used as badges by both King and Queen, these bindings are often considered to have been made for Diane, whereas, in fact, they are simply those of French Royal books which were presented to her.

A very few bindings do, however, exist which were certainly made for Diane de Poictiers, and the whole style of these is radically different from that to be found on the contemporary French Royal bindings.

In the 'Bibliothèque Nationale' is a binding made for Diane de Poictiers [1] which bears as its chief ornament her coat-of-arms as widow, Brézé-Maulevrier impaled with Poictiers; the rest of the design is curiously impressed in outline, like that on the cover herewith, which, in many respects, it strongly resembles, although more thickly studded with small cyphers and badges, among which are bows and arrows, crescents single and triple, the monograms H with two C's, Diane's own two interlaced D's, and the King's crowned H. So this binding proves conclusively that

---

[1] *Chronique de Jean de Courcy-Bourgachard.* MS. Sixteenth century.

2

the Duchesse was allowed to use the stamps of both the King and the Queen on her own bindings.

Another binding in the same collection bears in a central cartouche the name DIANNA, and is otherwise beautifully ornamented with coloured fillets and gold tracery, while at each corner and in the spaces between the curves are crescents.[1] This is credited as having belonged to the Duchesse de Valentinois; but there appears to be no absolute authority for saying so.

Diane de Poictiers belonged to an ancient family of Dauphiné. She was married at the age of thirteen, in 1512, to Louis de Brézé, Comte de Maulevrier, Grand Seneschal of Normandy, and after his death she wore mourning for him all the rest of her life.

Her father, Jean de Poictiers, Seigneur de Sainte Vallier, was accused of complicity in the flight of the Constable of Bourbon in 1523, and Diane interceded successfully with Francis I. for her father's life. It was on the occasion of her visit to the French Court on this filial errand that she first met the Duc d'Orléans, second son of the King, a young man some twenty years her junior, who was so struck by her beauty and charm that from that time until his death her influence over him was all-powerful. On the death of his elder brother the Duc d'Orléans became Dauphin, and eventually succeeded his father on the throne of France under the title of Henri II. His admiration for De Brézé's widow, however, suffered no abatement, and in 1548 the King created her Duchesse de Valentinois.

The Court of Francis I. had been kept for a long time in a state of unrest because of the rival charms and ambitions of the Duchesse d'Étampes and Diane de Brézé, considerably older in years but the especial favourite of the heir to the throne. Between these two ladies and their intrigues Catherine de' Medici had plenty to do to keep the peace. When Henri became king, Diane persuaded him to banish the Duchesse d'Étampes from Court. She had embittered the last years of Francis I., and intrigued with Foreign Powers so as to provide friends for herself on his death. It is probable that if Henri had not been unwilling to impair his father's memory he would have dealt much more severely with her than he did ; but, among other punishments, he took away her jewels and gave them to Diane. It is supposed that Francis I. alluded to the Duchesse d'Étampes in the celebrated distich which he wrote on the window at Chambord :

> Souvent femme varie
> Mal habil qui s'y fie !

when he was there with his sister Marguerite d'Angoulême.

---

[1] *Ptolémée*. Geographiæ libri viii. Lyon : 1541.

ON THE BINDING OF THIS VOLUME

During the whole of the reign of Henri II., the Duchesse de Valentinois exercised much political power, and aroused much jealousy by reason of her influence over the King; but it seems that she never meddled in the same mischievous way that the Duchesse d'Étampes had meddled; indeed, as far as can be seen, her power was always used for good. The King eventually made her 'Grande Sénéchale de Normandie,' and allowed Philibert de l'Orme, the Royal architect who had built the Tuileries, to design her beautiful house, the Château d'Anet.

On the accidental death of Henri II. in a tournament in 1559 Diane retired to Anet, and lived there, occupied in charitable works, until her death in 1566. Her life in retirement appears to have been of the quietest and simplest character, and such happiness as she could enjoy was found in the beautiful house and gardens which the King had given her. She enjoyed almost perfect health, is said to have always washed in cold water, and to have risen at six in the morning and gone out riding. On her return she went to bed again and read until mid-day.

Much has been written concerning Diane de Poictiers, and much difference of opinion expressed with regard to the real position she held at the French Court. Some authorities consider that the sole secret of her undoubted influence over the King was the fact that he knew and appreciated the ability and wisdom of her counsels. The King invariably showed her all the respect properly due to a lady of high rank many years his senior, and marked his sense of indebtedness to her by the gift of titles and property. Other authorities, among them De Thou and Brantôme, take a different view of the situation, and explain the circumstances differently. Thus, the difficulty of unravelling the knot of the cyphers on the bookbindings finds its analogy in historical records.

The binding which has been chosen as a model for this Number of the ANGLO-SAXON REVIEW covers an edition of the 'Architecture' of Vitruvius, printed in Paris in 1547, and now in the Bodleian Library at Oxford. It is in white leather, possibly deerskin, and adorned with badges and cyphers used by the Duchesse de Valentinois. In their original state many of these badges and ornaments appear to have been coloured, some of them white and some of them silver, or grey, or black; but the colour has largely chipped off, and become so uncertain and obliterated that I have considered it safer to reproduce the design in outline only. The middle ornament is that of three interlaced crescents flanked by two bows with broken strings, while above and below are quivers crossed by a single arrow. The crescents and bows show often enough on bindings made for Henri II.; but, as far as I have observed, the quiver never appears on any bindings other than such as were made for Diane herself.

4

CYRIL DAVENPORT

Enclosing these emblems is a fillet cleverly interlaced in ovals and rectangular forms, ending laterally in two bold foliated arabesques; a single crescent ornaments each corner; and at the top and the bottom is the much-discussed monogram supposed to be that of Diane and Henri. According to my theory, this monogram was originally used by Henri as Dauphin, and in this way the D crept in, which fitted so well with Diane's humour that she practically adopted it as her own, and certainly it is usually considered to stand for Henri and Diane.

The Duchesse de Valentinois had a fine taste in bindings, and it is much to be deplored that in England we possess so few that undoubtedly belonged to her.

'THE MOST GORGEOUS LADY BLESSINGTON.' BY JOHN FYVIE

HOSE who are old enough to remember certain characteristic products of early Victorian literature known as 'Books of Beauty' and 'Keepsakes' —wherein portraits of living beauties, by the most distinguished artists, were accompanied by a good deal of rather inferior letter-press—may perhaps have some recollection of the immense vogue enjoyed by their distinguished editor, so felicitously described by eccentric Dr. Parr as 'the most gorgeous Lady Blessington.' For nearly twenty years Lady Blessington's name was constantly before the public. She was the author of sixteen or seventeen books which had a considerable, though fleeting, popularity; for fifteen years she was Editor of the fashionable *Annuals* already referred to; for nineteen years her house in London was the habitual resort of all who were most distinguished in literature, politics, science, and art; her entertainments were luxurious and splendid; and she was, moreover, a remarkable beauty, whose fair fame had been tainted by the breath of scandal. Widely divergent views of her character have been presented to us. Mr. Grantley Berkeley, for example, paints her as an immoral, illiterate, unscrupulous adventuress; while her latest eulogist, Mr. Fitzgerald Molloy, makes her out an almost perfect saint. The whole truth respecting certain episodes in her life is not, and is never likely to be, known; but the story which her biographer had to tell is at least as romantic as that of the heroine of any of her own novels.

Marguerite, who was born on September 1, 1789, was the third child, and second daughter, of Edmund Power, a 'squireen' of Knockbrit, near Clonmel, in co. Tipperary. As a child she seems to have been remarkable—first, as the one plain member of an exceedingly handsome family; and secondly, as an improvisatrice, whose precocious powers of story-telling were the wonder of the neighbourhood. Her mother appears to have thought less of her children than of her pedigree; 'Me ancestors, the Desmonds,' were her household gods, and their deeds and prowess her favourite theme. Whether her father was equally proud of his ancestors is not on record; but, whatever they may have been like, he can hardly have been a credit to them. He was known far and wide as 'Buck Power,' and also, in consequence of his habit of swaggering about in buckskins, top-boots, lace ruffles, and white cravat, by the name of 'Shiver-the-Frills.' He was a man of extremely violent temper, verging on insanity; and when he was appointed magistrate for Waterford and Tipperary he provoked hatred amongst all around him, besides being a terror to his own family. His days and nights

6

were spent in the congenial occupation of riding about the country, accompanied by troops of dragoons, hunting down the unfortunate and misguided 'rebels,' who, not unnaturally, retaliated by burning his store-houses, destroying his plantations, and killing his cattle. In 1807 he was tried for the murder of a peasant whom he had shot, and narrowly escaped being convicted. No pay attached to his office, but visions of a prospective baronetcy inflamed his cruel zeal, and likewise induced him to indulge a profuse and reckless hospitality which did much to bring him to ruin.

By the time she had arrived at the age of fourteen it became evident that Marguerite was not to be without her share of the family beauty, and she had already shown herself to possess something more than the average of the family intelligence. About this time two officers of the 14th Regiment, then stationed at Clonmel—Captain Murray and Captain Farmer—paid her marked attention. After a short acquaintance, Captain Murray proposed marriage to the young lady, but she blushingly declined, on the ground that she was far too young to think of such a thing. The other cavalier, perceiving that the young lady herself was none too favourably disposed towards him, made his proposal to the father, who, without so much as troubling to acquaint his daughter with the fact, instantly accepted Captain Farmer as his future son-in-law. Tears, entreaties, prayers, were of no avail, and at the age of fourteen and a half Marguerite was married to a man whom she detested, and who, moreover, was reported to be subject to fits of insanity of so violent a character as to endanger the safety of those around him as well as his own. In after years she told Mr. Madden, her future biographer, that her husband frequently treated her with personal violence, that he used to strike her on the face, pinch her till her arms were black and blue, lock her up whenever he went abroad, and often leave her without food until she was almost famished. Grantley Berkeley tells another story, and expresses much pity for ' poor Farmer,' who, he considers, was driven to drink and other excesses by the vagaries of his little minx of a wife ; but what authority he had for any such statement does not appear. At any rate, three months after their marriage, when Captain Farmer was ordered to rejoin his regiment on the Curragh of Kildare, Marguerite refused to accompany him, and returned to the house of her father. This was in March 1804. Finding herself an extremely unwelcome guest, she soon left her father's house ; but what happened to her, or how she lived, during the succeeding twelve years has not been ascertained with any degree of certainty. Her sister, Mary Anne, who prefixed a memoir to Lady Blessington's posthumous story, ' Country Quarters,' professes her inability to give any account of this period. All she can say is that :

7

'THE GORGEOUS LADY BLESSINGTON'

Mrs. Farmer resided principally in England, in the most complete seclusion, indulging to the utmost her natural love of study, to which she devoted the greater portion of her time.

Grantley Berkeley, as is usual with him, places the worst possible construction on the matter, and not obscurely hints at very scandalous doings, but, as before, he quotes no authority for his statements. In 1807 she appears to have been, for a time, with some friends at Cahir, and, in 1809, in Dublin. But by the first-named year the ugly duckling had developed, at the age of eighteen, into so swanlike a beauty that Sir Thomas Lawrence was induced to paint her portrait. Nine years later, in 1816, we find her established, with her brother Robert, in a house in Manchester Square, London. Her sister says:

> She received at her house only those whose age and character rendered them safe friends, and a very few others on whose perfect respect and consideration she could wholly rely. Among the latter was the Earl of Blessington, then a widower.

In October 1817, Captain Farmer was killed by a fall from a window in the course of a drunken orgie with some of his friends in the King's Bench Prison; and four months later the happily-released widow became Countess of Blessington. Lord Blessington was an Irish landlord with a rent-roll of £30,000 a year, and a strong propensity for profuse and extravagant expenditure, a disposition which his newly-wedded wife was only too ready to encourage. She was generous to lavishness, says her sister. Every member of her family instantly felt the change in her fortunes, and, notwithstanding their unkind treatment of her, her now ruined parents were supported by her in comfort to the end of their days. As a young man Lord Blessington had been devoted to the drama, was a familiar figure in green-rooms, and had swallowed the flattery which told him he had himself a first-rate talent for the stage. He had erected a theatre on his estate, and frequently had actors and actresses down from Dublin during the shooting season. But the performances do not appear to have been altogether satisfactory, for we learn that a set of mock resolutions was drawn up for the benefit of the actors, of which the following —levelled principally at Crampton, who was always imperfect in his part—may serve for a specimen: 'That every gentleman shall be at liberty to avail himself of the words of the author in case his own invention fails him.' Whether Lord Blessington had any histrionic talent or not, he had certainly acquired a pronounced taste for theatrical costumes, gaudy dresses, and gorgeous ornaments, which he indulged in various ways to the end of his life. When he took his wife to Mountjoy Forest, immediately after their marriage, she found that he had had her private sitting-room 'hung with crimson Genoa silk-velvet, trimmed with gold bullion fringe, and all the furniture of equal richness.' But she had no notion of burying herself in an Irish country-house, however splendid, and in a very short time we find them back in London, where, to use Grantley Berkeley's words, at the age of twenty-eight she blazed like a meteor upon the town in a magnificent mansion in St. James's Square; and for the next three years her rooms were nightly crowded with people of distinction—royal dukes, cabinet ministers, wits, painters, poets, actors and authors, who thronged to pay their homage to her 'gorgeous' charms. Lord Blessington seems to have been a naturally amiable man, with many good qualities, and was bright and lively enough, if not particularly brilliant. In 'Moore's Diary' for 1819 there are many entries such as 'Dined at Lord Blessington's,' or 'Called to-day upon Lord Blessington, and sat some time with him'; and occasionally we find quoted a specimen of his lordship's Irish humour:

R. Power and I dined at Lord Blessington's. Lord B. mentioned a good story of an Irishman he knew, saying to a dandy who took up his glass to spy a shoulder of mutton, and declared he had never seen such a thing before, 'Then, I suppose, sir, you have been chiefly in the *chop line.*'

But at the age of forty, according to Mr. Madden, he was *blasé* and exhausted, and Lady Blessington persuaded him to try an extended continental tour. Accordingly, in August 1822, they left London. 'No Irish nobleman probably,' says Madden, 'and certainly no Irish king, ever set out on his travels with such a retinue of servants, with so many vehicles and appliances of all kinds, to ease, to comfort, and luxurious enjoyment in travel.' They went by easy stages. While in France, Lord Blessington persuaded young Count D'Orsay to join them on their tour; and we may presume the inducements held out were of no ordinary character, for D'Orsay at once resigned his commission, although the French army was then under orders to invade Spain; and in February 1823 set out with them for Italy. April and May were passed at Genoa, in almost daily intercourse with Lord Byron, affording Lady Blessington abundant opportunity for recording her conversations with the poet, which she publishes in book form some ten years later. Moore tells us in his life of Byron that Lady Blessington 'conferred most important services' upon his noble friend, in that she half revived his old regard for his wife, and, by her admonitions, placed something of a check on the composition of 'Don Juan.' But it seems probable that Moore had no authority other than her own for the statement, and that she somewhat over-rated her own influence. The company of the Blessingtons was, however, an evident pleasure and relief to Byron, and to Count D'Orsay, in particular, he took a great liking.

From Genoa they went to Rome; but the Eternal City did not

please her ladyship. In her diary she says she was driven from Rome by the excessive heat, and, although without fear for herself, by apprehensions that the prevalent malaria might attack some of those dear to her. Her friend and biographer, Madden, rather unkindly remarks on this that Lady Blessington, both in conversation and in writing, was just a little bit given to posing, with a view of acquiring the esteem of others by an exhibition of her altruistic virtues, and suggests that there were more weighty reasons for her hurried departure from Rome. 'All the appliances to comfort, or rather to luxury,' he says, 'which had become necessary to Lady Blessington, had not been found in Rome. Her ladyship had become exceedingly fastidious in her tastes. The difficulties of pleasing her in house accommodation, in dress, in cookery especially (!), had become so formidable, and occasioned so many inconveniences '— that, in short, he is inclined to regard the malaria scare as an after-thought. Naples, however, was found to be her ideal city, and she was fortunate enough to secure the Pallazzo Belvidere for her temporary residence. In 'The Idler in Italy' she describes this palace with some enthusiasm :

A long avenue entered by an old-fashioned archway, which forms part of the dwelling of the *intendante* of the Prince di Belvidere, leads through a pleasure ground, filled with the rarest trees, shrubs, and plants, to the Pallazo, which forms three sides of a square, the fourth being an arcade that connects one portion of the building with the other. There is a courtyard and fountain in the centre. A colonnade extends from each side of the front of the palace, supporting a terrace covered with flowers. The windows of the principal salons open on a garden, formed on an elevated terrace, surrounded on three sides by a marble balustrade, and enclosed on the fourth by a long gallery, filled with pictures, statues, and bassi-relievi. On the top of the gallery, which is of considerable length, is a terrace, at the extreme end of which is a pavilion, with open arcades and paved with marble. This pavilion commands a most enchanting prospect of the bay, with the coast of Sorrento on the left, Capri in the centre, with Nisida, Procida, Ischia, and the promontory of Misenium to the right ; the foreground filled up by gardens and vineyards. The odour of the flowers in the grounds around the pavilion, and the Spanish jasmine and tuberoses that cover the walls, render it one of the most delicious retreats in the world. The walls of all the rooms are literally covered with pictures ; the architraves of the doors of the principal rooms are oriental alabaster and the rarest marbles ; the tables and consoles are composed of the same costly materials ; and the furniture, though in decadence, bears the traces of its pristine splendour.

Her ' most gorgeous' ladyship also adds that there is a chapel and a billiard-room; and yet she was not altogether satisfied. Although the rent of the place was extravagantly high, and the Blessingtons only proposed to stay a few months, they called in an upholsterer and went to much further expense in providing a variety of luxurious additions before they felt they could settle down in the Neapolitan palace in comfort. Creature comforts, however, were by no means the only things which her ladyship desired—and got. As Madden says, when she visited Herculaneum, she was accompanied by no less an authority than Sir William Gell ; when she examined museums and art galleries, she was shown over them by Unwins, the painter, or Westmacott, the sculptor, or Milligan, the antiquary ; when she paid a visit to the observatory, it was in the company of Sir John Herschell, or the famous Italian astronomer, Piazzi.

A desirable and highly appreciated addition to the party at the Palazzo Belvidere was young Charles James Mathews, a youth of twenty, then just out of his articles to Pugin, the architect, and afterwards to become so famous on the stage. Lord Blessington, whose income ought certainly to have been multiplied by ten to keep pace with his notions of expenditure, had proposed, immediately after his second marriage, to build a castle on his Tyrone estate, and had asked young Mathews, with whose father he was well acquainted, to prepare plans for him. For a couple of months, Mathews says, he led a charmed life, diplomatically acquiescing in all the whims of Lord Blessington, who wanted to design the castle himself, and kept suggesting alteration after alteration. The castle was never built. But Mathews had his fill of stag-hunting, rabbit-shooting, fishing, and sight-seeing, and was heartily sorry when the fun was over. However, Lord Blessington did not abandon the project, and as he wished to have the plans completed under his own eye, Mathews went out to Italy for this purpose, and appears to have had another good time of it for nearly two years. He describes the party which he found domiciled at the Pallazo Belvi-dere :

Lady Blessington, then in her zenith, and certainly one of the most beautiful, as well as one of the most fascinating, women of her time, formed the centre figure in the little family group assembled within its precincts. Count D'Orsay, then a youth of nineteen, was the next object of attention, and, I have no hesitation in asserting, was the beau-ideal of manly dignity and grace. He had not then assumed the marked peculiarities of dress and deportment which the sophistications of London life subsequently developed. He was the model of all that could be conceived of noble demeanour and youthful candour ; handsome beyond all question ; accomplished to the last degree ; highly educated, and of great literary acquirements ; with a gaiety of heart and cheerfulness of mind that spread happiness on all around him. His conversation was brilliant and engaging, as well as instructive. He was, moreover, the best fencer, dancer, swimmer, runner, dresser ; the best shot, the best horseman, the best draughtsman of his age. . . . Then came Miss Power, Lady Blessington's younger sister, somewhat demure in aspect, of quiet and retiring manners, contrasting sweetly with the more dazzling qualities around her.

Mathews does not give us a full-length portrait of the Earl, but from an odd touch, here and there, we learn that his lordship 'always cuts his own hair with a pair of scissors !'—(it is difficult, by the way, to imagine what else he could have cut it with) ; and that he was so susceptible of cold that, according to D'Orsay, he would detect a current of air caused by a key being left crossways in the keyhole of a door ! The whole party frequently sailed about

the Bay of Naples in the *Bolivar*, which Lord Blessington had
bought from Byron before leaving Genoa. Sometimes they would
be becalmed from dusk until two or three o'clock in the morning,
and then Lady Blessington and D'Orsay would relieve their tedium
by bantering the poor captain of the yacht. He was a naval
lieutenant, named Smith, who had a grievance against the Admiralty
for not having 'posted' him fifteen years before, and they fooled
him to the top of his bent regarding his claims to promotion, and
the disgraceful lack of patronage for real merit. D'Orsay would
say, in his broken English, 'Ah, my poor Smid, tell Miladi over
again, my good fellow, once more explain for Mademoiselle Power,
too, how it happens that Milords of the Admirals never posted you.'
And the unsuspecting Smith would again and again be induced to
make a ludicrous exhibition of himself, while they all listened without betraying their intense amusement by so much as the ghost of
a smile. Lady Blessington had a very pretty talent for grave banter,
and much skill in drawing out an extravagant or eccentric person
into a display of oddity or absurdity; but Madden says that she
did this with such singular skill, tact, finesse, and delicacy of humour,
that pain was never inflicted, so that while she and those in the
secret were intensely amused, the victim seldom suspected that any
trick was being played upon him. Their stay in Naples was prolonged to two years and a half, and at the end of that time they
left suddenly, for some reason or caprice not specified.

It was at Florence, in May 1827, that Lady Blessington first
met Walter Savage Landor. He had known Lord Blessington
when the latter was still Viscount Mountjoy, and now, in the spring,
and until the end of the autumn, he went every evening from his
villa and spent it in their society, soon forming what her biographer
calls 'the strongest attachment that comes within the legitimate
limits and bounds of literary friendship.' In December of this
year, Lord Blessington's only legitimate daughter, Lady Harriet
Gardiner, then aged fifteen years and four months, was taken from
school in her own country, brought to Italy, and there, within a
few weeks of her arrival, married to Count D'Orsay, a man, whatever his attractions may have been, whom she had never previously
seen, and who had never until now set eyes upon her. Madden,
who was a medical man, says that when, on the death of his only
legitimate son in 1823, Lord Blessington executed a document
making D'Orsay his heir on condition of his marrying either of the
testator's daughters; he was of unsound mind. But he nowhere
hints that Lady Blessington ever had a word to say against the
arrangement.

In 1828 the whole party set out on a leisurely progress home-
wards. They proposed to stay some time in Paris, and accordingly
rented the best house they could find, which happened to be the

JOHN FYVIE

splendid mansion of Maréchal Ney. Besides the enormously high rent which he paid for this palace, Lord Blessington's expenditure in adding to its decorations and furniture was on a scale more commensurate with the income of a Rothschild than with that of an Irish landlord. In 'The Idler in France,' published in 1841, Lady Blessington described its gorgeous furniture and upholstery for the edification of the British public. 'Such carpets!' she exclaims, and well she might:

> The principal drawing-room has a carpet of dark crimson, with a gold-coloured border, on which is a wreath of flowers that looks as if newly culled from the garden, so rich, varied, and bright are their hues. The curtains are of crimson satin, with embossed patterns of gold colour, and the sofas, *bergères, fauteuils*, and chairs, richly carved and gilt, are covered with satin to correspond with the curtains. Gilt *consoles* and *chiffonnières*, with white marble tops, are placed wherever they could be disposed, and on the chimney-pieces are fine *pendules*.

Our present notions of household decoration are widely different from what were in vogue in the early Victorian period, and the mere recital of her ladyship's dithyrambic account is enough to make William Morris turn in his grave! Another drawing-room, we are told, was decked in 'blue satin with rich white flowers'; but it was in the decoration of Miladi's *chambre à coucher* and dressing-room that Lord Blessington and the upholsterer endeavoured to surpass themselves. She was not allowed to enter these rooms until they were quite finished; what she then saw is described as follows:

> The bed, which is silvered instead of gilt, rests on the backs of two large silver swans, so exquisitely sculptured that every feather is in alto-relievo, and looks nearly as fleecy as those of a living bird. The recess in which it is placed is lined with white-fluted silk, bordered with blue embossed lace; and from the columns that support the frieze of the recess, pale blue silk curtains, lined with white, are hung, which, when drawn, conceal the recess altogether. . . . A silvered sofa has been made to fit the side of the room opposite the fireplace, . . . pale blue carpets, silver lamps, ornaments silvered to correspond. . . . The *salle de bain* is draped with white muslin trimmed with lace . . . the bath is of white marble, inserted in the floor, with which its surface is level. On the ceiling . . . a painting of Flora scattering flowers with one hand, while from the other is suspended an alabaster lamp in the form of a lotus.

She goes into raptures over all this 'perfection of furniture,' which she considers 'chastely beautiful.' It is certainly remarkable for its costliness, and also for the fact that the Parisian upholsterers completed the decorating and furnishing of the whole mansion in three days. Madden grimly remarks on it that Lord Blessington was actively co-operating with other absentee landlords of his order in laying the foundations of the Encumbered Estates Court in Ireland! But he did not live to see the result of his prodigality. In the early part of the following year he suddenly died, and all his honours became extinct. It was then discovered that he had

13

reduced his rentals by about one third, and that his estate was otherwise much embarrassed. When he came into his property it was worth £30,000 a year; when he married his second wife it had fallen to £23,000; and when Madden wrote his biography of the Countess in 1855, all that remained was some £600 a year, which was then enjoyed by Charles John, Lord Blessington's illegitimate son. But this is anticipating matters. For the moment, Lady Blessington's jointure of £2000 a year was safe; and in the belief that she could very largely augment her income by the efforts of her pen, she came to London in 1831, and established herself in a handsome house in Seamore Place, Mayfair.

By way of a beginning, she tendered her services to Colbourn's *New Monthly Magazine*, then edited by Thomas Campbell; and S. C. Hall, the sub-editor, was sent to interview her on the matter. None of her suggestions for subjects appeared to him to be very promising; but in course of conversation she related an anecdote or two about Lord Byron, and Hall said: " Why not put on paper your stories about the great poet? ' This was the origin of her ' Conversations with Lord Byron,' which first appeared serially in the *New Monthly*, and afterwards, in book form, in 1834. The earliest contemporary notice of her at Seamore Place occurs in the diary of Crabb Robinson, who notes that, on September 28, 1832, he went by Landor's desire to see Lady Blessington, and that he found her to be a charming and very remarkable person :

> Lady Blessington is much more handsome than Countess Egloffstein, but their countenance, manners, and particularly the tone of voice, belong to the same class. Her dress rich, and her library most splendid. Her book about Lord Byron (now publishing by driblets in the *New Monthly Magazine*) and her other writings give her in addition the character of a *bel esprit*. Landor, too, says that she was to Lord B. the most devoted wife he ever knew. He says also that she was by far the most beautiful woman he ever saw, and was so deemed at the Court of George IV. She is now, Landor says, about thirty, but I should have thought her older. [She was forty-three.] She is a great talker, but her talk is rather narrative than declamatory, and very pleasant.

In 1833 appeared her first novel, ' The Repealers '; and in the summer of that year occurred what was the first of a series of pecuniary misfortunes, a burglary at Seamore Place, when a thousand pounds worth of plate and jewellery was carried off and never recovered. She had furnished the place with her accustomed splendour, and proceeded to entertain largely. Haydon's Diary for November 27, 1835, says : ' Everybody goes to Lady Blessington's. She has the first news of everything, and everybody seems delighted to tell her.' A month later he records a good story which he heard her tell :

> She described Lord Abercorn's conduct at the Priory. She said it was the most singular place on earth. The moment anybody became celebrated they were invited. He had a great delight in seeing handsome women. Everybody hand-

some he made Lady Abercorn invite; and all the guests shot, hunted, rode, or did what they liked, provided they never spoke to Lord Abercorn except at table. If they met him they were to take no notice. At this time 'Thaddeus of Warsaw' was making a noise. 'Gad,' said Lord Abercorn, 'we must have these Porters. Write, my dear Lady Abercorn.' She wrote. An answer came from Jane Porter that they could not afford the expense of travelling. A cheque was sent. They arrived. Lord Abercorn peeped at them as they came through the hall, and running by the private staircase to Lady Abercorn, exclaimed: 'Witches, my Lady! I must be off'; and immediately started post, and remained away till they were gone.

Lady Blessington's first 'Book of Beauty' appeared in 1833, and in December of that year she complacently informed Moore that its sale had beat Miss Landon's by 2000 copies. In the following year her 'Conversations with Byron' were republished in book form; in 1835 she issued 'The Two Friends'; and in 1836 her 'Flowers of Loveliness.' About this time also appeared the first of the annual 'Gems of Beauty,' which she edited for a period of five years.

The best account of Seamore Place and the society which gathered there is to be found in a volume entitled, 'Pencillings by the Way,' in which a lively and picturesque, but somewhat indiscreet, American writer, N. P. Willis, gave his countrymen a graphic account of all the notabilities whom he had interviewed during an extended European tour.

In a long library, he says, lined alternately with splendidly bound books and mirrors, and with a deep window of the breadth of the room, opening upon Hyde Park, I found Lady Blessington. The picture to my eye, as the door opened, was a very lovely one; a woman of remarkable beauty, half buried in a *fauteuil* of yellow satin, reading by a magnificent lamp suspended from the centre of the arched ceiling; sofas, couches, ottomans, and busts, arranged in rather a crowded sumptuousness through the room; enamel tables, covered with expensive and elegant trifles, in every corner; and a delicate white hand relieved on the back of a book, to which the eye was attracted by the blaze of its diamond rings.

Willis thought her by no means unlike her portrait in the 'Book of Beauty,' though he considered she was more like the picture by Sir Thomas Lawrence, painted when she was eighteen. At the time of his visit her age was forty-four, but although he could see she was 'no longer *dans sa première jeunesse*,' he guesses her to be something on the sunny side of thirty, and certainly one of the most lovely and fascinating women he had ever seen. He was invited to attend her evening receptions during his stay in London and relates that, on his first visit, 'Smith, the author of the " Rejected Addresses," with a cripple's crutch in his hand, and a pair of large india-rubber shoes on his feet, kindly told him who and what all the other celebrities were.' It must have been an unusually small party, for we hear only of Henry Bulwer, who had lately published his book on the state of France, of a German prince with a star on his breast, who was vainly trying to understand what the others were saying about a recent speech of O'Connell's, of the

Duc de Richelieu, and, of course, the splendid D'Orsay. Towards midnight the exquisite author of 'Pelham' was announced, and then ensued a flood of brilliant talk which lasted until three in the morning. At that hour, says Willis, 'the "Rejected Addresses" got upon his crutches, and I sallied out with him, thanking Heaven that, though in a strange country, my mother tongue was the language of its men of genius.' Later, he was at a dinner-party in the same house and listened to Moore's sparkling talk through the whole evening, until at last, with great difficulty, the latter was taken to the piano, when 'after two or three songs of Lady Blessington's choice, he rambled over the keys awhile and sang "When First I met Thee" with a pathos that beggars description. When the last word had faltered out, he rose and took Lady Blessington's hand, said good-night, and was gone before a word was uttered.' On another occasion, he found young Benjamin Disraeli sitting in the window, with the last rays of the daylight reflected from the gorgeous gold flowers of a splendidly-embroidered waistcoat, patent leather pumps, a white stick with a black cord and tassel, a quantity of gold chains about his neck and pockets, and a thick mass of jet-black ringlets falling over his left cheek almost to his collarless stock. 'He talked,' says Willis, 'like a racehorse approaching the winning-post, every muscle in action, and the utmost energy of expression flung out in every burst.'

Seamore Place must have been a quite sufficiently expensive house to keep up. But Lady Blessington conceived that she had a mission in life which required a much more extensive establishment for its proper development. She believed that it was her mission to bring together intellectual men of the most varying and diverse opinions—statesmen, lawyers, authors, artists, journalists—in order to promote among them, by means of personal acquaintance, some measure of good-will, charity, and toleration. And Count D'Orsay, ably seconding her in this by no means despicable ambition, desired to extend its scope on international lines, with the idea that many of the causes of national prejudices, jealousies, and antipathies might be removed by social intercourse. With this object in view, she removed to Gore House, Kensington, which was decorated and furnished with great magnificence in the early part of 1836.

Gore House stood where now stands the gigantic Albert Hall. It was originally tenanted by a government contractor, who is said to have been so stingy that he would not expend a single penny in keeping its garden in order. Its second tenant was the philanthropist, William Wilberforce, who delighted to sit under the shade of the old trees in the garden and meditate on the beauties of nature, 'as if I were two hundred miles from the great city,' and who tells us that he walked to it from Hyde Park Corner, 'repeating the 119th Psalm in great comfort.' Then came Lady Blessington and Count

D'Orsay, and for thirteen years the house was the scene of some of the most brilliant entertainments in London. And after their departure, Monsieur Soyer, of culinary fame, after getting young George Augustus Sala to cover the walls with original paintings in a bizarre and rather grotesque style of magnificence, opened the house as a restaurant 'for all Nations' during the Great Exhibition of 1851. Lady Blessington spoke of it as her country house, 'being a mile from town'; and in those days this was scarcely a misnomer, for the house was surrounded by about three acres of grounds, 'full of lilacs, laburnums, nightingales, and swallows,' and containing some fine old walnut and mulberry trees. Concerning Lady Blessington as hostess, and the society which she gathered about her, there is much diversity of opinion. Charles Greville seems to have been in the habit of dining there pretty frequently, although neither the lady nor the majority of her guests seem to have been altogether to his taste. He notes in his diary on February 17, 1837, that he dined at Gore House to meet Lords Durham and Brougham :

> There was that sort of strange *omnium gatherum* party which is to be met with nowhere else, and which for that reason alone is curious. We had Prince Louis Napoleon and his A.D.C. He is a short, thickish, vulgar-looking man, without the slightest resemblance to his Imperial uncle, or any intelligence in his countenance. Then we had the ex-Governor of Canada, Captain Marriott, the Count Alfred de Vigny (author of 'Cinq Mars,' &c.), Sir Edward Lytton Bulwer, and a proper sprinkling of ordinary persons to mix up with these celebrities.

On another occasion he remarks on the drollery of seeing Lord Lyndhurst, the most execrated of the Tories, hand-and-glove and cracking his jokes with two prominent Radicals. The house, he says, is furnished with a luxury and splendour not to be surpassed ; the dinners are frequent and good ; D'Orsay does the honours with a frankness and cordiality which are very successful ; and there is no end to the men of consequence and distinction in the world who go there occasionally. But all this, he thinks, does not make society in the real meaning of the term, and he will allow the house no merit but that of being singular. He finds a want of conversation, of easy, quiet interchange of ideas and opinions, and the reason is, in his opinion, that 'the woman herself, who must give the tone to her own society, is ignorant, vulgar, and commonplace.' Her literary success is a puzzle to him, for, he says, he never met a single person who had read any of her trashy books, and nothing could be more dull and uninteresting than her conversation. On the other hand, Henry Reeve, who, on a point of literary culture and taste, at any rate, is a more competent authority than the mordant diarist, says that Lady Blessington had a good deal more talent and reading than the other gave her credit for, that she was well read in the best English authors, and even in translations of the classics. The talent to which she owed her success in society, he says, was an incomparable tact and skill in drawing out the best qualities of her guests. Surely that was no mean gift? What Mr. Greville terms her vulgarity might, in his opinion, be better described as Irish cordiality and *bonhomie*. Madden, whose acquaintance with Lady Blessington extended over a long period of years, says that she seldom spoke at length, and consequently never bored her guests; that she was always more ready to draw them out than to shine herself, and that such was her skill in this art that, like Mirabeau's ideal lady, she could draw wit out of a fool. At the same time, he says, she could be admirably bright, lively, and humorous, and the witchery of her beautiful voice, her ringing laugh, and frequent outbursts of exuberant mirthfulness, contributed not a little to her powers of fascination. Walter Savage Landor used to say that he remembered no pleasanter time of his life in Italy than the summer evenings passed with the Blessingtons in the Casa Pelosi, on its terrace overlooking the Arno. And in Forster's Life of him we are told that Gore House was the place in which Landor's happiest London life was passed, for it was that in which he felt the least constraint, and knew he should always find the warmest welcome. Mr. Forster says:

> Its attraction to those who had familiar admission there was even less the accomplishments and grace of its mistress than her trueheartedness and constancy in friendship, and no one had reason to know this better than Landor. Again and again he dwells on it in letters to his sister. From the splendour of its mansion, the taste and order of its interior, the extent and beauty of its pleasure grounds, its company of men the most distinguished, and of opinions the most various and opposed—he comes always back to its central charm, the unaffectedness and warmth of heart that presided over all, and yielded to every one who entered it his greatest enjoyment.

There was, however, one regrettable peculiarity of the society at Gore House. Although Lady Blessington appears to have by no means wanted for cordial women friends, ladies were never present at her dinner-table, or her evening receptions, on account of the scandal created by her living in the same house with Count D'Orsay, and the rumours which had got abroad concerning her previous conduct. In S. C. Hall's 'Memories of a Long Life' there is a fine specimen of the confused and illogical, not to say hypocritical, way such matters are treated in this ultra-moral country. Hall considers that Count D'Orsay was so little guided by principle that he could not expect general credit for the purity of his relations with Lady Blessington; 'yet,' says he, 'I think he might honestly have claimed it.' 'But,' continues this virtuous gentleman, 'there was no doubting the fact' [for which, however, he does not adduce a tittle of evidence] 'that she had been the mistress, before she became the wife, of the Earl of Blessington.' Wherefore—and this is the extraordinary way in which British respectability accommodates

itself to its environment—'Mrs. Hall never accompanied me to
her evenings, *though she was a frequent day caller.*' Apart from the
interpretation of them, moreover, the facts of the case as regards
Lady Blessington's relations with D'Orsay have not always been
correctly stated. The writer of the articles, 'Countess of Blessington' and 'Count D'Orsay,' in the 'Dictionary of National
Biography,' for instance, in the one article states the case with
either unconscious or else carefully calculated ambiguity (to say
nothing of making two further misstatements in the same sentence),
while in the other article he contradicts what he says in the first.
In the Lady Blessington article we are told that:

> Count D'Orsay meanwhile, who but a few months after his marriage had been
> separated from his young wife, had for the last dozen years [*i.e.*, previous to 1848]
> been *living at Gore House with the Countess of Blessington.*

But in the D'Orsay article the same writer says:

> They lived scrupulously apart, though within easy distance. While the
> Countess had her home in Gore House the Count occupied a villa next door,
> No. 4 Kensington Gore.

Count D'Orsay was not separated from his wife a few months
after their marriage. They were married in 1827, and lived
together, with Lord and Lady Blessington, until the Earl's death
in 1829. And when Madden returned to England, and visited
Lady Blessington at Seamore Place in March 1832, he says most
distinctly that 'the Count and Countess D'Orsay were then residing
with her.' The precise date of the separation is of course a matter
of no particular moment, but it was probably not long before the
date, in 1838, when he executed an agreement relinquishing all his
interest in the Blessington estates in consideration of a sum of
money paid down to himself, and the application of the bulk of it
to the benefit of his creditors. It is quite true that for a short
time Count D'Orsay lived in a villa adjoining Gore House, but he
afterwards domiciled himself with Lady Blessington—though not
quite a dozen years before 1848. Lady Blessington writes to her
friend the Countess Guiccioli, from Gore House, on August 15,
1839, saying:

> Your friend Alfred [*i.e.*, D'Orsay] charges me with his kindest regards to you.
> He is now an inmate at Gore House, having sold his own residence; and this is not
> only a great protection, but a great addition to my comfort.

At this date, Lady Blessington's age was fifty, and Count
D'Orsay's thirty-eight. If not precisely his mother-in-law, she was
the widow of his father-in-law, and, according to the evidence at
our disposal, had stood towards him *in loco parentis* for the past
sixteen years. Miss Power, Lady Blessington's sister, says that
Lord Blessington loved D'Orsay with a parental affection, that he

'THE GORGEOUS LADY BLESSINGTON'

had promised D'Orsay's mother never to abandon him, that with her dying breath that mother had extracted a similar promise from Lady Blessington, and in the young Count her sister had found the son that Nature had withheld from her, and had therefore bestowed on him that tenderness with which her heart overflowed. And we know that when the hand of death was upon him, D'Orsay said to Madden respecting Lady Blessington, the tears all the while pouring down his face, 'She was to me a mother! a dear, dear mother! a true loving mother to me!' But, of course, people will continue to draw their own conclusions according to their several ways of thinking.

For ten years, from 1839 to 1849, D'Orsay did the honours of Gore House; and during the whole time of her residence there Lady Blessington's literary activity was indefatigable. Besides the various *Annuals*, the editing of which must have been no sinecure, she produced 'The Confessions of an Elderly Gentleman' in 1836, 'The Victims of Society' in 1837, 'The Confessions of an Elderly Lady' in 1838, 'The Governess,' 'Desultory Thoughts and Reflections,' and 'The Idler in Italy' in 1839, 'The Belle. of a Season,' a story in verse, in 1840, 'The Idler in France' in 1841, 'The Lottery of Life and other Tales' in 1842, 'Strathern; or, Life at Home and Abroad,' which first ran as a serial in the *Sunday Times*, in 1843, 'Memoirs of a Femme de Chambre' in 1846, 'Marmaduke Herbert; or, the Fatal Error,' in 1847, and, after her death, a story which she had completed, entitled 'Country Quarters,' was published in 1850. For six months in 1846 she had also been employed by the *Daily News*, at a salary of £500 a year, to supply that recently established newspaper with 'exclusive intelligence.' As far back as 1835, it may be remembered, Haydon noted in his Diary that Lady Blessington always had the first news of everything; and it is not much to be wondered at if, like other purveyors of early and exclusive intelligence, she occasionally heard of things which never happened at all. The hoax about Lord Brougham's death, which elicited such a host of criticisms and panegyrics on his life and character in all the papers in 1839, was first made public at Gore House, and thence spread abroad over the kingdom, although it cannot be said to have been originated by Lady Blessington. A letter purporting to be from Mr. Shafto (but, without a doubt, written by the volatile peer himself) setting forth the particulars of Lord Brougham's death by a carriage accident, was received by Mr. Alfred Montgomery. Mr. Henry Reeve says:

Mr. Montgomery brought the letter to Lady Blessington's—at Gore House, where I happened to be, and I confess we were all taken in by the hoax. Montgomery went off in a post-chaise to break the news to Lord Wellesley at Fernhill; and meeting Lord Afred Paget in Windsor Park he sent the news to the castle.

JOHN FYVIE

The trick was kept up for twenty-four hours, but the next day I received a note from Brougham himself, full of his usual spirits and vitality.

When Lady Blessington removed to Gore House she seems to have imagined that her jointure of £2000 a year, together with the profits of her literary work, would be amply sufficient to meet all conceivable liabilities. What these profits amounted to cannot be ascertained with certainty. The writer of her Life in the 'Dictionary of National Biography' quotes Jerdan as his authority for the statement that 'for nearly twenty years' she earned an income of between two and three thousand a year. Jerdan, however, says nothing about twenty or any other period of years; and his estimate of something midway between two and three thousand *per annum* is based on the questionable assumption that her well-arranged parties enabled her to make favourable terms with publishers, and also to obtain the bulk of the contents of her *Annuals* from private friends without payment. Her sister's estimate is probably much nearer the mark. 'I believe,' says Miss Power, 'that for some years she made on an average somewhat about £1000 a year,' although some years produced a good deal above that sum. It may go without the saying that an income of anything like this amount was far from sufficient to maintain the flunkies, the carriages and horses, which were the talk of London, the dinners, the entertainments, and other extravagances of Gore House. It must be remembered also that Lady Blessington had some half-dozen members of her family entirely dependent on her. In 1845 the potato blight in Ireland seriously reduced the value of her jointure. In 1848 she lost £700 by the failure of Charles Heath, the engraver. Then there were Count D'Orsay's difficulties to be perpetually reckoned with. Soon after his arrival in London he had been arrested for a debt of £300 to his Paris bootmaker, and he had been accumulating fresh debts ever since. We are told that Lady Blessington was exact, and even economical, in household matters, regularly examining accounts and keeping a constant eye on orders to tradesmen. But paltry economies of this kind could make little difference when her scale of expenditure was fixed at probably double the amount of her income. Madden says that the light-hearted happiness of the Italian period was conspicuous by its absence from the society of Gore House. And we find the Countess indulging in unwontedly gloomy 'reflections,' such as: 'Many minds that have withstood the most severe trials have been broken down by a succession of ignoble cares,' and 'friends are the thermometers by which we may judge the temperature of our fortunes.' From a letter of 1848 we learn that her diamonds were in pawn; and early in 1849 there were unmistakable indications that the inevitable crash was imminent. D'Orsay's liabilities were enormous. From a schedule drawn up by himself it appears that they amounted to £107,000 due to ordinary creditors, and about £13,000 more to private friends. Tradesmen had been only too pleased to give him credit for the sake of the immense advertisement which the report of his patronage gave them, but, of course, they were not content to wait for ever; and for some time he had been in such danger of arrest that he could not venture outside the house and grounds except on Sundays. For two years Lady Blessington had lived in constant apprehension of executions, and precautions had been carefully observed at the outer gate and hall door to prevent the entrance of any suspicious-looking person. At last, however, an ingenious sheriff's officer effected an entrance in a disguise, 'the ludicrousness of which,' says Madden with tantalising reticence, 'had some of the characteristics of farce.' He represented a house dealing in silk, lace, Indian shawls, and jewellery, to whom £4000 was owing; and, of course, a cloud of other claimants, bill-discounters, money-lenders, jewellers, tax-collectors, and others followed in his wake. As soon as the Countess heard of the entrance of the sheriff's officer, she sent up to D'Orsay's room to tell him he must immediately leave England; and on the following morning, with his valet and a single portmanteau, he set out for Paris. Lady Blessington and the two Miss Powers left for the same destination a fortnight afterwards.

Gore House was given over to the auctioneers. Those who are curious about such coincidences will be interested to note that Lady Blessington began her literary career in 1822, with a little book containing a fictitious sketch of the ruin of a large house in one of the fashionable London squares, and the sale by auction of all its magnificent furniture and costly ornaments. That career ended in 1849 with an auction at Gore House and the sale of what the auctioneer's catalogue described as:

> Costly and elegant effects, comprising all the magnificent furniture, rare porcelain, sculpture in marble, bronzes, and an assemblage of objects of art and decoration, a casket of valuable jewellery and bijouterie, services of rich chased silver and silvergilt plate, a superbly fitted silver dressing-case; a collection of ancient and modern pictures, including many portraits of distinguished persons, valuable original drawings, and fine engravings, framed and in the portfolio; the extensive and interesting library of books, comprising upwards of 5000 volumes; expensive table services of china and rich cut glass, and an infinity of valuable and useful effects; the property of the Right Hon. the Countess of Blessington, retiring to the Continent.

Lady Blessington's French valet wrote to tell her that they were selling catalogues all day long, and that during the five days the things were on view more than 20,000 persons went over the place. He adds: 'M. Thackeray est venu aussi, et avait les larmes aux yeux en partant. C'est peut-être la seule personne que j'ai vue réellement affecté en votre départ.' Prices at the sale ruled low. Landseer's spaniel picture fetched only £150 10s., and his sketch of Miss Power £57 10s. Sir Thomas Lawrence's portrait of Lady Blessington brought £336, and D'Orsay's of the Duke of Wellington

£189. The two latter were bought for the Marquis of Hertford, and may now be seen in the Wallace Collection at Hertford House. The net amount realised by the sale fell short of £12,000. Lady Blessington did not long survive the breaking up of her home. On June 4 in the same year she died suddenly of an apoplectic attack, due to an enlarged heart, in the sixtieth year of her age. She was buried at Chambourey, near Saint-Germains, in an odd mausoleum, designed by D'Orsay, in which, three years and two months later, he was buried also.

Whether Lady Blessington's books were altogether such trash as Greville would have us believe is a matter on which there may be some difference of opinion; but it must be admitted that, with the solitary exception of the 'Conversations with Lord Byron,' they have had their day and completely ceased to be. Her character was far from flawless, but there is no doubt that some of the aspersions cast upon her were entirely undeserved. And, on the whole, but little exception need be taken to the terms of the epitaph which Barry Cornwall wrote for her tomb: 'In her lifetime she was loved and admired for her many graceful writings, her gentle manners, her kind and generous heart. Men famous for art and science, in distant lands, sought her friendship; and the historians and scholars, the poets, and wits, and painters of her own country found an unfailing welcome in her ever-hospitable home. She gave cheerfully to all who were in need, help and sympathy, and useful counsel, and she died lamented by many friends.'

CORONATION MUSIC
BY FREDERICK J. CROWEST

HE musical aspect of Coronations will be among the matters possessing more or less interest in view of the great historical business in our country's affairs that lies immediately before us. The crowning of monarchs—even if we limit the matter to our own country—compels a great deal of ceremonial, religious and civil; not a little of which must be observed when our present King comes happily to be crowned. The object of this sketch is to mark the part that the divine art has played hitherto in coronation ceremonials more particularly in England—and it has almost invariably been a great incident.

In the first place, music at the crowning of kings has Bible warranty, which is not very surprising. The instance of Solomon being raised to the kingship introduces the first record of coronation music among the Hebrews. The not altogether unpicturesque scene of this ceremony is characteristic of the crude methods of the race. Zadok the priest and others went down and brought Solomon, mounted upon King David's mule, to Gihon.[1] Then and there the eventful ceremony was performed. 'And Zadok the priest took an horn of oil out of the tabernacle and anointed Solomon. And they blew the trumpet, and all the people said, "God save King Solomon." And all the people came up after him, and the people piped with pipes, and rejoiced with great joy, so that the earth rent with the sound of them.'[2]

Prior to this event the judges had been elected to their judge-ships; Saul and Daniel had been made kings over the people; but the Bible is silent respecting the music—if any—used on these occasions. Music or none—it must be remembered that Hebrew music was a rough, noisy element, remarkable for quantity rather than quality. The timbrel, trumpet, cymbal, pipe, buggab, and shawm were coarse and noisy, however manipulated, and it is con-ceivable that this consideration tended to eliminate music from a ceremony which seems to have been quite a quiet, religious service. Warlike, 'dwellers in tents,' inured to restless pursuit and war, rather than to the cultivation of composed social modes of life, the Hebrews cultivated little delicate music.

In Elisha's era, when Jehu the son of Jehoshaphat was anointed King of Israel, Ahab's house was the scene of great commotion. Amid it all, however, the servants 'took every man his garment, and put it under him on the top of the stairs, and blew with trumpets, saying, "Jehu is king."' When Jehoash was crowned—

---

[1] 1 Kings i. 38 *et seq.*
[2] The crown seems to be missing, but it is possible that with the Jews this was among the insignia of royalty.

here the crown is mentioned—the officials put the crown upon him, and anointed him, while all the people present 'clapped their hands and said, "God save the King."'

Now to England. From the time that Æthelbert, the first converted king among the Saxons, was invested with kingly authority, or from that year [785] when Egfirth was 'hallowed to king '[1] down to the coronation of a monarch whom we all hope to live to see anointed as Edward VII., sums up pretty well the whole of English history.

Æthelred II. was crowned on Easter Sunday 978, when an order of service was used which probably provided the pattern for the coronation ceremonials of all subsequent Saxon 'kings of England. The account of this function is preserved in the Cotton MS.[2] Simple, beautiful prayers were used; there was an anointing with oil, girding with sword, and the placing upon the head of the crown to the words, 'May God crown thee with a crown of glory, and with the honour of justice, and the power of fortitude; that by the grace of our [3] benedictions, with right faith and abundant fruit of good works, you may attain to the crown of an everlasting kingdom, through His bounty whose kingdom shall endure for ever and ever.' The royal sceptre and rod of virtue having been handed to the King, there were prayer and the blessing—after which there was the Mass.

Instrumental music, even to the extent of the organ, was in so crude a state that scarcely anything in the shape of orchestral music was possible. What music there was would have been entirely vocal, probably unaccompanied. The Mass service would afford some scope here; but, as harmony was little known, the vocal music would have been lugubrious, at least to modern ears. The Mass was rendered most probably to a Gregorian plain song, or *canto fermo*, which, sung as it was in unison by priests and monks, was probably more convincing and startling than beautiful.

Never before had there been a more unanimous call to the throne than when 'All folk chose Eadward to King '[1042]. 'The choice expressed the full purpose of the English nation to endure no king but one who was their bone and their flesh.'[4] Never was an election and coronation to kingship more popular. At this period the consecration of a king in England was not a mere pageant, but a rite of the utmost moment, partaking almost of a Sacramental character. 'Eadward was crowned at Winchester on Easter Day, April 3, 1043, by Archbishop Eadsige, Ælfric of York and most of the other prelates of England assisting. On this

---

[1] Augustine having introduced the Roman service here (597), the proceedings were doubtless rendered in the Latin tongue.
[2] A. S. Chronicle.   [3] The assembly of bishops.
'History of the Norman Conquest' (Freeman), v. ii. p. 4.

occasion, we are told, the Archbishop [Canterbury] gave much good exhortation both to the newly-made King and to his people.' We hear nothing of the music performed, although the ceremony must have been a brilliant one, judging from the number of foreign ambassadors present, and the exchange of costly presents (even to ships with sterns and prows of gold) between king and princes. The English chroniclers at this period, and long after it, are not greatly addicted to detail, and music itself was at so low an ebb, vocally and instrumentally, that little could have been accomplished in this direction. Eadward possessed an underlying fondness for foreign Churchmen, and it is not unlikely, therefore, that such music as was drawn into the service was rendered in the best possible way that Gregorian music could be rendered in those days.

'To thee, Harold my brother, I commit my kingdom,' were among the last words of Eadward, and as the Witan approved, Harold was crowned king on January 6, 1066. It was a great occasion. In one breath there was a king's burial and a king's coronation.[1]

Of all the gorgeous rites celebrated by Kings and Prelates beneath the vaults of the West Minster [says a great historian[2]] the two-fold rite of that great Epiphany which haste and urgency may well have rendered the least gorgeous of them all, is that around which the national memory of Englishmen may well centre most fondly. The first royal burial, the first royal consecration, within the newly hallowed temple, possess an historic interest and an historic import beyond all those which have followed them.

Although for three hundred days masses, psalms and hymns were sung at Eadward's tomb, all this devotion did not blur the rejoicings at Harold's coronation. Harold was consecrated, Ealdred being the celebrant and not Stigand, as the historical tapestry shows. Two bishops led the King-elect (with processions of choristers singing hymns) to the high altar of St. Peter's at Westminster, and thus the rite began. We know the tenour of at least one of these hymns. It was that Harold might be strengthened and exalted, and that mercy and truth might go before his face.[3]

Christmas morn, 1066, witnessed the sight of a monarch awaiting to be crowned who spake not our ancient tongue, and knew not the speech of England. Geoffrey, bishop of Coutances, therefore, put the question whether the assembled crowd consented to the consecration of the Duke of Normandy, in French. 'Yea, yea, King William,' was the immediate response that rang loud through the minster. The northern primate, Ealdred, Archbishop of York, was the actual celebrant, for Stigand, Archbishop of Canterbury, had refused to pour the holy unction on the head of

[1] 'Le Roi est mort ; vive le Roi.'
[2] Freeman, 'History of the Norman Conquest,' v. iii. p. 28.
[3] Maskell.

26

an usurper and a man of blood. Led by the two Archbishops, William the Conqueror passed to the royal seat before the high altar, where the *Te Deum*, which had been sung over Harold, was now again sung over the Norman Duke.

Suddenly all was confusion. A fire had broken out in the buildings surrounding the minster, and the congregation rushed from the church. The King-elect, with the officiating prelates, clergy, and monks of the Abbey alone remained before the altar. And they trembled. Yet while the flames were raging around outside, the rite went on. Litanies and hymns were sung, and prayers intoned. Then William took the oaths, the holy oil was poured upon the royal head, and the Norman Conqueror stood there a consecrated English king.

William II. (Rufus) was crowned at Westminster, September 29, 1087, the ceremony being taken by Lanfranc—the first Norman Primate, and Wulfstan—the one remaining Saxon bishop. Stephen, Henry I. and II., Richard I., and John were crowned with much the same ceremonial. Never had there been such a joyous day as when Queen Maud, the descendant of Alfred and Consort of Henry I. was crowned in the Abbey. At Stephen's coronation the kiss of peace was forgotten and the Host given at the Holy Communion suddenly disappeared. An evil omen in the shape of a bat was seen fluttering through the church, and inconveniently circling round the throne at the coronation of Richard I.[1]

The advent of the House of Plantagenet in English history was by no means unfavourable to music—many of the kings and queens having distinctly musical talent. Isabella—the Consort of King John [1190–1216], for instance, kept her musical retinue—one of whom Ambrose 'the songster' had the honour of singing the hymn, *Christus Vicit*, at her unction and coronation. For this he received the not inadequate pay of twenty-five shillings, a sum which Lackland, giver of English liberty, may, or may not have paid for her. What other music was performed at this coronation is unknown, but as the service would have included the Mass of the old religion, rendered in monotone, it could hardly have been much.

Henry III. was twice crowned—once at Gloucester, and again at Westminster, on his marriage to the beautiful Eleanor. It was in this reign that the King provided the notable addition to the insignia of all future coronations—even the famous stone chair which exists in the Abbey to-day, and in which, if all goes well, Edward VII. will assuredly sit. The first English Monarch to sit in this august seat was Edward II., crowned on Shrove Sunday

---

[1] This is the first coronation of which any large detailed account is given by historians. Hovenden and Matthew Paris both describe it fully.

1308; and every English Sovereign from that time has been in-augurated upon it—save Queen Mary.[1]

Henry V., the hero of Agincourt, evinced distinct musical taste quite early in life, and there is an entry in the household book of his grandsire, John of Gaunt, showing that a payment was made for strings purchased for Henry's harp before he was ten years old. He was not only a performer on the harp and organ, however, but also a composer, who took great delight in Church harmony, which he practised assiduously on the organ. One admirable notion he possessed concerning music, one which, even to-day, is as rare as it is desirable. He had a wholesome aversion to all noisy music, and at his coronation in Westminster Hall, in 1413, he would hear of no other instruments than harps being employed. Of these there was quite an army. 'The number was exceedingly great,' says a chronicler,'[2] 'the sweet strings of the harps soothing the souls of the guests by their soft melody.' Wagner was unknown then, and the modern German school had yet to come. It manifests, it must be allowed, excellent taste on the part of this monarch to have preferred a wholesale sweep of harp music to the barbarous noise of trumpet and drum which obtains even to-day whenever an opportunity is provided at our public functions for the introduction of a little music.[3]

At the coronation of Henry VI. and Queen Margaret of Anjou, music formed a great feature. Westminster Hall resounded to the strains of a huge band of harpers, in addition to which there were five minstrels of the King of Sicily, who came to England especially for the occasion and were paid £10 each. There were besides two of the Duke of Milan's musicians, who pocketed five marks each upon this auspicious occasion.

At Henry VII.'s coronation the Yeomen of the Guard, familiar to us as 'Beefeaters,' first appeared. Henry VIII. was crowned with prodigious splendour, and even this was surpassed when, on Whitsunday, June 1, 1533, Archbishop Cranmer crowned Anne Boleyn. On this occasion a choir of men and boys even stood on the leads of St. Martin's Church and sang new ballads in praise of Her Majesty. None of Henry's other queens were crowned. At Henry's coronation the customary mass was consider-ably abridged, for it was discovered 'that many points of the same were such as by the laws of the nation were not allowable.'

Mary was crowned after the Roman faith, the ceremonies being performed according to the old custom. Oglethorpe, Bishop of

---

[1] Mary declined to sit in the chair lest it had been polluted by her Protestant brother's presence therein !   [2] Thomas de Elmham.

[3] This king even took his minstrels away with him on his honeymoon with Catherine of Valois, and while at Corbeil sent to London to John Bore, harp maker, for two new harps for the queen and himself (Ellain).

FREDERICK J. CROWEST

Carlisle, crowned Elizabeth[1] in Westminster Abbey—the Archbishop of York declining to officiate and the Primacy of Canterbury being vacant. The service was partly in Latin and partly in English.

On the occasion of the coronation of King James II. and his Queen,[2] on April 23, 1685, the musical (*i.e.*, choral) part of the proceedings devolved upon the following bands of musicians:

(*a*) 'The twelve Children of his Majesty's Chapel-Royal in their Surplices, with Mantles over them of Scarlet Cloth.'

(*b*) 'The Choir of *Westminster* in Surplices with Musick Books in their Hands, the youngest first.'

(*c*) 'The Organ-blower, in a Short Red Coat with a Badge on his Left Breast—viz., A Nightingale of Silver-gilt sitting on a Sprig; The Groom of the Vestry, in a Scarlet Robe, with a Perfumery-pan in his Hand, burning Perfumes all the Way from *Westminster Hall* to the Choir-door in the Church.

(*d*) 'One of His Majesty's Musicians, in a Scarlet Mantle, playing on a Sackbut; One of his Majesty's Musicians, in a Scarlet Mantle, playing on a double Courtal[3]; One of his Majesty's Musicians, in a Scarlet Mantle, playing on a Sackbut.

(*e*) 'Thirty-two Gentlemen of his Majesty's Chapel Royal, in Surplices, with Mantles over them, Four-a-Breast.

The procession formed, 'the drums beat a march, the trumpets sound several levets and the choirs sing all the way from the Hall to the Church, usually this known Anthem, "O Lord, grant the king a long life," &c.' So ran the Official Court Circular when James II. and his royal Consort were crowned.

The other anthems on this occasion were: (1) 'I was glad when they said unto me'; (2) 'Let thy hand be strengthened'; (3) 'Come, Holy Ghost'; (4) Zadok the Priest'; (5) 'Behold O Lord our Defender'; (6) 'The King shall rejoice'; (7) 'God spake sometimes in visions'; and (8) 'My heart is inditing of a good matter.' In addition to this music the Litany,[4] and *Te Deum* were sung. Another musical feature was this. When the Queen entered, the choir, the King's scholars of Westminster School, in number forty, all in surplices, being placed in a gallery adjoining to the great organ-loft, entertained her Majesty with the short prayer and salutation *Vivat Regina* [naming her Majesty's name], continuing to do so until the entry of his Majesty into the choir, when they sang in like manner *Vivat Rex*, giving his Majesty's name.

[1] Sunday, January 15, 1558.
[2] The procession was abandoned on the score of economy, but more than £100,000 was laid out in dressing the Queen.
[3] A short sackbut or bassoon.
[4] This was done by the Bishops of Oxford and St. Asaph. The Archbishop officially orders it to be read, and did so on this occasion; but, nevertheless, it was sung or intoned.

29

CORONATION MUSIC

It will be observed that there were eight anthems sung at James II.'s coronation, but this was due to the extra 'waits,' consequent upon the consort's coronation at the same time.

Charles I.'s coronation was a chapter of *contretemps* and ill omens—even to the sermon text—'I will give thee a crown of life,' uncomfortably suggestive, which evil forebodings even the substitution of a white satin robe for the usual purple one did not avert. There was an earthquake at about two o'clock in the afternoon, which Baxter, a boy at school, who later wrote about Charles II.'s coronation, says : 'Did affright the boys, and all the neighbourhood.'

At the coronation of Charles II., King of Scotland, England, France and Ireland 'as it was acted and done at Scoone,' the first day of January, 1651, there was no provision for music. The minister of the kirk at Scoone had matters pretty much his own way, and beyond the singing of Psalm XX just before the Blessing the proceedings were only enlivened periodically by the people shouting, with a loud voice, 'God Save the King.' His coronation in England—April 23, 1661—on the contrary was marked with all the reckless gaiety of the Restoration. Archbishop Juxon performed the anointing, and the utmost care was taken to follow the old patterns as far as they could be remembered. A writer of the day says 'the anthem sung by the quire was "Sadoc the Priest," &c.' Matthew Lock composed the whole of the music for the public entry of Charles II. and had received the appointment of Composer in Ordinary to the King.[1]

The estimable and engaging Pepys relates that on this 'Coronaicon' Day 'the King passed through all the ceremonies of the Coronâcon, which to my great grief I and most in the Abbey could not see. The crowne being put upon his head, a great shout begun. . . . But so great a noise that I could make but little of the musique.'[2] When the King went out of the Hall it fell a raining and thundering and lightening as I have not seen it do for some years ; which people did take great notice of.'[3]

Much the same musical order and observance as that attending James II.'s raising to the kingship was followed at the coronations of William III. and Mary, April 11, 1689 ; Queen Anne, April 23, 1702 ; George I., October 20, 1714 ; and George II. and his consort, Queen Caroline, October 11, 1727. Queen Anne was carried to her coronation on account of her gout. George I. could not speak English, and the ceremonies had to be explained to him in Latin, for his enlighteners could not speak German. No wonder a wag observed that 'much bad language passed between them !'

[1] 'Relation of His Majesty's Entertainment passing through the City of London to the Coronation,' April 22, 1661. (Ogilby.)
[2] 'Diary' (Pepys), v. i. p. 220.   [3] 'Diary' (Pepys), v. i. p. 222.

FREDERICK J. CROWEST

The only Coronation Music worthy the name may be said to be
Handel's four 'Coronation' anthems—'Let my hand be strengthened,' 'My heart is inditing,' 'The King shall rejoice,' and
'Zadok the Priest.'[1] These have held their own from the day they
were written—September 11, 1727—and one or more of them have
been performed at every coronation ever since.

On the accession of George II. in June 1727 Handel was given
the honorary titles of Composer to the Court and Composer to the
Chapel Royal, for which he had no regular salary, although fees
were paid to him on special occasions. It must not be forgotten,
however, that the 'mighty Saxon' was secured of an income of
£600 a year for life, made up of two pensions of £200 each given
him by Queen Anne, and a salary of the same amount as music-
master to the young princesses.[2]

George II.'s coronation took place at Westminster Abbey on
October 11, 1727, on which occasion Handel's four coronation
anthems beginning with the now well-known 'Zadok the Priest'
were performed with a large orchestra. These anthems, like
Handel's 'Te Deums,' are made up principally of massive writing
of five, six, and seven vocal parts. On the coronation in question
the singers were all English, being members of the Chapel Royal
and Westminster Abbey choirs. Twelve boys and thirty-five men
choristers were employed, the solos being sung by Francis Hughes,
John Freeman, John Church, Samuel Wheely and Bernhard Gates.
A new organ (which the King afterwards presented to the Abbey)
was built for the occasion by Schröder, and was a very fine instrument. At the placing of the crown on the head of the new
monarch there was, we are told, 'an accompaniment of instrumental music of every sort'—which we may take to mean the full
orchestra, and at the conclusion of the ceremony the anthem 'My
heart is inditing of a good matter' was sung.

Dr. Croft, who as Court composer-organist, and Master of the
Chapel Royal, was organist on this occasion, paid for it with his
death. At any rate he died in this same year, and his biographers.
commonly attribute his death to an illness contracted at the coronation of George II.

In the case of the coronation of George III. a proclamation had
been issued to the effect that it was his Majesty's intentions that
the Queen should be crowned at the same time that he was, and,
for the celebrating of the coronation feast, Westminster Hall was.
to be laid open throughout. Special structural arrangements for·

---

[1] It was in connection with the composition of these anthems that it is stated
that the Bishop of London selected and sent some texts to the composer, but that.
Handel took offence and wrote to the bishop, saying, 'I have read my Bible well, and.
will choose for myself.'

[2] 'Handel' in 'Master Musicians' series.

31

the service were deemed necessary on this occasion. Over the north
gate a balcony was erected for musicians, trumpeters, and kettledrums; while in the centre, over the end, was fixed a noble organ,
at which was the Abbey organist.

With the scene of the ceremony changed to the venerable pile
of Westminster Abbey, the musical portion of the proceedings
opened with the drummers and trumpeters who had preceded the
procession on its way to the Abbey turning upstairs into their
gallery over the entrance door of the Abbey. Then the ceremonies
proceeded. The choir, prebendaries and dean, on their entrance,
fell off to the left, while George III. and his Queen entered the
church. The children and gentlemen of the Chapel-Royal afterwards proceeded to their seats on each side of the area before the
altar; the remainder of the vocal music retired to a high gallery
over the south side of the same, and the instrumental to one on the
north side of the area next the pulpit. On this occasion the
coronation service immediately commenced by the Westminster
choir singing Purcell's anthem, 'I was glad when they said unto
me,' during the singing of which their majesties passed through the
body of the church. At the conclusion of the anthem, the choristers
passed on to their gallery at the back of the choir. Then the archbishop made the presentation : 'Sirs, I here present unto you King
George the Third,' &c.—at the end of which were loud acclamations of 'God save King George the Third.' The final presentation
being reached a flourish of trumpets concluded that part. Their
majesties now being seated in their chairs of state, another anthem
was sung by the choir—'The King shall rejoice in Thy strength.'
The Litany followed, being on this occasion sung by Dr. Edmund
Keene and Sir William Ashburnham, the Bishops of Chester and
Chichester, duly vested, while the choir of Westminster took the
responses or people's part to the accompaniment of the organ.

The third anthem was 'Come, Holy Ghost,' sung by the archbishop and the choir to the music of Turner. As his Majesty
removed into the ancient coronation chair to be anointed, the choir
sung Handel's coronation anthem, 'Zadok the Priest.' After the
'anointing' and 'blessing' a fifth anthem was sung, 'Behold, O
God, our Defender, &c.,' during which while there took place the
ceremony of presenting the spurs and sword. After the consecration
and when the crown was set upon the King's head, there was a
fresh flourish of trumpets while the assembled congregation shouted
'God save the King'—a shout that was taken up vociferously
outside and in St. James's Park. The *Te Deum*, 'We praise Thee,
O God,' followed; there were two more anthems, the eighth and
ninth, the drums and trumpets then flourished, and the people
shouted 'May the King live for ever.' A choral Communion
Service immediately succeeded, at which the choir sang a beautiful

setting of the words : 'Let my prayers come up into Thy presence as incense, &c.' Such was the music at the ecclesiastical portion of George III.'s coronation festival.[1]

When George IV.[2] was crowned, the trumpets struck up the air of 'God save the King' as the monarch, splendidly attired, wearing a plume of ostrich feathers surmounted by a black heron's plume, entered Westminster Hall, prior to the ceremony in the Abbey. For this, in addition to the choir of Westminster in their surplices, there were the children and gentlemen in surplices and scarlet mantles four abreast. During the procession from the throne in Westminster Hall to the great steps in the Abbey, the anthem, 'O Lord, grant the king a long life,' &c., was sung in parts by the choristers, the intervals being filled up by his Majesty's band playing, the sounding of trumpets, and the beating of drums, until the arrival in the Abbey.

The coronation service itself opened with the anthem 'I was glad when they said unto me.' On this occasion the Communion Service was read, the people speaking the responses to the Commandments. The *Veni, Creator Spiritus* hymn, Handel's anthems, 'Zadok the Priest,' and 'The King shall rejoice,' and *Te Deum* were sung in the same parts of the service, as upon the occasion of Queen Victoria's coronation. At the earlier coronation, and while the medals were scattered, the choir sang the 'Final Anthem with instrumental music of all sorts '—'Blessed be Thou, Lord God of Israel.' At its conclusion drums beat, the fifes and trumpets sounded, and all the people shouted, crying out :

> 'God save King George the Fourth,
> Long live King George
> May the King live for ever.'

At the banquet which followed this coronation, whereat, by the way, the Lord Chancellor said, ' They would have drunk a subject's health with three times three, and ought to have drank the King's health with nine times nine,' the choir of Westminster sang the anthem 'God save the King.' When they came to the words

---

[1] It need hardly be said there was a banquet in Westminster Hall. The dishes were provided and sent from the adjacent temporary kitchens, erected in Cotton Garden for this purpose. No less than sixty haunches of venison, with a surprising quantity of all sorts of game were laid in for this grand feast. The King's table was covered with one hundred and twenty dishes, at three several times served up by the gentlemen-pensioners. During the feast the King's Champion in white armour and on a fine white horse challenged and threw down his gauntlet, which not being taken up the Garter King of Arms proclaimed the King's styles in Latin, French and English.

[2] The dawn of day saw the metropolis of England in military occupation, and had a stranger not possessed of any previous knowledge of the events which had been passing, approached at that moment, he might have mistaken London for a conquered city in which the governing powers were at war with the people.

CORONATION MUSIC

'Scatter his enemies,' and 'Frustrate their knavish tricks,' the assembled multitude rose as one and continued their shouts and acclamations for several minutes.

Strange to say George IV. took more interest in the music to be performed at his coronation than do monarchs generally.[1] A grand rehearsal of the music performed on Thursday, July 19, 1821, took place upon the previous Monday, upon which occasion the King-elect suggested many alterations and improvements. At his Majesty's command the 'Hallelujah' chorus from the *Messiah* was added to the selection already made, and was performed on the entrance into the Abbey. By his Majesty's desire, too, 'God save the King,' and 'Non nobis, Domine' were rehearsed preparatory to the banquet in Westminster Hall. During the rehearsal his Majesty found that the instrumental part of the band was too powerful for the vocal. The King therefore commanded that the voices should be strengthened, and this took place as far as the extent of the orchestra would permit. At the end of the rehearsal George IV. was pleased to express his gracious approbation of the persons employed musically upon this important occasion. He particularly complimented Messrs. Attwood and Knyvett, the composers of the two new anthems, on the talent which they had displayed.

It appears that the anthem, 'Blessed be Thou, Lord God of Israel,' with music by Kent, was a peculiar favourite with the King. To this, Kramer, the master of the King's band of wind instruments, added orchestral parts which greatly pleased the monarch.

Some of the names of musicians present on this occasion are interesting now, getting on, as we are, to a hundred years from the occasion itself. Mr. Shield, the master of the King's State Band appeared as conductor, and led off the whole of the band. Mr. Kramer appeared at the head of twenty-nine wind instrument performers. Mr. Knyvett was the organist, while Mr. Cramer was appointed to lead the band upon this memorable occasion, and had

---

[1] The King, it would appear, had studied the ceremonies of his coronation much more diligently than had his attendants, for he corrected a terrible mistake in which the Marquis of Salisbury fell in being out of place—a matter which the Deputy-Garter soon put right. George IV. smiled while this was doing, but it evidently was a matter of consequence to him that no error in form should for an instant find place in the ceremonial of his coronation. Strange that in his anxiety for regularity and precedent he should have forgotten how completely his queen was out of her place. Poor Caroline! Party spirit was mainly to blame for the situation. Imagine a newspaper throwing this comment in the King's face : ' It was deplorable that the coronation of "the first gentleman in Europe" should have been prefaced by the grossest of insults, offered under his presumed sanction to a woman—his own wife, and the second person in point of rank in his realm. Yet although the queen was not present, despite all her appeals, Mr. "Tom" Cribb, and a few other pugnacious spirits were observed ! '

34

the honour of having eight other leaders of bands to play under him. Such names among the stringed instrumentalists as Smart, Spagnoletti, Calkin, Mountain, Crosdie, Lindley, Dragonetti and Hill will be of interest to all music-lovers. Hawes, Sale, Welsh, Greatorex, Turle, Knapp and Horn are not unknown names either in English vocal music-lore.

William IV.'s coronation took place on Thursday, September 8, 1831—an occasion when much fuss and capital were made out of the incident of the Duchess of Kent's, and the presumptive heiress to the crown, Princess Victoria's absence from the ceremony—an absence that was occasioned, not by any feelings of disrespect to the King, but by the temporary indisposition of her Royal Highness. It was a poor affair in every way, for the bluff rough-and-ready sailor King had no taste and no wish for display; indeed, he put it seriously to Earl Grey, the Prime Minister, whether the coronation service could be dispensed with. Economy in the public purse was being mooted—so there was no procession and no banquet.

At the coronation of our late beloved sovereign Victoria (June 28, 1838), the musical part of the service was excellent and impressive. Her Majesty on entering the west door of Westminster Abbey was received with the anthem—'I was glad when they said unto me we will go into the house of the Lord,' sung by the choir. At the moment when—

> '. . . . opposing freely
> The beauty of her person to the people,'

the 'recognition' took place there were loud, simultaneous, enthusiastic shouts of 'God save Queen Victoria,' the sounding of trumpets, beating of drums, and, finally, the National Anthem rendered by band and people.

After the 'first oblation' the Litany was read, not sung; as, too, was the Nicence Creed. Preparatory to the 'anointing' ceremony the hymn *Veni, Creator Spiritus* was sung by the choir, the Archbishop of Canterbury reading the first line. Then followed Handel's anthem—'Zadok the priest, and Nathan the prophet, anointed Solomon King; and all the people rejoiced, and said: God save the King, long live the King, may the King live for ever. Amen. Hallelujah.' After the 'putting on of the crown,' and when the tumultuous shouts, which all but made 'the vaulted roof rebound,' had died away, there followed the anthem—'The Queen shall rejoice in Thy strength, O Lord.' There was then the 'presenting of the Holy Bible,' after which the Benediction and the singing of the *Te Deum* by the choir. Another anthem—'This is the day which the Lord hath made,' succeeded the 'homage,' which, being ended, the drums beat, the trumpets sounded, and all the people shouted:

CORONATION MUSIC

God Save Queen Victoria.
Long live Queen Victoria.
May the Queen live for ever !

At the conclusion of the celebration of the Sacrament, Handel's sublime 'Hallelujah; for the Lord God Omnipotent reigneth' was given.

At Queen Victoria's Coronation, every one capable of sound judgment in the matter was disgusted to see Sir George Smart pitchforked into the position, as organist, where Mr. James Turle [1] should have been. Turle was young, and above courting what is known as 'influence'; but, he was in the full vigour of his intellect and ability; and Smart could not hold a candle to him as a church musician—whether as a composer or organist. Smart, however, was a favourite in certain exalted circles—although not of her late Majesty, who protested strongly (albeit in vain) at the favouritism shown to the older musician.

From an old coloured print of the 'Form of Procession to the Coronation of the Sovereigns of England,' the musical element takes the following order: Fifes, Drums, Drum-major, Trumpets, Kettledrums, Trumpets, Sergeant-trumpeter, Children of the Choir of Westminster, Children of the Chapel Royal and Choir of Westminster, Groom of Vestry and Organ Blower (Organist), Two Sackbuts and a Double Curtail, and the Gentlemen of the Chapel Royal.

The rite itself, it may be added, is of great antiquity. A coronation service of uncertain date, but as old at least as the eighth century, is still extant. The *Anglo-Saxon Chronicle* represents Offa's son, Egfirth, as having been 'hallowed to King' in 785. In the same authority we find distinct records of the consecration of Edgar, Ethelred II., Edward the Confessor, and Harold II. to the kingly office with the same rite. And the two essential parts of the ceremony—the placing of the crown on the King's head and the anointing—had then been fully established. The ritual used at Ethelred II.'s coronation has survived, and contains both the essential parts and the form of oath taken by the King. With differences of detail the ceremonial has not materially changed since the Conquest. The chief variations have been in the oath. Till 1308 this pledged three things only—peace and reverence to God and Holy Church, justice to the people, and the removal of the bad and upholding of good laws. At Edward II.'s coronation it became more comprehensive and precise, and took the form of question and answer. No vital alteration was made for centuries in the body of the oath, though liberties were taken in Tudor and Stuart times with its wording. Once the ceremony marked the

---

[1] One of the writer's early masters, and a true disciple of the Purcell School of English Musicians.

36

FREDERICK J. CROWEST

beginning of the new reign; it afterwards came to be regarded
as giving the King a sacred character, making him the Lord's
anointed, against whose authority it was an impious act to raise
one's hand. It ought to be something more than a mere pageant
as many of the more immediate coronations have been. Possibly
—and it would be worthy the new century if it should be so—
Edward VII.'s coronation will mark a new state of things in this
direction.

Of coronation music generally a good deal might be said if
we stepped out of the arena of English music, but that is rather
beside the purpose of this sketch. Nearly all the great masters
have written something in this vein, and not a few operas exist in
which the coronation ceremony is introduced more or less vividly
and extensively. One such is Meyerbeer's *Le Prophète*, the 'Coronation March' of which is known to every music lover, especially
those who play the organ and pianoforte. Many of the musicians
of foreign Courts have had occasion to write coronation music, and
not a few of the army of lesser composers have tried their hand
with such a *pièce d'occasion* as a 'Coronation March.'

CASTLE NONCHALOIR
BY THE EARL OF CREWE

N distant days of old romance,
 Three hundred happy years ago,
There lived a gentleman of France,
 A kindly Gallic Gallio;
No courtier fine, no roystering blade
 Athirst *se faire trop valoir*,
But humorous, and slyly staid,
 The lord of Castle Nonchaloir.

His porch an open welcome gave
 To every jovial passer-by,
The scullion hummed a drowsy stave,
 The ban-dog blinked a peaceful eye;
Unchecked the prying ivy crept
 To dress with green the old *manoir*,
The rose-leaves littered all unswept
 Across the lawns of Nonchaloir.

Lulled by the homely stir of bees,
 The summer noon seemed half awake,
The anglers took their gentle ease
 Beside the lily-bordered lake;
' *Bien fol*,' went up the fitful song,
 ' *Qui veut ce qu'il ne peut avoir !* '
Their longest day was not too long,
 The merry guests of Nonchaloir.

Within, the genial host proclaimed
 A truce from all untimely things;
Imperious reason shrank ashamed,
 Shrill controversy closed her wings;
Who dragged down dulness from the shelf
 To conjugate the verb *sçavoir*,
Might surely look to find himself
 Outside the pale of Nonchaloir!

They never summoned Love to find
 The hidden keys of hell and heaven;
If knights were gay, and ladies kind,
 No more was sought, no more was given;
No need to dim delightful eyes
 By vows of reckless high *devoir*,
They wooed Decamerone-wise
 Beneath the elms of Nonchaloir.

THE EARL OF CREWE

We know those ancient folk were fools,
    We trade from wisdom's garnered store,
We learn a hundred thousand rules,
    And preach a hundred thousand more ;
We flaunt our broad phylacteries—
    The vasty thought, *le grand espoir*—
Scarce condescending to despise
    The graceless sloth of Nonchaloir. ·

And yet—and yet—, when hurrying feet
    Pursue the fever-race for gain,
When clamorous mart and seething street
    Are choked with Mammon's haggard train ;
When sect and party shriek and fret,
    And ply their sorry *rouge et noir*,
Some eyes will strain with dry regret
    Far back to Castle Nonchaloir !

THE GIFT OF PITY
BY ROBERT BARR

WHEN Paul was Prince of Salerno, that town attracted all the roisterers of the land, for the wine was good, the inhabitants gay, and no man was ever clapped in jail because of a frolic. Music resounded from the city hall, as the Prince had turned out the councillors and installed players in their places, saying there were more laws now in existence than people would keep, and that small profit accrued from adding to the list of statutes. The place was sparkling with lights at night, and, to the fishers on the sea, looked like a necklace of diamonds strewn along the coast. There was not lacking in the district a variety of pleasure, and Salerno put forth a challenge that it could consume more wine in the twenty-four hours than any city of its size in the world, which challenge remained uncontested while Paul lived, for, when it came to drinking, he was able himself to turn the scale in favour of his own principality, a wholesome quality in a ruler, that endeared him to his loyal subjects. Paul held the privilege of putting to death whomsoever he pleased within his own dominion, as was right and proper, but he seldom exercised this power, being an easy-going man, permitting many to live who might, with advantage to the world, have been eliminated. If Paul saw a gloomy face in Salerno, he was prone to have the sour fellow scourged into better humour, and was always amazed that the more severe the whipping, the less did its recipient seem inclined to that laughter which the Prince so dearly loved, and if the man howled, his Highness was apt to shake his head and aver that this was but a contrary world after all, when even the lash, well applied, could not spur a person toward mirth.

Paul, when he came to his own, was the patron of all good fellows, if they but showed some trace of merit, and it was his boast that Salerno would yet rival Rome and Florence in the fine arts. But, as they say still in Salerno when they speak of him, a man may begin with a laugh and end with a sigh, and it is strange that if you read of the Prince now, it will be in the records of that Church which in early life he so jauntily flouted, and those who caroused with him then, would have been astonished to learn how near he came to be included in the category of the saints. We may start in the race with a fine flourish of our heels, but we never know in what condition we shall breast the cord at the finish.

Paul's palace stood high over the town, every night a blazing beacon-light of pleasure ; music and laughter floating down from it, echoed back by the revels of the city itself, for as the prince is, so are the people. At the other end of Salerno, also highly placed, was the castle of the painters, built by Paul to house them, with a lofty studio, the like of which was not to be found elsewhere in Italy, and consequently upon no other spot on this fair earth. Here was every appliance for the use of picture-making; Rome sneeringly said, every appliance except genius, of which the Imperial city claimed a monopoly.

Florence held that an immense studio and pampered painters did not necessarily produce great pictures, and Paul replied, 'Wait and see.'

At the head of this art school Paul had set the imperious Rufino, lured from Venice by the compensation of a doge and the retinue and lodgings of a king. Hither then flocked art students, to the delight of Prince and painter, and Rufino, hating both Rome and Florence, echoed his potentate's words, 'Wait and see.' If the coming artist was to be produced, Rufino was resolved he should hail from Salerno; and Rufino was a determined man, stopping at nothing to accomplish his ends, with the cruelty of the Venetian, the determination of the Roman, and the hard polish of the Florentine; a man not to be baffled, who, in spite of his qualities of despot, was simply adored by his followers. But one student dared contradict him; this was young Andrea Farnenti, who had come on foot, begging his way, from Perugia, that he might take advantage of the lavishness of Prince Paul, for he had no money to support himself at Rome or elsewhere. The arrogant Rufino took at once to the lad, who came in upon him footsore, gaunt and starved, but with eyes aglow with enthusiasm for his calling. The master gave the pilgrim immediate place in the studio, although to do so he curtly refused admission to a rich and titled fop who had been recommended by no less a person than Paul himself, to whom the fop, indignant that a pauper should be preferred to a noble, made complaint to his Highness. The latter threw back his head and laughed boisterously, crying:

'By God, there are *two* rulers in Salerno, and I am the lesser. Fling away your maiden brushes, my lord, and join the minor Prince in his palace routs, choosing as I do the colour of nature as preferable to all the pigments of art. By my soul, I shall not interfere with Rufino, who may yet daub me a picture the world will go down on its knees before.'

Andrea soon justified Rufino's selection. He possessed the creative spark of genius, as yet untrained, and the master's preference for him was marked by all the school. The youth had northern courage in his veins, and sometimes when the master's insolence became undue, Farnenti would front him valorously and say such contumely was not to be borne by free men, while the others held breath, expecting his demolition. Rufino's dark eyes would blaze suddenly with Neapolitan anger, then the coolness of the Venetian lagoons came upon him, and with a shrug of the shoulders or a sinister smile he allowed the unexpected opposition to pass in silence. Andrea was warned by his comrades that some day he might go too far and court annihilation, but the youth modestly said he hoped such would not be the case, for he loved the master and hoped not willingly to offend him.

Prince Paul was a thorn in the side of the Church. He was too powerful to be grappled with by force, too well beloved by his people to be undermined by craft, too philosophical to be overcome in argument, too frivolous to be touched by appeal, too fearless to be affected by the terrors of excommunication, too independent to be browbeaten in his own Court; all-in-all a difficult man to deal with. If angered, he might well cudgel every monk from his principality. Indeed, he seemed to care as little for an abbot's robe as for a beggar's tatters, so far as the rod was concerned. He thought monks should drink and be jolly fellows, and it must be admitted that too many of the brethren under his rule most cordially agreed with him. His sumptuous table never lacked a holy friar or other churchman who could toss flagon with the best of them, and if he did not rollick forth a song, was unstinting in applause when one was melodiously sung. The monks within the Prince's confines were disinclined from one reason or another to protest against his conduct, their motto being, ' Let well alone.' To their eternal credit, then, be it recorded that the good fathers of Amalfi undertook this ungracious task of expostulation. Their detractors may say that it was safe enough, because the ruler of Amalfi was a lord paramount with whom Paul would think twice before he gave ground for quarrel, even if he wished to have trouble with a close neighbour, which, it was well known, he did not. So the monks came along in solemn procession, passed thus chanting through the streets of Salerno, and so to the Prince's palace.

Paul received the serious men with great hilarity, ordering in seven hogsheads of wine, amid the laughter of his boon companions, under pretence that the fraternity had come to drink with him, and that the supply needs be ample.

' O Prince of Profligates ! ' cried the leader of the holy men, and surely his beginning could hardly be called conciliatory, ' we are not come hither to carouse with you or with your sinful band, but to make protest in the name of our Holy Church against the immoral life you live, to the scandal of the land.'

Paul had thrown a leg over the arm of the great chair of state in which he sat, a most undignified position in which to receive a sober delegation, and a cynical smile curved his fine lips, for he cared little for churchmen, except those who sat at his table and were the last under it. His nobles watched him keenly, hoping their chief would not become suddenly angry with these meddlers, or that the monks would be less lavish with their censure than at the opening.

'Good father,' said the Prince genially, ''tis not a question of morals at all.'

'Sir, of what is it a question, then?' asked the monk.

'It is solely a question of wine. The grapes about Amalfi seem to have taken on some of the sourness of your distinguished Order, while the grapes we crush possess all the warm mellow character of their over-lord. Had Amalfi our wine, Amalfi were the centre of joy, and I should be heading an embassy begging you to lead a better life. Were Salerno compelled to drink your wine, we would be arrayed in sackcloth and powdered with ashes. Improve your vintage, good father, rather than attempt to improve me, and view life through the golden medium of an excellent wine. 'Twould marvellously clarify your vision, I warrant you. The Founder of your cult made good wine for the marriage feast; better, it is written, than all that had gone before. Well, we follow Him closer than do you, and will have only the best.'

'Blaspheme not the Christ, O Paul of Salerno, or your pride shall be humbled. Crucify Him not afresh by your ribaldry, lest He call you before Him, terrible in judgment.'

And this saying, thundered forth with that threatening majesty of tone which is the sonorific gift of some stern churchmen, had a palpable effect on all present, even upon the Prince himself, for each there, though a roisterer for the day, hoped to die in the faith, at some long postponed time, when wine or women were less tasteful to the lips. And the saying was long remembered, bestowing later upon Amalfi an odour of prophecy as lasting as it was unmerited, for the good man spoke indignantly on the the spur of the moment, with no thought of forecast.

'Ah well,' said Prince Paul, with some attempt at nonchalance, 'charity also is a virtue of our common Church, surely taught by our Saviour. Do not forget that one of my name, now a saint in your calendar, persecuted the Church, which I never did, and that his reform was admittedly complete. Therefore, reverend father, practise charity and pray for me, so that my ultimate redemption may redound to thy credit. You see I have faith, a most saving grace.'

'Faith without works is dead,' quoted the father, unflinching. He liked not to be contested with upon his own ground, in the presence of his own flock.

'Then let us add good works to faith and make the combination complete,' cried the jovial Prince, as if this were an easy problem, happily thought of and speedily performed. 'How would the gift of a thousand golden crowns to the famous monastery of Amalfi commend itself as a step in the right direction toward the regeneration of the second wicked Paul?'

The churchman's forbidding face perceptibly softened, and his followers smacked their lips as if they had been moistened by that excellent wine of which the Prince boasted. Paul's humorous eye twinkled as he noted the eagerness of shepherd and flock.

'I doubt not 'twould be accounted, when blessed by our prayers, as marking progress toward salvation.'

'I am rejoiced to hear it,' replied the Prince, 'but even in accomplishing our own redemption we must be cautious lest we throw temptation in the way of our fellows and jeopardise their souls, equally precious as our own. Yellow gold is as seductive as the yellow wine of Revello, therefore shall I not pay the money to the monastery, but denude myself of the dross by offering a prize of a thousand crowns for the best pictured head of the Christ, which painting I will bestow upon Amalfi to the eternal glory of the place, only hoping that Salerno will have the credit of producing it.'

To this proposal the monks demurred. They were already well supplied with pictures, they said, while the money would come useful by making possible certain long-needed additions and alterations.

The Prince smiled, but was firm. It was suggested that he might present an image of silver to the value of the thousand crowns, and thus patronise art while at the same time he enriched the convent with bullion, valuable to melt in time of trouble.

'We in Salerno are no silversmiths like the hammering mechanics of Genoa,' replied the Prince. 'It is the picture or nothing, for the solid metal would but tempt ravishers from without or promote corruption within, and we will not pave our way to heaven with disaster to our fellows, monk or layman. Quote to them, Sir Prior, the saying regarding the love of money and the root of evil. I disburse the gold, art is stimulated, and the brethren are inspired by a noble painting—surely a threefold consummation, admirable in scope and completeness. And furthermore, to commemorate a season of joy and good comradeship, we will make a Christmas gift of it. Next Christmas Day shall be devoted to the painting of this picture. You hear, Rufino? The prize is open to the world and you shall be the judge of the competitors. I know you as too true an artist to allow anything but merit to sway your choice, and while we hope Salerno wins the contest, still, if the money goes north, the picture comes south, and that will be our consolation. What say you, Prince of Painters?'

''Tis a most munificent endowment, your Highness,' cried Rufino in his stentor voice; then rapping out a great oath, to the scandal of the monks, he smote his huge fist on the table, and swore roundly that Salerno would make an effort toward it, but that the best man should win, wherever he hailed from. 'Nevertheless, your Highness,' concluded Rufino, 'one day is too short a time in which to paint a worthy picture. Let it be finished by Christmas

Day, or then begun, but I should not advise your Highness thus to limit the time of its production.'

'Not so, Rufino. Save us all from fire! We may cause a miracle to be done in Salerno. I will do my part toward such an outcome by giving a great feast on Christmas, and would invite our pious visitors from Amalfi, did I not know they will prefer to forward this wonder of a picture by holding service in their chapel on Christmas Day. And an admirable arrangement we make of it: they fast and we feast, so through starvation and repletion we should accomplish something between us.'

With this the monks were fain to depart contented, although Salerno drank not a cupful less wine because of their mission.

Rufino gathered his pupils and followers around him in the great studio, his fierce eyes aglow because of the challenge flung forth to the artistic world. He told them of the splendid generosity of the Prince, withdrew all leave to visit the taverns of the town until the picture was finished ; the studio, he said, must now become a very monastery in strictness of discipline, and any student who disobeyed, did so under pain of instant dismissal from the select coterie.

For a few days before Christmas all was activity within the huge studio. The students were busy stretching canvases and preparing panels. Workmen placed a heavy log athwart the floor near the upper end of the room, at the spot formerly occupied by the model-stand, and in the timber they mortised an oblong rectangular hole. Finally there was fitted into this socket, slightly inclined from the perpendicular, a massive wooden cross.

Rufino had given his orders and had disappeared. On the morning of Christmas he returned, and, with gloomy brow, surveyed the result of his command. Everything being apparently to his satisfaction, he withdrew a roll of parchment from his mantle, strode to the door, and nailed the document against the panel. At first the students thought it was some list of rules to be observed, but as Rufino stood away from it, they saw, in red wax, the seal of the Prince, like a blotch of coagulated blood in contrast with the pallid leather. As it was undoubtedly posted up for scrutiny, although Rufino said nothing, they read it silently. It was a State paper delegating to the Court painter power of arrest, imprisonment without trial, life or death over all not noble within the domains of the Prince until such time as the painting was completed.

The young artists looked gloomily at one another, thinking this warning was directed against themselves, well knowing that Rufino was not a man to be trifled with, and here was evidence that for the day at least he had supreme authority to do what he pleased, his victim losing even the right of appeal to the Prince.

Rufino had brought back with him some half a dozen stalwart

mountaineers, low-browed ruffians, who now stood in a ragged group, lowering upon the daintily-dressed students, gazing upon this visible embodiment of unreasoning force.

Rufino, with his own hand, bolted the outer doors, then said to his brigand following :

'Lower that cross.'

The men lifted the heavy timber from its cavity and laid it prone upon the beam. The painter now opened the door of an inner room, and led forth a bare-footed, bare-headed man, who stared bewildered around him, unused to the novel circumstance in which he found himself, his large appealing eyes filled with a vague fear. At sight of him, a ripple of applause went up from the enthusiastic students. Here, in the flesh, was an ideal figure of the Christ, with head and face that could not have been bettered. This, then, had been the result of Rufino's absence and search, and a most admirable conclusion it was.

The painter, with the exactitude of knowledge that pertains to the expert, draped about the trembling form a loose white robe, and placed on his head a twisted bramble chaplet, then stood back to admire his handiwork.

'Excellent, excellent !' murmured the students with unanimous approval, while the haunting eyes of the man followed every movement of the black-browed Rufino.

'Nail him to the cross !' commanded the painter.

The outlaws fell upon the terrified model, threw him back downward on the outstretched arms of the intersecting timbers, and, amidst excruciating screams, drove the cruel spikes through flesh and wood, with a celerity that was almost merciful.

'Lift the cross into place,' cried Rufino in a voice that pierced the tempest of agony. 'Now, gentlemen, to your canvases—to your canvases. There is your model.'

From the time that Rufino's purpose became understood, freezing horror struck all action from the group of students who were witnesses of his action. Now his heated command melted the spell that enchained them. The majority, tutored in the painter's unquestioned despotism, flew to their easels ; several remained fearhelpless, watching wide-eyed the gruesome spectacle ; one strode forward.

'Love of God ! Signor Rufino, take that wretch down,' beseeched young Andrea Farnenti.

'Get to your work, sir,' roared the painter.

'It is past bearing ; the act of a demon, not of a man. Take him down, I implore you.'

'Sir, to your brushes. I'll have no interference from you or any other. He hangs to the cross until he is painted.'

Andrea appealed wildly first to the mountaineers, who laughed

at him, then to his fellow students, who dared not brave the anger of
their master.

Rufino, with teeth-held lip, stood watching the young man's
frenzy, the quick flush of anger at opposition mounting higher and
higher in his swarthy face. Nevertheless he restrained himself
marvellously.

'Enough of this,' he said, panting. 'What is the agony—the
life or death—of one hind—of a thousand such, compared with the
production of an undying picture? To your task, Andrea.'

'Never while that tortured spectre hangs there.'

The abutment of self-control gave way, and a hot lava-stream
of words poured forth, Rufino's menacing eyes blazing.

'To your work, you whimpering hound, or, by the living God,
I shall nail you in that man's stead.'

The calmness which had so abruptly deserted the elder man
seemed to fall on the younger. He spread out his arms and replied
in low tones:

'Do so, Rufino, and I will stop my whimpering. Rather for me
the place of principal than of witness.'

An imperious gesture by the painter indicated that he was
about to carry out his threat, but a low growl from the students
warned him of growing rebellion. They gathered themselves
behind Andrea, and one of the oldest tore down the Prince's proclamation from the door. Rufino curbed himself as a strong man
checks back a bolting horse. Common sense had not been entirely
submerged by rising passion. To precipitate a conflict between his
mountain desperadoes and his class was not the action that would
result in the painting of a great picture, and the scant time at their
disposal was flying. The wily diplomacy of the born Italian came
uppermost.

'Andrea, and the rest of you, listen. It is you who are pro-
longing this man's pain, not I. There he stays until he is painted.
If you refuse to work, then my doors are open for you to leave. I
myself will paint the Christ, and I have little sentiment to waste on
the model. But if you set yourselves to this glorious accomplish-
ment I swear he comes down the moment you have finished. That
is my utmost concession. Now paint or go.'

'You promise to release him when I cry I have done?' shouted
Farnenti eagerly.

'Yes. Yes. I have already said it. But your word of honour
that you do not slight your work.'

'Agreed, agreed!'

Andrea threw himself feverishly upon his task, tears streaming
unheeded down his cheeks. Now the native genius of the youth
backed by the skill acquired under Rufino's stern teaching was his
helper, and he wrought as painter never wrought before. The model

47

had ceased his ineffectual outcry, and merely moaned piteously from time to time. Once or twice he swooned and his head fell helplessly forward, then pain revived him and he groaned aloud. The light was beginning to wane, when Andrea startled the silent room by springing to his feet and crying aloud almost in the very words of the Saviour:

'Master, it is finished!'

'On your honour?'

'On my honour. Not another stroke can I add to it.'

Instantly, at a wave of Rufino's hand, the cross was lowered, and the limp body removed from it as tenderly as might be. A cup of wine was held to his pallid lips, and with wailing murmurings he came slowly back to life and pain. Rufino caused him to be carried into the room from which he had emerged, and, as the door was bolted upon him, said significantly, 'We may need him again.'

But Rufino failed to reckon on the open window and upon the crafty temporary insanity his cruelty had implanted in the ill-used man. The victim climbed stealthily out, bent on one thing only— an appeal to the Prince and its consequent vengeance upon the painter.

Three women, gaudily dressed, were dancing up the main street of Salerno, arms intertwined, garlands of flowers in their flowing hair, for Christmas festivities were at their height. Their gay lilt mingled with the laughter of their followers. Suddenly the song was frozen on their lips and they stood still in the road paralysed with fear. Down towards them in the centre of the thoroughfare strode a figure, with arms outstretched, for thus only could the burning palms be cooled. The lurid evening light reflected from the glowing sea, glorified the agonised face, ghost-white save for the drops of blood that trickled from the headdress of thorns. His robe of snow seemed to shine in the gathering darkness, and each step in the dust left its mark of crimson.

'Accursèd! Accursèd!' cried this apparition. 'Accursèd be Salerno and all within its walls!'

The revellers fell to their knees, calling on their forgotten God for mercy. Thus the forlorn human shape journeyed through the town, in the enchanted luminous haze of the dying day, transfigured by its magic, leaving the terror-stricken population in a mown swath behind him as if he were the veritable Reaper of Death with his swinging scythe.

All unheeding the effect he produced, the man made straight for the well-guarded portals of the palace. He met with no opposition. Pikes that would have crossed to prevent the unauthorised passage of any other fell clattering to the pavement; sentinels, set there to challenge and dispute, prostrated themselves face downward on the flags; servants fled shrieking.

ROBERT BARR

Prince Paul, already wine-drenched, sat, a jovial host, at the head of his table, a prelate on one hand, a warrior on the other, with a hilarious company down each side of the long board. Constellations of wax candles shed their brilliant starlight from vaulted timber roof and the rectangular horizon of the cornice. The air was resonant with jest and laughter. Nevertheless there was some slight trace of annoyance on the Prince's brow, for the third course was overdue, an unheard-of dereliction where prompt service was taken for granted. Of what could the henchmen be thinking? Why was the progress of the feast impeded? The eyes of the Prince were fixed on the crimson curtains of heavy Sorrento silk that hung over the doorway, but no servitor parted them, and his Highness frowned at the unwonted delay. Nevertheless ill-humour, from whatever cause, rarely remained long with the light-hearted Paul, and remembering his duty to his guests, he shook off all trace of it, rose to his feet and uplifted a flagon.

'Nobles and gentles,' he began.

The uproar subsided, and a murmur of applause rang along the table, drinking-vessels clattering on the planks.

'His Highness speaks. The Prince! the Prince! Silence for the Prince,' was the cry.

Paul bowed to his enthusiastic guests and continued : 'We are gathered here to-night to celebrate in befitting manner the most auspicious anniversary of the year, duly honoured by all godly princes and people, in palace and in hovel. We commemorate Christmas, the birthday of our Saviour, and therefore I propose to you a suitable toast, to be drunk from brimming measures. Nobles and gentles, I give you Jesus Christ, first on earth and second in heaven!'

Now, this was going too far even for that impious gathering, for although, as has been said, they lived freely, all hoped for absolution and salvation at the end. The daring toast was received in dense silence, several furtively crossing themselves. A Christmas revel was all very well, but even a prince should not drag in a sacred name, except, of course, by way of an oath. It was the portly prelate who ventured to give voice to the general sentiment. The good father rose to his feet, a little unsteadily, for he was top-heavy with the potent liquors so lavishly bestowed upon him, but he spoke with all the gravity of the half-drunken and all the dignity of the highly-placed churchman.

'Your Highness, it is not seemly that you should link the name of our Lord with a drinking toast, as you might that of a favourite beauty of your Court.'

'And why not, your reverence? 'Tis my way of paying honour : you with your beads, me with my flagon ; each according to his habit.'

THE GIFT OF PITY

'With all deference, your Highness, 'tis an unheard-of thing, not to be lightly undertaken in a Christian land.'

'Sir Priest, that is a woman's reason,' cried Paul angrily, made stubborn by his potations, forgetting he should be host first and ruler afterward. 'Has the feminine gown of your Order banished all masculine vigour from your brain? 'Twas never done, say you. Very well, let's set a precedent, which is the privilege of princes. Not link a good name with good wine? Out upon such a sentiment! Christ Himself, if He were here, would sanction me. Did He not change slavish water into noble wine that the feast might be merry? Do you contravene your own teaching? Give me logic, not cant phrases.'

'Your Highness threatens an act of sacrilege.'

'Bald assertion, divorced from all proof. I say 'tis an act of worship, and my pronouncement is as good as yours.'

'Thou shalt not crucify Christ afresh. Peter the Apostle returned to Rome and martyrdom that our Lord might not suffer again. Beware, O Paul the Prince, lest worse befall thee!'

Despots love not contradiction, and this continued opposition maddened the master of Salerno, the more as he saw that his courtiers sympathised with priest and not with Prince. He was accustomed to carry all his following with him in a controversy, and now he gave reins to his wrath, shouting aloud words long remembered with dismay in Salerno, bringing fear to the most hardened listener around that ribald board. The stalwart Prince seemed majestic in his anger as he raised the beaker high above his head, and roared forth in tones that echoed from the vaulted roof:

'Name of God! Have I lived to learn that cravens surround me, frightened by a myth? Then, O Christ, I alone have the courage to drink to you. If I do wrong, paralyse this strong arm ere it bring the wine to my lips—if you can! Now for the second miracle of the wine!'

A shiver of abject apprehension ran through his audience at this bold defiance, and, as all eyes were turned upon him in grim foreboding, they saw the right arm tremble and the drops of wine, like blood, lip over the flagon's brim and splash on the marble floor. The Prince's stare became wild and fixed, his under jaw dropped, he breathed like a man in apoplexy, and the flagon fell with a startling crash on the stone, as he staggered back, bringing his hands to his head. The crimson curtains had parted: there stood before him, white against red, a vivid representation of the Great Tragedy, which none but Paul at that moment saw, and he, dazed, thought at first it was a vision made from the fumes of wine, till, drawing hand across his straining eyes, the picture still remained.

Several sprang to their feet.

'The Prince, the Prince! Look to the Prince. He is stricken. He is ill. Support him.'

'Merciful God,' prayed the prelate, 'visit not Thy just resentment upon Thine anointed. He knew not what he said.'

Then upon the commotion struck a hollow voice that changed the tumult into panic:

'Accursèd city and thrice-accursèd ruler! Prince of Salerno, behold your work!'

The scene which followed found no one there sane enough to record it. No two present agreed regarding its details. The monkish chronicle is tinctured with incredibility through the evident belief of the writer that the apparition was supernatural, and the equally evident desire to bring the lesson home to all readers of the manuscript. Women shrieked and fell unheeded to the floor; benches were overturned; men drew swords only to let them clang nerveless to the marble tiling; then all dropped to their knees in a fervour of prayer and supplication. The Prince, arms outspread upon the table and head buried in them, moaned for mercy, and there remained all that tempestuous night.

The wounded man, sanity slowly returning to him, became affected by the wave of emotional terror he had occasioned. The myriads of lights dazzled and bewildered him. He began to realise that he was in the lion's den; that the potentate he had braved was lord of life and death and torture. He could not understand why his words and appearance should have so demented those proud nobles who listened and saw, but he feared the reaction and their vengeance. He dimly understood that here was a Court at which no serf like himself could expect either justice or mercy, and an eager desire to escape took possession of him, before worse might ensue. Silently he stole back between the curtains, and passed unheeded through deserted corridor, cloister, archway, square, and outer gate. Thence eastward and up, to the comparative safety of his native mountains, seeking a hiding-place for a time.

In the studio, at the other end of the town, a very different scene was being enacted, those gathered within its walls having no knowledge of the escape of their victim or the uproar in city and palace. Rufino, his purpose accomplished, sought now to soothe the ruffled spirits of his pupils. Seeing the effect his tyrannous action had had upon those who might have been expected to subordinate everything to the success of their craft, he began to fear the outcome if any account of it filtered through to Prince and people. He spoke to his silent auditors about the lasting glory of their profession, admitted his own heart was so thoroughly imbued with love of it, that perhaps he thought too little of the methods he had that day made use of. However, a guild must stand together, and he expected support from his following. He asked from them,

51

therefore, a pledge of secrecy regarding the work of that Christmas Day, and this they somewhat sullenly granted.

'And now,' he cried with an assumed jauntiness, 'before the light fails, let us see if your results have justified my cruelty.'

Each easel, with its square burden, was taken by its owner from the group and placed in line with the others, where the light would fall fairly on the pictures; then Rufino, with the artists behind him, passed along before the sketches commenting and, for the most part, commending. The work pleased him, and confirmed him in his opinion, never swerved from, despite their womanish shrinking before pain, that much depended on a perfect model. At the last he came upon the painting by young Andrea Farnenti, the artist standing moodily by his easel, unheeding the chatter of his more volatile comrades or the grave criticisms of the master.

Rufino became silent as he looked upon the final canvas. Here was a portrayal of human agony such as even he had never seen in all the thousands of pictures he had viewed during his life in the very homes of finest art. Silently he took off his broad bonnet and stood uncovered before it. Every pupil knew that here at last was the masterpiece, even before the judge spoke.

Rufino unclasped the long robe of his office and let it fall from him.

'Place the mantle on Andrea's shoulders,' he said in a low voice. 'I am no longer master; he is supreme. Andrea, forgive me that I spoke coarsely to you. Still, I was in the right and you have proved it. The skill to do this great work you have had partly from me, but your genius has mixed with your pigments the divine element of Pity, and the grace and pleading of Pity shines forth from every brush-stroke.'

The young man, his face flushed, stepped forth and spoke eagerly:

'Do I, then, get the thousand crowns?'

At this unexpected question a chill seized the enthusiasm of those who listened, for where true art is under consideration, the question of money should not thrust itself forward. There were a few moments of painful silence, then Rufino answered coldly, with a shrug of his shoulders:

'I suppose so, for it is not likely that the equal of this will come even from Imperial Rome itself. You may be poor, Farnenti, but, if you viewed it aright, this moment of triumph is not to be weighed against all the coin ever struck.'

'My poverty has nothing to do with it, Signor. I would finger the money no more than if it were the thirty pieces of silver. Nevertheless I thank God it comes to me, that it may go instantly to endow for life the poor wretch who was tortured that I might paint.'

ROBERT BARR

Thus it came about that Salerno grew to be the most pious city in the realm; that the peasant got his thousand crowns; and that Amalfi received its picture, which later, during an invasion, was riven from the monastery and so became lost to the world, as if to show that nothing is lasting, bought at too great a price of pain.

WAR CORRESPONDENCE AND THE CENSORSHIP UNDER ELIZABETH

BY JULIAN CORBETT

IKE so many other things which we regard as essentially modern, war correspondence made its first appearance under Elizabeth. Of course, there were no newspapers, and therefore no regular war correspondents. It is true there exists in the British Museum, heading the list of old newspapers, a little journal, which is dated 1588, and contains an account of the defeat of the Spanish Armada. But this, though it long retained its honourable position unquestioned, now lies with its shameless pretence exposed in a little note declaring it to be a forgery. Still, though regular newspapers had not yet taken the field, pamphlets were opening the way for them, and every one who had a public end to gain, from the Secretary of State down to the latest craze-monger, used the press freely. It was a pushing—we may even say, an advertising—age. The great Queen herself on occasion could play to the gallery, and the most high-minded of her servants, whether military or civil, were not blind to the stimulating force of popularity with the man in the street.

It was towards the end of the reign that the practice became pronounced, and the first time we find a marked instance of its vulgarising the old pomp of war was on the occasion of the expedition which Lord Howard of Effingham and the Earl of Essex led against Cadiz and the Spanish Treasure Fleet in 1596. It was an occasion nicely fitted for the new machinery. The composition of the staff, in which almost every faction that disturbed and enlivened Cynthia's court was represented, was the outcome of a compromise—or shall we say a truce ?—that had behind it a long tangle of intrigue too intricate to be unravelled here. Suffice it to remember that the main threads were an active personal rivalry for the Queen's supreme favour between Essex, Ralegh, and Sir Robert Cecil. In order that the full power of the country might be put forth once more against the reviving power of Spain, the three had agreed to bury the hatchet and act in cordial co-operation. They did so loyally enough, for, after all, each of them was first an Englishman and a patriot ; but it would be hard to deny that each hoped for some marked personal advantage out of the great national effort that was being made. For Cecil's personal position, a comparative failure of the expedition would probably be best. It would raise the 'scribes' over the heads of the 'men-of-war' and throw Elizabeth back again into the hands of her diplomatists. For Essex and Ralegh, on the other hand, a brilliant and lucrative campaign was essential, and their relative position would largely depend on the share of glory which each could credibly claim.

JULIAN CORBETT

Besides the opposition between the civil and military elements of the Queen's Court, the personal rivalry between Essex and Ralegh typified another. This was the natural antagonism which existed amongst the 'men-of-war' themselves—between the soldiers and the sailors—the 'land faction' and the 'sea faction,' as they were spoken of at the time. In this relation Lord Howard himself was involved. As Lord High Admiral he was in duty bound to see justice done to the sea-service, and, in spite of his lofty desire to hold the balance true, his natural bias cannot but have been emphasized by the fact that a young soldier of little experience had been joined with him in command of the expedition on equal terms. At sea he took precedence, but in shore operations he had to give place to Essex. So here was the antagonism between the soldiers and the sailors beginning at the top of the tree and extending downwards. The subordinate commanders were, of course, equally concerned ; for, beside the fact that they were divided by the nature of their profession, some were followers of Essex, some friends of Ralegh, and all of them supremely anxious to come out well in the eyes of Cecil, who was to be left at home unhindered at the Queen's ear. To add to the excitement, it was known before the expedition sailed that Drake and Hawkins had failed in the West Indies, and that both of them were dead. To the man, therefore, who could make the greatest mark in the coming campaign, Drake's cloak in all probability must fall, and in the eyes of the country he would dominate the situation as the personification of the military spirit of the day.

Here, then, was a typical opportunity for the press to play a part, and so alive were the leading commanders to its possibilities that each of them except Ralegh appears to have attached to his person a gentleman with a ready pen. For Ralegh the precaution was unnecessary. In all England there was no hand so skilled in such work as his own. If the brotherhood of war correspondents desired to choose a patron saint, a primitive type and mirror of the qualities and defects that are popularly ascribed to them, it is hard to say whom they could more fitly canonise than the author of the famous Cadiz despatches.

As it turned out, the expedition fully justified the commanders' foresight. It was not an entire success. Cadiz itself was taken by a brilliant and daring *coup de main* carried out by Essex in person and Sir Francis Vere, his chief of the staff. But the sailors, although they defeated the Spanish war fleet, failed to secure the throng of richly laden merchantmen which it had tried to protect, and the whole of them were given to the flames by the Spaniards themselves. Cadiz itself produced no ransom nor substantial plunder, and though Essex was for holding it, the Council of War, mainly by the influence of the sailors, decided it must be evacuated. An

55

equally unproductive descent on the South Coast of Portugal was followed by an attempt on the Treasure Fleet, but this too was given up as impracticable, and the fleet set its course for home with some glory but little else. Now the Queen loved glory, but her level head was not to be turned by any amount of it from a careful contemplation of the balance-sheet. In this case, whatever might be said of the glory, the balance-sheet was as bad as could be, and every officer at once felt the importance of persuading people at home that the glory was his, and the balance-sheet the fault of his colleagues. What is more, every one knew the game his fellow was going to play, and hence followed one of the most diverting episodes in Elizabeth's reign—the astute struggle of all those romantic old figures to be the first to get at the press.

In those days it was not the practice for commanding officers to write detailed despatches. It was preferred to send home an officer with little more than a general letter saying that he was cognisant of all that had happened, and could be trusted to give a full and fair account of the operations. The man chosen was naturally one whom the general regarded as devoted to his interest, but at the same time, for his credibility's sake, it was necessary that he should be a *persona grata* at Court, and not too well known as a blind partisan of anybody's.

The man selected on this occasion was unexceptionable. He was none other than Sir Anthony Ashley, the Secretary-at-War to the expedition, an officer who was looked upon as specially representing the Queen, and whose duty it was to observe and report the general behaviour of the commanders, and particularly to keep an eye on the plunder, that the Crown might not be defrauded of its fair share. No one could object to such a choice. Essex even regarded him as a special admirer of his own, and had himself knighted him after the capture of Cadiz. Still he managed to have associated with him one of his most violent partisans, Sir Gelly Meyricke. These two men were detached home when Cadiz was evacuated, but long before they could reach Plymouth the expedition had run rapidly down hill. There was at last a *sauve qui peut*, and every one had loosed his hound in full cry for the London printers.

The man whom Essex had ready for the occasion was an Oxford don, one Mr. Henry Cuffe, a gentleman of a good Somersetshire family, and a scholar of some distinction. He had been fellow of Trinity, and having lost his fellowship for slandering its founder had been subsequently given another at Merton. A few years later he was made professor of Greek, and had only left the University two years before to enter the Earl's service as one of his secretaries. This man Essex instructed to draft a full account of the whole campaign, incorporating in it certain notes which the Earl drew up with his own hand on points of which Cuffe was not well informed. When the draft was complete it was submitted to Essex, who again with his own hand made the final corrections.

Cuffe's instructions are highly interesting, and may be safely taken as a type of those received by the other competitors in the race. He was to carry the draft with all possible speed to London and to use every endeavour 'that it should with the soonest be set in print both to stop all vagrant rumours and to inform those that are well affected of the truth of the whole.' But on no account was either the Earl's name or his own to be used. The authorship was to be kept a profound secret, and special pains were to be taken that no friend of the Earl's was to be mentioned in connection with it, 'either openly named, used or insinuated, so that not the slenderest guess could be hazarded as to who was the penman.' In other words, he was to get into print an account of the campaign which gave the largest share of the credit to Essex, and which at the same time must not arouse a breath of suspicion of its having been written or even inspired by the Earl. To this end Cuffe proposed to have the whole draft rewritten by some one not-too closely connected with his chief, and the fair copy so made was at once to be carried to 'some good printer' with orders to publish it 'in good characters and with diligence.' To further allay suspicion, he proposed to give the pamphlet a title, or 'preface' as he called it, which would lend it the air of a private letter from the front. This was the favourite device on such occasions, and several of the other commanders' productions are also in epistolary form. It was a device that could only have deceived the vulgar and the antiquaries of future generations who have spent a deal of curious learning and diligence in trying to discover the identity of these supposititious correspondents.

The 'preface' or title which Cuffe had in his mind is a fair example of the kind of thing usually adopted. As drafted by him it ran as follows: *A true relation of the action at Cadiz the 21st of June under the Earl of Essex and the lord admiral sent to a gentleman in court from one that served there in good place.* The expedient was transparent enough, but, to do Cuffe justice, it must be said that he was not satisfied with it. The security of anonymity was not enough for the Greek professor. He preferred something more directly misleading. To this end—with no compunction that appears—his idea was to approach Sir Philip Sidney's old friend Fulke Greville. He held a unique position at Court—something of the Queen's tame cat—and without offending anybody or joining any party he had managed to live on in the sober distinction of his old intimacy with Sidney and in mild favour with his mistress. If he could only be persuaded to allow his initials to appear as those of 'the gentleman at Court' to whom the letter was supposed to be addressed, the thing would be done and Cuffe's version of the affair would go

57

forth to the world lambent with the pure radiance of a spirit beyond reproach. One wonders that a man of Cuffe's talent thought it necessary to ask permission for so trifling a service, but his delicacy is more easily comprehended when we follow the remainder of his plan. Plainly it was that Greville was to be asked to lie about it. If he consented to appear as the recipient it must be on the clear understanding that he was not to disclose the identity of his supposed correspondent. He was to pretend not to know, and Cuffe had the necessary lie ready cut and dried for him. When questioned on the point he could easily say that he had received the letter with a batch of others by the first messenger that arrived, but that the initials with which it was signed (and these Cuffe suggested should be ' D. T. or some other disguised name ') gave him no idea who had written it. Still he had thought it of some literary merit, and as competent persons to whom he showed it had vouched for its accuracy, he had been persuaded to make it public, and in this way it had ' fallen into the press.' It was not too plausible a story, but Cuffe seemed to think it would serve if Greville could only be induced to tell it. In case he refused to have anything to do with the deception, some other initials were to be chosen, such as ' R. B.,' ' which some,' as Cuffe said, ' no doubt will interpret to be Beale.' Robert Beale was a well-known civil servant who at this time held an office under the Council of the North, but clearly was not exalted enough for Cuffe to think it necessary to get permission for making free with his initials.

With these details neatly arranged in his head Cuffe hurried ashore. It would seem he thought himself in the first flight, but it was not so. There was a man already away on the London Road, a servant of Lord Thomas Howard, and he was the first to bring the news. Whether he too carried a draft for the press we cannot tell. There is no reason to believe he did, for stout Lord Thomas was one of the few great figures of that time who never seemed to care a straw for his own reputation or for anything but fighting Spainards and doing his duty to the Queen. If he ever appears in the quarrels of his hot-headed colleagues it is always as a mediator trying to bring them to their senses. Still his man seems to have done his best for the ' sea faction ' and to belittle the exploit of Essex and the soldiers. He was also ' a creature of Throckmorton's,' Sir Walter Ralegh's turbulent brother-in-law, and Essex's friends in London believed he had been hurried forward on purpose to throw cold water on the whole conduct of the campaign, and yet to gain all the credit of the little that had been achieved ' to the sea-service and in that to Sir Walter Ralegh above all others.'

Whatever it was the man brought with him, his presence rendered Essex's agent in London very anxious to get something with which they could set to work to counteract the impression he was making. But they were destined still to wait. The Earl's messengers had yet to deal with one more cunning than themselves. This was the official despatch-bearer, Ashley. Apparently, when Cuffe reached Plymouth he found him and Meyricke already landed. Meyricke, it seems, had already been astutely got rid of, for Ashley had persuaded him to remain at Plymouth to look after the prizes and plunder as the ships came in. He thus had the field clear, and was about to start for London when Cuffe appeared. It was annoying enough, but Ashley was equal to the occasion. He was privy to the Earl's design, and, as we have seen, Cuffe was given to understand he could trust him implicitly, and suspected nothing. The motto of the brotherhood is still ' All's fair in love and war correspondence,' and Ashley was of the same opinion. For him it was easy to act upon it with the unsuspecting Oxford don. It was arranged that the two should ride to town together the following morning, and before Cuffe was ready Ashley started without him. Once away he did not draw rein till he reached Ashburton, some forty or fifty miles on the London road. We can see him there sitting down with a chuckle to make his apologies to the Earl's men and further secure that he should not be overtaken. He wrote a joint letter to them both. To Cuffe he said:

I know you take it somewhat unkindly (though causeless) that I left you, being better horsed than you ; but necessity hath no law, for my hard fare did enforce my extraordinary haste, and I am now gone, lingering a little before out of that town of Plymouth by very easy journeys, not doubting but you, Mr. Cuffe, will surely overtake me, considering I never ride by night nor more than forty miles by day till I come to Court, where, if I arrive before yourself, I dare undertake to make you a sufficient excuse, where it shall need, serving all turns till I may see you and may have further conference. . . . From Ashburton, the 28th of July, 1596. Mr. Cuffe, you shall be sure to find me at Salisbury or Andover at the furthest.

Then he folded his letter complacently and addressed it on the back, ' To the right worshipful my very loving friends Sir Gelly Meyricke Knight and Mr. Cuffe or either of them,' adding this note, ' I pray you haste King away if he be not drunk and the oil prize, that I may dispatch all ere my return.' Then he rode on.

Cuffe was at this time some thirty-six years old, young enough to overtake Ashley if his horse were good enough, but his heart must have failed him or else he saw a speedier way ; for, two days after Ashley gave him the slip, he was at Portsmouth, whither presumably he had gone by sea, hoping to get even with his rival that way. Thence on the morning of Friday, July 30, he started on a desperate ride for London. The roads were vile, a ' very ill and intolerable way,' he complained, but he rode on manfully, feeling worse and worse the farther he went. As night came on, he says, he was so weary he could hardly sit on his horse. By the time he reached a place he calls ' Crook' he was dead-beat. It was not without shame he gave in, for, as he said, it was no great journey, being not above fifty-three miles; but besides his weakness, as he explained, he had fallen into a distemper with symptoms of ague, and he dared not risk going on. 'If I hold out,' he wrote to Reynolds, Essex's agent in London, 'one other journey will undoubtedly ensue.' It was a pity. He had done very well, and was hard on Ashley's heels. Ashley was not expected at Court till that evening, and he was himself within two or three hours ride of London.

Still he was not yet beaten. At Crook was Sir Robert Crosse, one of Drake's favourite officers, who had been Ralegh's squadronal vice-admiral in the late expedition. He too was on his way to town, perhaps actually bearing Ralegh's version of the campaign, but at any rate in the interest of the 'sea faction,' and he had been knighted at Cadiz by Howard and not by Essex. It does not appear whether the two had ridden together from Portsmouth or whether Cuffe had overtaken him, but in any case he meant to continue his way to London. It was not the messenger Cuffe would have desired, but there was no choice. So he decided to trust him with all his papers and with a letter to Reynolds detailing all the steps he was to take as soon as the draft came into his hands. Cuffe's packet was duly delivered within a few hours of Ashley's arrival, and he might have congratulated himself that he was not beaten after all. But the end was not yet. When Reynolds opened the parcel he found to his consternation that the precious draft was missing. He knew not what to think, and wrote off to Bacon, who was Essex's chief representative at Court, to give the alarm. All he could hope was that Ashley had got it, since Essex had written that Ashley was aware of what he was doing. This was the morning of August 1, the day Ashley appeared at Court. Later in the day Reynolds wrote again to Bacon to say he had wind of foul play, which, God willing, he would impart to him next morning. Meanwhile he sent him on Cuffe's letter to show there were only two explanations—either Cuffe had been careless and Crosse dishonest, and the later was the alternative he evidently suspected.

So, after all, Ashley had the field to himself. On Sunday he gave a full account of the expedition in his own words to the Council, and after dinner had the honour of repeating it to the Queen. Essex's men were beaten, but still they had no suspicion of Ashley's good faith. As soon as he was free, Reynolds got hold of him and asked him about the missing draft. It was all he could do, and Ashley was ready for him. Of course he knew nothing of it, but in the friendliest way in the world he told Reynolds in confidence that he had better look after it and have it set up with the greatest possible speed. There was not a moment to be lost, for the Council were going to publish an official version of their own, and for this purpose Cecil had impounded Ashley's own notes. Meanwhile he promised faithfully, on the duty he owed the Earl for all his favours, not to breathe a word of his secret.

With this Reynolds had to be content; but still he was at his wits' end till Cuffe suddenly turned up with the missing draft. It was not any dishonesty of Crosse's that was to blame, but either by an oversight or of purpose Cuffe had never given him the paper. Here, then, was still breathing-time. The official version was not yet out, and Reynolds hurried to the printers, but it was only to be confronted with the shadow of the third competitor, Cecil. By this time he had probably got wind of the various accounts that were flying home, and he had coolly taken precautions that his own should be the first. Amongst the papers that had reached his hands was a long account from Howard written to his father-in-law, Lord Hunsdon. Before it could be delivered the old Lord Chamberlain was dead. Thus Cecil got possession of it, and as it held the balance fairly true between the various officers, and generally suited his views, he decided to make it the basis of the official account, and before any one could get at a printer he had taken his precautions and was quietly editing it for publication.

Thus it was that when Reynolds reached the printing-office he was informed that they could not undertake his work. Through the Archbishop of Canterbury, who was then the press censor, they had received an inhibition from the Council forbidding them to print any discourse of the kind without special licence. In fact, Cecil had quietly secured the field to himself by the heroic measure of censoring the whole of the war correspondence without so much as looking at it. Reynolds flew to the Archbishop and showed him his manuscript. It was presented, without disclosing the Earl's part in it, as a letter sent by a gentleman in the army to Bacon. The Archbishop read it, kindly expressed himself very pleased with it as a literary performance, but regretted 'that he could not by himself give it passage.' Nothing could be passed except by order of the Council. Essex's men were now in despair. Whether or not they had any thought of applying to Fulke Greville as originally intended is not clear. Perhaps they had already done so. At all events, on the morrow he informed Cuffe that his scheme was known to the Government, and that he himself was charged by her Majesty to inform him that on pain of death he was not to publish anything about the campaign without her privity.

It was the last blow; the Earl's men were thoroughly beaten, and they all agreed it was Ashley who had betrayed them. No efforts availed to recover their position. Bacon, we are told, 'laboured in this point with all the affection, discretion, and secrecy he could, both with the Archbishop and the printers,' but all to no effect. The English press was closed to them. All they could do was to circulate as many copies as possible in manuscript and furnish the Scottish Government and the Ambassadors of France and the Low Countries with translations for publication abroad. Cecil had done the same, but here he had no power to prevent their fuller accounts superseding his own laconic communications, and with this small result of all their scheming they had to rest content.

All the other accounts so assiduously prepared shared the fate of Cuffe's. The only one besides the official relation founded on Howard's letter that was suffered to get into print was one prepared by Doctor Marbecke, the Queen's physician, whom she lent to Howard for the voyage. In a sadly eviscerated form it was put in type for Hakluyt's ' Collection of Voyages ' in 1598, but eventually it was suppressed as being too favourable to Essex, and the edition appeared without it. Ralegh's own account lay still-born till it was discovered and printed by his grandson. Sir Francis Vere's account appeared in his ' Commentaries ' in 1657. The account by Sir William Monson, who was Essex's captain, did not see the light till long afterwards, when it was published amongst his ' Naval Tracts.' Others still in manuscript lie scattered up and down the country in various libraries. The longest and best of them, written apparently by an officer of Ralegh's ship the *Warspite*, is at Lambeth Palace, where, perhaps, it may have rested ever since the reverend censor laid hands on it. Three others, all in epistolary form, are in the British Museum, and there is some reason to believe that one of them is a copy of Cuffe's draft. Another, prepared by a scholarly gentleman whom Sir George Carew, Master of the Ordnance to the expedition, had attached to his staff, is in the possession of the Duke of Northumberland at Alnwick. There are still others of less importance elsewhere, and there they lie in their virginity, monuments of Sir Robert Cecil's draconian ideas of the censorship, beside which complaint of the way it is exercised to-day seems bare triviality. Yet, when all is said and done, it must be recorded in justice to his house that the official version, which lies as he amended it in the Record Office, is probably the fairest and most impartial he could have adopted.

Of the whole affair it is hard for us to judge. Times and standards have changed, and, as we cannot help feeling, changed for the better. Laments over the ways of war correspondents and protests against the manner in which the censorship is exercised are abundant ; but when we feel them most acutely let us pause and remember that, in what we regard as the golden days of Elizabeth, generals and admirals, for their personal and political ends, schemed to do their own war correspondence behind the backs of their Government, and the censor who held the bridle upon the pens of these ' men of war ' was a prelate absorbed in the theological controversies of the time.

H. R. H. The Duchess of Cumberland.

From the Royal Collection at Windsor Castle.

Gainsborough.   From Photo: Engraving Co

ANNE LUTTERELL, DUCHESS OF CUMBERLAND. BY LORD RONALD SUTHERLAND GOWER

WENTY years ago admirers of Gainsborough—and who that cares for what is beautiful in art is not an admirer of that great artist ?—were astonished at the splendour of an unfinished portrait, lent by her Majesty the late Queen Victoria, to the Exhibition in the New Gallery in Regent Street, illustrating the period, in painting, of the Royal House of Guelph. This portrait, by Gainsborough, is a life-size presentment of the head of a strikingly distinguished *grande dame*, with a face of most refined beauty, of perfect contour, with speaking eyes, fringed by beautifully pencilled lashes. The features, such as the nose and the mouth, are painted with a skill known to Gainsborough alone. The lady wears her powdered hair brushed back from the forehead, and falling in graceful curls on either side of her comely neck. The upper part of the figure, as well as the hands and arms, are but roughly sketched, and the work gives one the impression of having perhaps been done at a single sitting.

This fine portrait came as a revelation to many, for few people, even of those who were well acquainted with the treasures of art at Windsor Castle, had ever seen it ; it used to hang in one of the bed-rooms, where it was to all intents and purposes unseen and unknown. Perhaps, owing to its unfinished state, it was not considered by the Castle officials worthy of a place in one of the State rooms or in the Great Corridor of the Palace, which contain so great and precious a quantity of paintings, sculpture, china, and artistic furniture. On referring to the catalogue of the Guelph Exhibition you will find this portrait styled ' Anne Luttrel (*sic*), Mrs. Horton, Duchess of Cumberland.' Here there was an error, for Anne's family name was spelt *Lutterell*, this manner of spelling having been adopted by a branch of the ancient family of Luttrell, which since the reign of Henry IV. have held the grand old Castle of Dunster in the north of Somersetshire among the rolling valleys of Exmoor, one of the most picturesque of the stately homes of England. This branch of the family, to which Anne belonged, had been settled for several centuries in Ireland, and had added an extra E to their historic name.

Little is known about Anne Lutterell, and her chief claim to distinction was that she was the wife of the Duke of Cumberland, and thus the sister-in-law of a British sovereign. The lives of good women generally present little interest outside their own family circle. They pass through the world without scandal and without adventure ; they grow up, they marry, they have children, or not, as Nature wills ; they have some good friends and few enemies ; and

63

after their allotted time on earth they lay them down and die, and there an end as far as things of this world can affect them. Fortunately for them, they are left outside the realm of the chronicles of local and town scandal and town gossip. To this class of respectable matrons belonged Anne Lutterell.

All that I have been able to glean about her (for that most gossiping of gossips, Horace Walpole, barely mentions her in his delightful letters) I owe to the great erudition of the most amiable and obliging of curators, Mr. George H. Birch, who, by his indefatigable labours, has made what was formerly the dullest of London museums—the Soane—one of the brightest and best worth visiting. Anne Lutterell, Mr. Birch informs me, was the daughter of Simon Lutterell, Lord Irnham, who was afterwards raised to the Earldom of Carhampton. Her first husband was Christopher Horton, of Catton Hall, in Derbyshire, a well-to-do squire. This marriage appears to have been a very happy one, for Mrs. Horton had not only good looks but also was blessed with an amiable character. She had the sorrow of losing her only child, a daughter, and her husband, who was devoted to her, within a fortnight of each other. Mr. Horton was dying when the little child died, and the poor wife was obliged to conceal their loss from him.

Some time after this double bereavement Mrs. Horton went to Brighton (the Brighthelmstone of that day), where she met Prince Henry, Duke of Cumberland, younger brother of George III., a feeble and dissipated youth, who had been brought up amid vicious surroundings, and (what was worse) by a mother who caused her children much unhappiness. Prince Henry fell head-over-ears in love with the handsome widow, and on November 1, 1771, the young couple ran away together to Calais, where they were secretly married.

When the Duke's mother, the Princess Dowager of Wales, heard of her son's match, her fury knew no bounds; her indignation being shared by the bridegroom's brother, George III., and his Queen. Writing to George Selwyn in that year, Lord Carlisle says : ' I hear Mr. Delaval met the Duchess of Cumberland at Calais, and kissed her hand.' She said it (not, I presume, the hand kissed) ' was disagreeable at first, but she should soon be used to it.' The marriage was legal, as the Royal Family had been specially exempted from Lord Hardwicke's Marriage Act by the King himself, who had declared that it was an indignity to the Princes of the Blood Royal to be placed on a level with the rest of his subjects. The marriage of the Cumberlands was, therefore, additionally unpleasant to the haughty young monarch, whose annoyance was further increased by the Duchess of Cumberland's brother, Colonel Lutterell, being returned just at this time to Parliament as member for the county of Middlesex.

LORD RONALD SUTHERLAND GOWER

The King sent orders to Prince Henry that he was not to appear at Court, and he also instructed his representatives at foreign Courts not to receive the Duke and Duchess. At the end of November the newly-wedded pair returned to England, and were permitted to live at Cumberland Lodge, in Windsor Park, but without the guard of sentries. For all his obstinacy, George III. had a vein of good nature in his character, and but for the influence of his wife, who never forgave what she considered a derogation in royal dignity, would, it is believed, have become reconciled to his brother. But Queen Charlotte was implacable; her sense of Court and royal etiquette had been cruelly tried by the marriage of two of her brothers-in-law to subjects, and she would not hear of forgiveness being extended to the Cumberlands.

We get some glimpses of the Cumberlands in Leslie's 'Life of Sir Joshua Reynolds.' One day in the month of April 1772 the Duchess is sitting to the President for her portrait, and the Duke accompanies her to Leicester Fields. George III. was not famous for the happiness of the questions he put to his subjects, but in this respect his brother Henry was even less happy. The Duke enters Sir Joshua's studio, 'blundering and swearing and stumbling over easels and stretchers' (to quote Leslie's account of this visit), and upon his wife whispering to him that he should say something to the President about her portrait on the easel, the only remark he can muster up, as he stares at the canvas upon which his pretty wife's face was 'laid on,' was, 'What, eh! so you always begin with the head—do you?'

It was owing to Anne's second marriage that the Royal Marriage Act was drawn up: it passed both Houses of Parliament in March 1772. This measure declared it illegal for all the descendants of George II. to contract marriages without the royal consent given under the Great Seal, but that such descendants, if over twenty-five years of age, could marry without the royal consent if they gave twelve months notice of their intention to the Privy Council, unless both Houses of Parliament disapproved the proposed match within the twelve months.

Of the Duchess, Horace Walpole writes: 'She has the most amorous eyes in the world, and eyelashes a yard long, coquette beyond measure, artful as Cleopatra, and completely mistress of all her passions and projects.' But this, I think, was written in 'Horry's' most exaggerated style. That Anne Lutterell was 'mistress of all her passions' is praise indeed; but I no more believe that she was a coquette, or as 'artful as Cleopatra,' than I believe she had eyelashes a yard long.

Her second husband had also been married before, his first wife being Olivia Wilmot, of whom nothing is known. The *soi-disant* Princess Olivia of Cumberland of a later day claimed to be descended

THE DUCHESS OF CUMBERLAND

from this first marriage of the Duke of Cumberland ; but she had no proofs to support her claims. The Duke died in 1790, unmourned, his love for his wife being the only trait of interest in his vacuous character. His widow lived until 1803.

There are two other portraits of the Duchess by Gainsborough besides the unfinished one of which such a beautiful reproduction is given here. One is a life-size full-length in her robes ; the other is a delightful little painting in which she is walking through a wooded glade with the Duke, whom she overtops by a good head or more. This is one of those subjects in which Gainsborough excelled, combining vivid portraiture with exquisite landscape, and it was one of his earliest portraits of the Royal Family. The two unfinished portraits of the husband and wife were probably never seen by the public until they were shown in the New Gallery in 1891. Gainsborough, whose magic brush could make even George III. look interesting and Queen Charlotte distinguished, has in this fine sketch of the Duke given the King's brother the manner and bearing of a gentleman.

The name of Cumberland has not been a lucky one in the House of Guelph or to those royal dukes who have borne it. The title received an evil lustre from the uncle of Anne Lutterell's husband, William Augustus, that Duke of Cumberland who has left the most unenviable record of any English prince, and whose nickname, 'The Butcher,' popularly given him because of his barbarous suppression of the Scottish rebellion of the 'Forty-five,' will cling to him for all time. Prince Henry himself was too characterless to be bad, but he in no way added dignity to the title. In the next generation his nephew, Ernest Augustus, created Duke of Cumberland by his father, George III., was by far the most unpopular Prince of his time. If we may judge from the memoirs of the time, there is little doubt that, had he succeeded his brother William IV. upon the throne, his reign would have been the shortest in our history, so universally detested was he by all sorts and conditions of men. Fortunately for England, the Duke of Cumberland's elder brother, Edward, left a daughter to whom her uncle's crown descended—one who lived through a long and honoured life, and by whose pure home, and perfect conduct, both in matters political as well as social, the Monarchy again received the respect and loyalty of the nation. That sovereign has made the name of Victoria illustrious throughout the world-wide dominions over which for sixty-one years she was the beloved and honoured monarch.

H.R.H. The Duke of Cumberland.

From the Royal Collection at Windsor Castle.

Gainsborough   Swan & Slater Engraving

H.R.H. The Duke of Cumberland.

From the Royal Collection at Windsor Castle.

Gainsborough pinxt.   Swan Electric Engraving Co.

THE CITY IN THE SAND
BY ROBERT HICHENS

AND is curiously fascinating. Children love it. Before we have built our first castle in the air most of us have built our first castle in the sand. We have felt, with a keen delight, the shining grains sifting through our eager little fingers. We have made nests for ourselves in sand, or graves, or robbers' lairs. Over ramparts of sand we have looked forth upon imaginary enemies. From sandy watch-towers we have played Sister Anne. Stretched upon warm sand we have known our first waking dreams—dreams that were made musical by flowing seatides, that were filled with the white light, the ethereal innocence of foam. Never does the sun shine so brightly in a child's eyes as when it shines across sand. No flower is so beautiful to the child as the little lonely rose that blows in sand, the nomad flower that seems to have paused to enjoy a sweet siesta in some long journey towards a hidden clime. Nature speaks her first words to the child most clearly in the Paradise of the sand. For air is the very voice of Nature, holding her soul and all her secrets, and the air that travels, so lightly, so fervently across the plains of the sand is keen with the magic of all central things and humours.

I have felt the fascination of sand in many places, the fascination of its exquisite monotony, of its delicate colour, of its warmth and golden softness by day, of its pale ghostliness by night. On English seaboards I have exulted in its firm beauty, walking along the verge of the waves. Beside the little rills of Ismailia, as twilight fell over the spectral shrubberies, and absinthe-coloured lights in the Canal heralded coming ships, I have looked towards that antique country whose wonders and whose glories the sand has held so long and parted from so reluctantly. Beyond the minarets and cupolas of Cairo I have tried to learn the secret which the sphinx knows, and the sand. With Monsieur Naville at Thebes I have heard the love-songs of Nubian labourers, and, bending down over the sand, have seen the bright, whimsical figures of long dead dynasties emerge from their sand seclusion of how many hundred years. At Margate I have watched the desecration of the sand by human happiness with all its paper bags. And in the Sahara I have seen the mirage which comes surely from the soul of the land, and is a faint and passing exhibition of its powers and of its many secrets. In the Sahara, too, I have dwelt in a city of the sand, one of the most barbaric and tumultuous cities which a traveller can visit, yet a city full of pathos and of dreams, alive sometimes with music that is mysteriously beautiful, passionate often with a love that has its hand upon its knife-hilt.

Tougourt is as strange as Tetuan, and has advantages which are

67

denied to that walled abode of typhoid, dead cats, and living leather-workers. It contains an inn where one may put up without much fear of fever, though with a certainty of sand and a probability of mosquitoes. The language of Paris may be heard there now and then. It is possible to sip an *apéritif* in anticipation of the evening meal. And for those Europeans whose consciences are heavy with sin there is a most kindly priest, whose good offices in another direction I have the utmost occasion to remember. For he it was who took me to visit the grimy tents of certain remarkable Sahara ladies on the huge sand-hill which towers beyond the city.

The approach to Tougourt is most impressive. It was towards nightfall in January when I drew near, after a four-days journey in the Sahara, alone with Arabs and far from any trace of civilisation. I had left the dancing black children of Mer'ier behind me, those laughing troops of boys in snowy white and girls in purple. I had said reluctantly good-bye to the ceremonious gardeners of Sidi-Amrane, whose life glides by in the palm thickets among the ripening dates. I had passed the sweet waters of Our'lana, the wild sandstorms of Chegga, and had seen beyond the white fringe of the great salt lakes the mirage of sailing ships die mysterious away. Now I heard the guard dogs barking to the first bright star, and the rustle of the horses' feet in the eternal sands. There was a tingling freshness of night in the air, a dying primrose light in the sky. The palm-trees were gone. The stony ground, tufted with dusty alfa, had vanished. We were in a vast world of sand, still, dreary, and pathetic; and far away a shadowy tower rose like a guide-post towards the sky, the great tower which dominates the mosque of Tougourt. The spaciousness of this desert world is so tremendous that it lays a spell upon the senses. The monotony of it is so complete that it is like a hypnotic touch quivering upon the soul. And the pigmy traveller creeping, like some little fly, across this wilderness of sand towards this hidden city is filled with a consciousness of insignificance which is almost overwhelming.

If he be at all imaginative, this consciousness abides.

The freedom and the passion of Tougourt, the fierceness of the life glowing, like some Nomad's fire, in the midst of the sandy solitude, the ample and barbaric manners of the people—now cruelly contemplative, now loftily ceremonious, avariciously polite, or maniacally excited—the wildness of the music and the dancing, the utter absence of what we call morals—all these facts smite upon the heart of the lonely European and prevent him from inflation. Jostled by Sheiks and Caïds, by Marabouts and plungers in artesian wells; by naked rascals who will not shrink before a provender of living scorpions; by negro giants, sand diviners, bronzed spahis and languid lovers of the hacheesh; he becomes aware that civilisation has its disadvantages, and learns to contemplate his tweeds with a chastened resignation. At moments, perhaps, he forgets them, and then he is happy.

In the guide-books you may learn something about Tougourt, or Tuggurt, as some people prefer to spell it. You may learn that the population is about seven thousand in an oasis of one hundred and ninety thousand palms, that the city is two hundred and four kilometres from the nearest railway station, that it is divided into quarters, occupied respectively by the citizens proper—I don't think I happened to meet any of them when I was there—the Jew converts to Islam, the negroes, and the foreigners; that it is built of burnt and sun-dried bricks, and that it is surrounded on every side by sand. You will find also that the garrison is native, and that there are scarcely any French in the place. Most of these few are officers. These facts, no doubt, are instructive and valuable. I soon forgot them and gave myself up to a barbaric dream, through which strange figures flitted—figures of women hung with golden chains and crowned with golden crowns, figures of dwarfs broad and bearded, muscular as Samson and diminutive as Little Tich, figures of Khodjas robed in orange brown, and of Kabyles in striped turbans and close-fitting jerseys of yellow and of red. And through my dream blew sand borne on the winds of the Sahara, filtered sand carried by little breezes from the palm-groves, stole sand moved by some process of Nature of which I was unaware. For the desert creeps about this city by day and by night, comes into the festivities when the tom-toms loudly beat, wanders to the doorstep of the dancers' abode as if to watch their antics, flies over the high wall of Monsieur the Aumonier's Court to play with his gazelles, lies at ease in the bath of the commandant in the palace on the hill, falls softly on the altar step of the Catholic chapel, and upon the red-brick floor of my bedroom in the inn; is to be found in the cage of the green parrot, Coco, who cries aloud in the arcade, in the Court of Justice where the functionaries of the Bureau Arabe gravely perform their duties, in the abattoir among the patient victims, in the Bain Maure where bronzed masseurs crack the sturdy limbs of the dwellers of the desert; everywhere and at all times, winter and summer, in calm and in tempest.

In Tougourt one eats, and dreams, and sins, and prays, and loves, and dances, and dies in sand. And one is buried in sand at the end of it all, unless one has escaped to a firmer region far from this empire of the sand and of the sun.

One realises what a speck in the sand the city is when one stands at the top of the great minaret, and looks down and then away to right and left. The huge-market place which sweeps round at right angles by the low arcades of the bazaars, and stretches up the hill to the barracks, and the imposing Bureau Arabe with its gigantic bronze cupola, its ornamented arches, its terraces and

parapets, is crowded with roaring camels, with merchants, with
actors, and with musicians. From here the hurrying people look
like excited dolls, the camels like toy monsters. The streets are
covered by palm-wood roofs to protect them from the sun of
summer, and above these roofs the pigeons are flying. On the flat
tops of the houses there are some lonely figures, women at work on
mysterious tasks, children in long robes flitting to and fro or bending over rubbish heaps in black and dingy corners. Goats skip
among them, cats bask in the heat, chickens scratch and flutter, and
pale dogs bark unceasingly. But how little it all means, this human
and animal life, to the watcher from the minaret—as little as our
fretful midge would mean to us if we leaned on the gold bar beside
the Blessed Damozel. For he sees the huge desert, the emblem of
eternity. In the near sands the tents of the nomads are scattered
thickly, each with its white or yellow dog tethered beside it. The
hedges of dried reeds make little avenues to the tent doors, pens for the
animals, or an odd semblance of tiny gardens, fairly secluded although
but few feet square. In the sun many stalwart forms are stretched,
shrouded in the mud-coloured patched robes the poorer Arabs
wear. Soldiers pass in and out to play cards with the women—
midgets, intent on trifling, petty pleasures. Everything that lives
and moves looks trifling and petty here, set in the leagues of whitish-
yellow sand. Even the groves of palms are as nothing. There
lie the graves in the Arab cemetery, out beyond the verge of the
city in the soft bosom of the sand. That swiftly-gliding black
thing, about the height of a pencil, is a religious fanatic praying
for the cemetery. If you were near him you would hear his voice,
praying loudly, buzzing prayers like a fly on a window pane in the
drowsy days of summer. By one white tomb—you can scarcely
see it from here—he makes many reverences and offers many suppli-
cations. Beneath it lie the bones of the Turcos who were murdered
by their own people in the revolution of 1871, fighting for their
masters, the French. All their names are inscribed upon it, and
this brief eulogy, half-covered by the sand grains:

> Morts au Champ·d'Honneur.
> Honneur et gloire.

They were children of the desert despite their uniform, their pledge of
fealty to conquerors over sea, a pledge sealed with their blood, and the
desert has them in safe keeping now. Their names are graven for
the rare traveller to read ; a fanatical Arab bows and wails above
them. But they are one with the sand, sunk far down, dispersed
in this great ocean whose waves roll away to the indigo line of the
horizon. Are their souls at ease among the roses in the paradise of
Allah ? The watcher in the minaret wonders. Then, from his height,
his eyes travel to the graves of the French who have died here, far

from the fair country all Frenchmen love so dearly; soldiers who have borne well the burden and heat of the African day, but have laid down the burden at last in this fierce land of the sun. They are there in the sand too, near to their dusky brothers. Over one tomb there is a cross, and the legend

ICI REPOSE

FABRIANI

JEAN BAPTISTE.

Who was he? What were his thoughts in dying here? Did he dread the nearness of his last sandy home, where the vipers nest and the pale pariah dogs roam drearily by night? How unforeseen are the fates of men, thinks the watcher in the minaret, as he casts one last look over the fascination of the Sahara, ere he turns to descend into the little, furious city.

The contrasts of Tougourt are amusing and abrupt. The first two buildings on either side of the broad road, which leads from the desert to the highest point of the town, are the dwelling of Monsieur the Aumonier, who takes care of the few French souls in exile here, and the great 'native *café* where all the dancers are gathered together. I remember, when I drove into Tougourt on my arrival, being struck by the humours of this situation. In the dying yellow light I saw Monsieur the Aumonier, standing at his door in his black soutane and a big white sun-helmet. His little white-and-yellow dog, Bous-Bous, stood contemplatively near him. On the opposite side of the way, well in the sand, was a frantic rag-bag praying aloud to Allah. She—it was a lady!—lifted her wrinkled, unwashed face to the evening star, wagged her head, from which black, braided tresses ornamented with fatma-hands depended, bowed her withered body, and cried her invocations. Behind her was the dancing house, yellow with light and shrill with music. Round its low door were gathered native soldiers smoking cigarettes. On the arm of one hung a most fearsome danseuse, her hands dyed red as if with blood, her spreading figure clad in scarlet and in gold tissue, her monstrous head smothered in feathers, many-coloured handker-chiefs, jewels, and strings of coins. Beyond the laughing soldiers, through the doorway, I perceived more heads of leaping women, ostrich plumes shaking, gold crowns glittering, red fingers fluttering like fingers of exulting murderesses. And with the music of the pipes was blended a piercing sound, a fierce tremolo ending in a peacock scream, as some rich Arab, carried away by the emotion of the moment, thrust a twenty-franc note among the turban folds of the master of the maids.

Above the flat roof of the dancing-house rose the wooden spokes of the palanquins, in which, when they have made enough money, the dancers are carried on camels to their tented dwellings

far distant in the south. They were black as the soutane of
Monsieur the Aumonier, who gravely regarded me as I passed by
between him and the wailing ragbag in the sand, the grandmother,
he informed me later, of the danseuse upon the soldier's arm.

In the winter, when the scorpions grow sleepy in the old walls
of the zgags, and the desert is alive with processions of date-laden
camels, the nomads descend upon Tougourt mysteriously as come
the yellow locusts on the winds. They camp in tents upon the
high sandhills round about, and invest us like a hostile host. The
seven thousand residents are swamped by this wild multitude, which
makes night golden with its camp fires, day vocal with its everlasting
chatter. These own children of the desert are very different from
the representatives of the many tribes whom one encounters at Biskra
and elsewhere in the comparatively civilised parts of Algeria.
Lean, filthy, almost black, hard and muscular as iron, their gaieties
are more brutal, their displays of feeling more wantonly unabashed.
Unveiled are their women, who sit at the tent doors weaving mats,
or idly waiting for custom. Withered mamas preside over the
distinctly unconventional proceedings of daughters who are often
brilliantly handsome, although obscured by layers of desert, which
—so Monsieur the Aumonier declared to me—are only removed
annually at the close of the Fast of Ramadan. When I beheld
these fashionable beauties, that epoch, though near, was not yet
fully come, and I was therefore compelled to summon up a spirit
of divination, to pierce in imagination beyond the seen to the
unseen, and to deduce from what obviously was, what presently
might be. Having achieved this feat, I agreed with Monsieur the
Aumonier, as we stood over our ankles in the sand, that, granted
the annual ablution, many of these ladies possessed the elements of
loveliness.

From the damsels on the sand hill let us pass, by night, into
the quarter where the decadents of Tougourt assemble after dark.
For there are decadents of the Sahara, minor poets, young gentlemen
who dye their nails with henna, and condescend to skirt dancing and
to the singing of songs which are distinctly morbid in tendency.
As the decadents of Paris have their cafés, so have the decadents of
the desert theirs. The one I visited is hidden under a black-browed
archway at the foot of the market place. It is called the Café of
the Smokers of the Hacheesh. Here, when the sun has set and the
fires of the nomads are warming naked limbs, comes Larbi the
sinuous dancer with his comrade Sahdah, the negro Ahmed Spaâ
of the Tribu of the Whites, Ben-Abid, who sings the songs of the
hacheesh, Kouidah, the boy who makes sweet music with two
spoons upon a piece of metal or a glass, Sadok, the holder of the
mighty pipe with the bowl of cocoanut, and many another devotee.
The door is very low; the place is small and very dark. Ceiling

and walls are black. Two candles, set almost on the floor, give a flickering illumination. The decadents crowd together cross-legged on the ground, many of them hooded, all wrapped in flowing robes. In the middle sit the pipe-holder and the musicians near the little furnace for the coffee. It is a hot and dreamy place, full of strange odours. Now some sweet incense burns or essence of rose is scattered. The smoke of the hacheesh floats up into the shadows and is lost, as the pipe circulates slowly from dusky hand to hand. The dreamers look at one another with heavy-lidded eyes and sway their bodies softly to and fro. Then Kouidah strikes his glass, and in a soft contralto voice murmurs 'Wurra-Wurra'; Aloûi, the minor poet, shakes his instrument of reeds; Safti plucks his guitar of goatskin backed by sand tortoise ; and Ben-Abid begins to sing to us of the dreams which hacheesh gives. It is an exquisite song with music like a dream, and Ben-Abid's voice is exquisite. The words begin with this sentence, sung in recitative:

> 'No one but God and I
> Knows what is in my heart ' ;

Then the refrain of Wurra-Wurra is murmured deep and low by all the decadents, and Ben-Abid tells of the dreams, strange, terrible, exultant, long almost as eternity that the drug of magic brings. Some one, hidden in the dark, beats softly on a tom-tom. The spoons tinkle on the glass like the plash of water falling. All the bodies sway. Then comes the recitative once more:

> ' The Gazelle dies in the water,
> The fish dies in the air,
> And I die in the desert sands
> For my love, for my sad love.'

By the door, where there is a little space, a white figure appears. It is Larbi dressed in a tight Zouave jacket and a long, pleated white skirt. And while the song continues, and the 'Wurra-Wurra' is whispered almost under the breath of the sleepy decadents of Tougourt, he performs his dance, a dance morbid and barbaric, very graceful, very drowsy. All his gestures are unfinished and suggestive, like the gestures of a sleeper whose soul is obscurely agitated far down below the layers of his sleep. His eyes are closed. His head quivers. His long, bare throat works. The moon peeps in at him under the black-browed arcade, and the great pipe of the hacheesh steals round from hand to hand.

As I go out the minor poet joins me. He is young, and quite the largest minor poet I have ever seen. His hue is peculiar, resembling that of a grey kid glove which has been exposed to the weather and has known hard times. He wears a pale-blue robe and has much aplomb. I find that he is quite accomplished. He has travelled, and he speaks French. He also tries to write in French, and shows me several minor poems in that language. They are naturally full of mistakes, but they contain some pretty phrases. They are very lovesick, and are addressed to various danseuses—to Halima, to Borria, to Aïchouch. The last is compared to a little viper of the sand, to a golden date, to a lotos flower, and to a squirrel. Like most minor poets, Aloüi is inclined to a vague impropriety in his verse. In one or two of his mournful numbers the vagueness vanishes and the impropriety remains. I forgive him, remembering he is an Arab. As he bids me good-bye and returns to the Café, I think again that he is quite the largest minor poet I have ever seen. He must be much over six feet in height. His head is like a cannon ball. His legs are sturdy as tree trunks. Yet he has something of the languishing air one knows so well in London, and the luscious smile, half-melancholy, half-saccharine, which, in every land, beseems the minor poet.

I breathe a prayer for his success, and seek my sandy pillow. It is a windy night.

In these dark and windy nights, when there is a drifting and dense fog of sand in the city, you must be careful if you walk abroad in Tougourt. Keep your revolver charged and within easy reach of your hand. The nomadic Arab is not the most trustworthy person in the world, and the important citizen is generally attended by a servant who is well armed.

The present Caïd of Tougourt is a short but imposing man with a pale skin, intelligent, penetrating eyes, a well-trimmed black beard, and a ruthlessly dignified manner. His health is delicate, for, some time ago, his life was attempted by poison, and he has suffered internally ever since. In the summer he travels to Europe to take his annual 'cure,' like any English premier or American millionaire. I found him an agreeable companion, though occasionally almost embarrassingly abrupt. For instance, one of my first conversations with him was something like this:

THE CAÏD. Do you have good health?
MYSELF. Thank you, yes. Do you?
THE CAÏD. Certainly not.
MYSELF. I am so sorry.
THE CAÏD. Sorrow cannot heal.
MYSELF. I hope it is nothing serious?
THE CAÏD. Yes, it is.
MYSELF. I trust you will soon be cured.
THE CAÏD. No: impossible. It is the effect of poison.
MYSELF. I am grieved.
THE CAÏD. I say again, grief cannot heal.
MYSELF. But I hope the doctors——
THE CAÏD. Hope is a poor remedy for a stomach overturned.
MYSELF. What I meant was——

ROBERT HICHENS

THE CAÏD. Your meaning is clear to me. And again I say that neither your grief nor hope can restore my stomach to its former condition.

MYSELF. [*Silence that might be felt.*]

The most famous and interesting inhabitant of the district of Tougourt is certainly Mohammed El Aïd Ben Ali Tidjani, Marabout, Zaouia de Tamacine. This majestic personage is one of the greatest Marabouts of Africa, and dwells in patriarchal state in the sacred village of Tamacine, surrounded by brothers, wives, children and adoring hangers-on of all sorts. I duly went to his palace to pay my homage. After a drive of two hours across plains of sand, I reached Tamacine, a village of dried mud and brick, surrounded by a high brown wall pierced with narrow loop-holes. Passing through a tunnel, and under an arch, above which was a window with an iron grille, I came to a great door of palm-wood, sheeted with iron. My attendant, Doud, struck upon it. A negro opened to us, and conducted us in silence through various courts, and under various archways, till we reached another door, on which was written, 'L'Entrée de Sidi Laïd.' This being un-barred, we mounted a winding stair and entered the reception room of the Marabout. Doud nearly had a fit, and I drew a deep breath of surprise, for here, in the heart of the desert, I found myself in an arched apartment containing positively tables and chairs, grandfather and cuckoo clocks, a writing bureau, and a mantelpiece on which cabinet photographs were carelessly scattered. Even as we gasped a cuckoo—most definitely Swiss—emerged from its wooden seclusion, and, in a voice quite startlingly European, proclaimed the hour of noon.

But more wonders were in store. The negro servant, having signed to us to be seated in two armchairs, glided away and returned almost immediately bearing a large box of polished wood, which he set down on the table near me. Doud's eyes were by this time round as full moons, and I also was considerably strung up. The negro opened the box and put in his hand. I heard a sharp click, and then upon our listening ears poured forth the strains of ' Come o'er the moon-lit sea,' from *Masaniello*. For a quarter of an hour, by the cuckoo clock, we sat to hear it. Then the negro ushered us into a second room, carrying the box with him, made us sit down once more, and again turned on ' Come o'er the moon-lit sea.' Another quarter of an hour passed by, and I was beginning to feel the monotony of sitting in the Sahara in Auber's perpetual company, when a second retainer arrived, and requested me to descend to the mosque, where the Marabout would receive me. We met in a sort of cloisters, and had a short colloquy through an interpreter.

The Marabout, who is a large and dignified old man with a

smiling, yellow face, was surrounded by a crowd of Arabs. His bearing was papal. He was clad in autumn-leaf tints, brown and yellow, and carried a tall staff from which hung green ribands. When he heard I came from London to visit him he seemed highly delighted, touched my hand and his lips, and took me himself to see the shrine over which he presides. This is the tomb of the venerated saint, Cheikh Sidi El Hadj Ali ben Sidi El Hadj Aïssa, who died in 1260. It lies in a small chamber under a cupola exquisitely decorated with Moorish work. Flags of different colours droop around and above it, and from the ceiling hangs a crystal chandelier. The tomb, which is surrounded by an iron railing, is covered with a red velvet pall, dusty with grains of sand. As I was leaving the Marabout said a hurried word to Doud, who then informed me that, feeling sure I wished to be polite, the Marabout desired me to know that he would consider it a delicate attention on my part if I gave him twenty francs.

I did so and took my leave.

That this sacred personage is not likely to come upon the parish just yet seems fairly certain. He is overwhelmed with gifts, and I was told that the day before I visited him he received, from a devotee of Tunisia, forty camels laden with barley, and that he kept not only the loads but also the camels which bore them.

It is very good to be a Marabout of Africa. But I suppose it is sometimes very bad to be a nomad of the Sahara. Two days before I left Tougourt, in the deep sand before Monsieur the Aumonier's door, I saw two old Sahara women grubbing patiently. I wondered why they grubbed. The next day, towards evening, I saw them again, still squatting there and turning the sand over in their withered hands. I asked the Aumonier what they were doing. 'O,' he said, 'they dropped a halfpenny there yesterday when they were coming from the market.' The coin was the Algerian equivalent of our halfpenny. On hearing this I gave each of the old women a copper and departed to my inn. But the next morning when, at dawn, I departed from Tougourt I found them both in the same place, still searching in the sand for the lost fortune.

I was sorry to go. Only some forty travellers visit Tougourt in the course of the year, and I daresay many of them think it dreary, comfortless, and savage. So, I suppose, it is. But it has a fascination all its own which cannot easily be forgotten. Its isolation in the endless wastes of sand, its barbaric life, its hordes of strange wanderers come up out of the south to spend their winter on the sandhills round about it, the glory of its sunshine, the glamour of its moonlight falling upon the bronze cupolas of its public buildings, upon its minaret, upon the wide market-place and the flat roofs of the zgags, the pathos of its music—whether sung by the decadents of the hacheesh café, or by the gipsies round their tents—the flickering gold of its camp-fires and the wild movements of its jewelled dancers—all these things stir the imagination of the traveller, and remain long in his memory.

The sun shone when I left Tougourt. In their terraced court all the dancers were asleep. But Monsieur the Aumonier was at his door and Bous-Bous stood contemplatively beside him.

'You will never come again,' said the Aumonier. 'You are leaving me alone with the sands and the scorpions. Good-bye.'

But I answered, 'Au revoir!' and I meant it most sincerely.

PERSONAL RECOLLECTIONS OF RUBINSTEIN. BY ALEXANDER McARTHUR

NTON RUBINSTEIN spent the best years of his life in searching for the *juste milieu*, not only in art but also in life itself. Up to the last, so great was the strength of his intellect and his optimism, he could scarcely be brought to recognise that he was hankering after a chimera. The declining years of his life were saddened and darkened, not by the conviction, as one might hastily suppose, that art and life as we know them are incapable of perfection, or that we are incapable of attaining perfection in either, but that he had not discovered the road to this perfection. He was at times almost childish in his hopefulness and his desire to right things. Our helplessness in relation to many of the inner mysteries of life and the perplexities of art had no existence for him. 'There is a way to avoid or remedy this or that evil,' he would say with a leonine toss of his head, when faced by evident confusion in existing conditions; and sometimes he really found this way.

In the early 'sixties the state of the musical tastes and musical ignorance in Russia was appalling. To-day, thanks to Rubinstein, Russia is foremost in musical progress. Had Rubinstein been less hopeful and less of an enthusiast and a worker, we might not have had Tschaikowsky, Rimsky-Korsakoff, Raichmanoff, Glazunoff, Liadoff, among composers, or Paderewski, Petschnikoff, Sapelnikoff, Essipoff, and Siloti, among executants—to name but a few of the brilliant galaxy of musical stars that have appeared in the firmament of Slavic art since the founding of the St. Petersburg Conservatory and the sister institutions at Moscow, Warsaw, and elsewhere.

Rubinstein was a born reformer. The desire to do something for humanity, and especially for art, amounted with him to a passion. Not to have done something useful in his life, to have lived without being of service to his fellows, he deemed the greatest curse that could fall upon him. Then, too, as one only too seldom finds with artists, there was complete absence of personal ambition in this desire of his. It was instigated and inspired only by a very rare and lovely philanthropy. Time and again he sacrificed his own artistic and pecuniary advancement to promote the welfare of some scheme of this nature, and the sum total of his financial help, could it be estimated, would represent a large fortune.

In 1862, Rubinstein, with the Grand Duchess Helen Pavlovna, sister of Emperor Nicholas II., Princess Elizabeth Witgenstein, Mesdames Verigin and Abaza, Count Matthew Vielgorski, Vassili

ALEXANDER McARTHUR

Kologrivov, the latter a landowner and chinovnik, who adorned, instead of, as is more usual, discrediting, the title of amateur, and Stasov, a musical critic, founded the Russian Musical Society, which to-day includes the symphony societies and conservatories of the various towns in Russia.

In 1867, after five years of gratuitous labour, Rubinstein threw up the directorship of the St. Petersburg Conservatory in anger, and spent over twenty years looking on in sullen discontent at things as they were under a new *régime*. Then, the wisdom of his advice and arguments becoming apparent, the committee of the Conservatory begged him to undertake the management once more, which he readily did. Rubinstein, having made an exhaustive study of the various musical institutions of Europe, was, outside of his genius and attainments, which placed him ahead of all others in Russia, peculiarly fitted for the post. The only question that puzzled him completely in his undertaking was that relating to the various methods of teaching singing. Those inside and outside of the Conservatory were always discussing this question and deploring the condition of the singing classes. Rubinstein heard what one clique in the Conservatory had to say, and he listened just as patiently to the several other cliques, and ended by being disgusted with all. He could not solve the problem himself. He was altogether dissatisfied with the work, and knew that it was a blot on the institution, and one for which, he frankly acknowledged, he could find no remedy. The singing classes of the Conservatory were his *bête noire*, and caused him absolute suffering.

I remember one evening finding Rubinstein in the hour before dinner sitting in semi-darkness before his study table, evidently plunged in the gloomiest of thought, for his cigarette was lying unlit in its holder. It was a miserable day in February. The snow outside was several feet deep; the wind was bitterly cold; and the leaden-hued sky that for four long months had lain as a pall over the city-on-the-Neva seemed gloomier, more depressing, than ever. Rubinstein tried to smile as a welcome to my arrival; but the attempt was a failure. His face was dark with anger; his lips were compressed. I dreaded that hour, for Rubinstein had unexpected faculties of making time pass unpleasantly for those about him when badly ruffled in his feelings. He drummed on the green baize cloth with his fingers. I sat on the edge of the writing-table, my back to the window, and did not say anything. On the days I went to dine with Rubinstein I always felt myself the happiest person in Europe ; but just then the atmosphere of that room, and Rubinstein's bent figure and frowning face would have oppressed the stoutest heart. Clearly there had been a row at the Conservatory. 'Why don't you smoke?' he thundered at length, as

79

he almost flung his cigarette case in my face. I lit a cigarette without a word : then I took up his cigarette and holder, and, lighting the former, handed them to him. I fully expected to have them thrown at me, for Rubinstein was far from polite when angry ; but to my surprise he took them quite gently, and just as soon as he had taken a few puffs, I said boldly : 'Bear with a sore head. If the world could only see the great Rubinstein now—Demon—(a name of mine for him, which he liked)—or I could photograph you and give it to Markoff for a painting in the Hermitage !'

Rubinstein was on the point of exploding several times ; but I kept on talking and puffing in his eyes the smoke from the cigarette.

'I wish I were as happy and careless as you are,' he said at length. 'You are happy because you are young, and youth spells ignorance. But I tell you—and mark my words, you will remember them fifty years hence—the best thing you could do, while you are young and ignorant, if you would save yourself suffering, is to go now and cut your throat.'

'You suffer as badly as that ?' I asked doubtingly.

'As you have no conception, that Conservatory is my crown of thorns. Everything is wrong. My time has been given for nothing. Sometimes I believe that half the world is peopled by idiots. I have lived to no purpose.'

'You cannot say that while there is left a prelude of Chopin's for you to interpret.'

His face brightened at once.

'And by the way,' I continued, going into the next room to the pianoforte, 'how does this phrase go ?' and I purposely played the phrase contrarily to his teaching. Rubinstein was by my side in a moment, and, pushing me from the key-board, sat down before the instrument.

Five minutes later he had forgotten his rage. He began to play the Chopin preludes, then some of the shorter pieces of Schubert, which he loved. In such moments, although it is hard to believe this, Rubinstein played as he never played for an audience, and an hour so spent with him was well worth a lifetime following of misery. At dinner on that particular evening, as rarely happened —probably owing to the weather—we were alone. I handed him a knife with which to cut his throat and mine if he so desired. He growled as he laughed, and then began to tell me what the trouble had been—a quarrel among the singing professors and his disgust with all their methods.

'I begin to think,' he said, 'that people are like birds : some sing and some don't sing, and their method is in their throats. One cannot make a nightingale out of a thrush. But the pretensions of these singing professors! That is what one cannot forgive, what makes me wild, for the less they know the more they pretend to know.

For three years during the ten months of a working year Rubinstein spent his entire life from nine until five, and at least two evenings weekly, at the Conservatory, superintending classes, teaching, and framing laws. During this time he wrote an elaborate memorial on the question of musical instruction in Russia—how it could best be promoted and advanced—which memorial lies in the archives of the library of the Conservatory at St. Petersburg. When Rubinstein had got things into the running shape he wanted, it fell short of his memorial although he made wholesale changes; but at last, when he had done all he felt he could do, he left Russia and settled for the best part of each year in Germany.

It was in Germany that much of his 'Gedankenkorb,' which in English signifies 'Thought-basket,' was jotted down. Rubinstein wanted to square himself and excuse himself to posterity. He felt he had done little or nothing for the future of art in spite of earnest striving; but he wanted at least to leave on record that he had striven. His 'Gedankenkorb' was born of vexation.

In his boyish years, especially during the months of his pecuniary difficulty in Vienna, Rubinstein had been an inveterate scribbler; but as he grew older literary aspirations forsook him entirely. He grew to detest writing; even a necessary signature was an annoyance. As religiously as Chopin, he avoided letter-writing; in fact, he corresponded only with his mother. He never attempted to answer a letter himself, invariably imposing that task on those of his friends or pupils whom he trusted. From this dislike of his it can be gathered that the jotting down of his 'Thoughts' was done neither casually nor for pastime. Rubinstein felt he had something to say, and, although at first sight these 'Thoughts' seemed somewhat tentative and confused, deep wisdom and varied experience prompted and inspired most of them.

All the known writings of Rubinstein, not including the memorial in the St. Petersburg Conservatory, if collected, would make but a medium-sized volume. They are an article on Music in Russia, written in 1860; a letter to the *Signale*, replying to the proposition that he should edit the classics; an article on Sacred Opera, one of a collection from 'Vor den Coulissen,' printed in the *Signale* of June 1882; his Autobiography, his 'Conversation on Music,' and his 'Gedankenkorb' or Thought-Basket.

Of these six pieces his 'Conversation on Music' is undoubtedly the most coherent in plan. Rubinstein is here quite fearless in his utterances. As a rule he talked freely on musical matters before his friends, but always with the proviso that his sayings should not be repeated or made public. He was wise in a sense in this. Take for instance his attitude towards Wagner, which by the malicious or the ignorant could be construed as the outcome of mere jealousy. This attitude was the source of much discussion among musicians; but the outside public knew very little about it till he himself made it public. However, only half of what he thought of the subject is given. Rubinstein detested the Wagner of the latter period heartily. He detested all Wagner's art theories, his pose, his innovations, and always predicted that his influence on the future of art would be most baneful.

The mere name Wagner uttered in his presence was as a red rag to a bull. Night after night as we sat round his dinner table, discussing various events and conditions of art, and especially music, he has given utterance to sayings that might fill a book. It was impossible to avoid the subject of Wagner and his theories; especially strangers, ignorant of Rubinstein's antipathy, were sure to hit on this very subject. It was on such occasions that Rubinstein had a rare opportunity to tear his passion to tatters. I hardly believe there was one single tenet of Wagner's that he did not attack vigorously. As to the Musik-Drama, he had hardly vocabulary enough to denounce it, employing French, German, or English words, when Russian terms failed him. 'Wagner had no understanding of music in its supreme essence,' he often said, 'or he would never have gone to the assistance of the other arts in constructing a Musik-Drama—he thereby acknowledges his poverty and limitations as a musician.' Sometimes, when discussing this subject, Beethoven's bringing in of words in the last movement of the Ninth Symphony would be brought forward as an argument for Wagner, and then Rubinstein would patiently explain, to the unutterable surprise of the new-comer, that, far from seeking assistance of poetry, Beethoven, after saying all that was unutterable in the first three movements of the symphony, had desired to say something 'utterable' in the last.

I have seen rabid Wagnerians come away from Rubinstein's dinner-table with a dazed, distressed expression that was comical. Fresh probably from one of the many shrines in Germany, having drunk to the full of the many traditions and theories of the great Bayreuth giant, and priding themselves on such knowledge, their reception at Rubinstein's hands was perplexing. The best of it was, too, that Rubinstein's arguments were forcible and convincing, and few intellects were capable of measuring a lance with him. On one occasion I saw a young disciple of Wagner, who had listened to and violently opposed Rubinstein's arguments at dinner, sit on a couch in a corner alone, after he had left the table, while the others played cards and drank tea. When it was time to go, the young German took his hat and coat mechanically from Matve, Rubinstein's valet, and went without a word of farewell to his host, so rapt was he in his own thoughts. An hour later the apartment was shut up for the night. Rubinstein laughingly related to us how he was forced to jump from his bed, throw on a dressing-gown, fearing fire, to find the young fellow pulling the bell and profuse in apologies, having returned to say good-night.

Rubinstein invariably insisted that Wagner had landed young musicians who sought to follow in his footsteps into a quagmire made up of all musical nastiness.

Although he made very vigorous statements anent Wagner and others, notably Berlioz and Liszt, Rubinstein was far from wishing to induce his pupils, as followers, to think as he did. In this respect he was the most broad-minded of musicians. Now and then an expression implying 'Et tu, Brute' might darken his eyes, as he watched the delight which Wagner's music gave to one or other of his pupils; but even so he much preferred a spirit of opposition to a slavish admission. Time alone, as he had so often said, would prove the wisdom or the folly of his belief in regard to Wagner's influence on art.

It was not to Wagner alone, however, that he objected; for, as he put it in his 'Gedankenkorb,' 'Creation in all branches of contemporary art seems to me like the electric light, bright illumination, but without fire.' This certainly is a statement that cannot be overlooked, or lightly taken, for it will surely make history in future decades.

Even the casual reader will be inspired and impressed, in Rubinstein's 'Conversation on Music,' by what he has to say about Beethoven's Ninth Symphony, on Beethoven as an opera composer (Rubinstein considered 'Fidelio,' the greatest opera ever written— surely a daring paradox), on symphonic music (on Bach, Bach, whom he worshipped), on Schumann, Schubert, Glinka, and Chopin— after whose name he writes *Finis musicæ*. The whole book is a very mine of thought and musical philosophy.

Paradox is too often the subterfuge of unknown writers as a bid for fame or notice. Rubinstein had no desire or ambition for either. Fame was his from his childhood, and his paradoxes come, therefore, from depth of thought impossible to corrupt or question. Rubinstein wrote as he felt and thought, and there was much of *naïveté* in both. Strange as some of his paradoxes are, they are all of them bound to excite controversy and incite deeper musical feeling on the part of his readers. Years ago, when he first expressed himself about Beethoven's Ninth Symphony he was laughed at. To-day half Russia thinks as he does, and in every musical centre he has followers.

There is a note of pessimism and world-weariness in all Rubinstein's writings that is saddening. They have the true Slavic

RECOLLECTIONS OF RUBINSTEIN

touch of melancholy. The evening of his life was cloudy. He
had lived too much, and at fifty was a man of seventy. His
intellect alone had grown stronger. For this reason he wanted
more from life and more from art-workers than either gave. He
was a musical Hamlet: the times were out of joint for him, and
he never could settle satisfactorily with himself the question
as to whether he was born a decade too late or a decade too
early.

People were constantly disappointing him. His house was a
centre for all foreign artists staying in St. Petersburg; and how
often we have listened to his expectations concerning this or that
artist, only to see in the end his silent gesture of contentment and
impatience when they had spoken their adieus, and Rubinstein stood
in the small vestibule of his hall thinking. Rubinstein was always
searching for talent and originality, and it was amazing how, after
each failure, he started afresh with the same enthusiasm, and was
always eager to welcome new comers.

In the last paragraph of his 'Conversation on Music,' he tells
us: 'I returned to my studio and remained standing there, meditating whether it might not be the musical Götterdammerung that is
now breaking upon us.' Those of us who saw him frequently
often noticed just such a pose. However, it never lasted long. He
was *blasé* only at times, and for short periods.

Probably there has never been a human being more puzzling in
individuality than Rubinstein. In one passage of his 'Gedankenkorb'
he tells us truly: 'I am in constant self-contradiction. I think
differently from what I feel. I am an atheist from a religious and
sectarian point of view; yet I am convinced it would be misery if
mankind had no religion, no church, no God. I am a Republican,
but realise that the proper government for men as they are is a strict
monarchy. I love my neighbour as myself, yet see that mankind
deserves little more than contempt.'

Rubinstein as an author was not ambitious. He wrote clearly,
concisely, and without frills. Having no desire to shine in literature, his efforts were all directed towards helping his fellows in an art
which he deemed the most difficult of all, an art towards which his
reverence was boundless.

The misfortune of music has hitherto been that it was outsiders, rather than practical musicians, who discussed and wrote of
it as an art. The sayings of a musician of Rubinstein's rank will
ever be of vast value and absorbing interest. It is a matter of
congratulation that, despite his dislike of literary work, Rubinstein
felt an imperative call of expressing his sentiments in print.

84

THE FIRST CHURCH OF THE RESTORATION, AMERICAN
BY RICHARD LE GALLIENNE

[I am compelled to disguise the names of the people taking part in the following story, as their real names are too well known in New York Society. Essentially, however, the story is true, as time will prove.]

S the Reverend Arthur Winslow stepped out on to Fifth Avenue at four of a May morning—to be precise, the morning of May 14, 1901—any one who had observed him would readily have understood why he, of all men, or rather all clergymen, should have been chosen for the remarkable revelation which had been made to him during the most momentous night of his life, a revelation with which his whole being was turbulently on fire. He dismissed the automobile which had been awaiting him since one o'clock—the automobile with which, as a fashionable divine, he did his district visiting—and turned toward the park. He needed to walk. As he strode away, with the vigour of an athlete, and 'the grace of a young god,' he paused once to look at the house he had left—a famous house, the owner of which was known for his combination of enormous wealth with exquisite taste. Probably no one ever passes the house without saying to himself, or his companion, 'That is Mulciber Jackson's house.' But, if that passer-by knew how much more that house means than he has the dimmest notion of, with what a different wonder would he gaze at it. The minister knew—that is he had known for an hour or two. He had often dined in that house before. He was quite accustomed to dining with millionaires. Was he not known as 'The Millionaire's Vicar?' Yet he had never had the smallest suspicion of what he now knew. Not a hint. The secret had indeed been well kept.

The world was all sensitive with the dawn. A mysterious purity was in the air. Fifth Avenue looked like some fairy-street just made in a dream. The indescribable eloquence of the silent coming of light thrilled the heart. From masses of sleepy mother-of-pearl, the sky changed to handfuls of fire-red opals, and spears of pure gold shot up here and there through the tumbled colours of the clouds.

Winslow had an impulse to go on his knees, right there in Fifth Avenue, before the august Light-Bringer, but he forbore; though the impulse showed the insight which had prompted the remarkable proposal which was filling his heart with the blended exhilaration of joy and fear. Within the seclusion of the park, the impulse grew even stronger. The vivid grass, almost phantasmal in the freshness of its green, the spiritual look of the trees—

FIRST CHURCH OF THE RESTORATION

'the trees about a temple'—the consecration which seemed mysteriously poured over the most ordinary object, affected him almost to the point of ecstasy. He looked at his Christian clothes with a strange smile. Had he been in a more secluded place, he would have torn them from him, and stood up naked in the dawn, a radiant young priest of Apollo.

Mulciber P. Jackson was one of those powerful ugly men whom women love; of massive build, and rough-hewn face, bearded as a rock is bearded with ferns and mosses, he was, at the same time, ponderously lame. He had a humour which was like the laughing of a volcano, and he could also, at times, suddenly reveal a charm of gentleness, tender as those surprising nooks of green that nestle in the fire-mountain's side.

His wife was the most beautiful woman in New York. As such, I presume she is not easily identifiable. Were I to tell you her real name, you would recognise her at once as the most beautiful woman in the world. The Mulciber Jacksons were somewhat mysterious in their origin. Of course, it was said that Mulciber Jackson was a Jew, or 'a Hebrew' as they politely say in America. It is one of the many privileges of all rich men to be credited with belonging to one of the two most remarkable races that have made human history, and still go on making it. Acute observers referred Mulciber Jackson to that other race, and there they were undoubtedly right; for he was certainly more Greek than Jew. His wife's face was pure Greek, as a woman's face is allowed to be. Some spiteful tongues said that Mrs. Mulciber Jackson imitated the Venus of Milo; but her beauty was too adventurous, too rich and strange, to merit the accusation. Even if Mulciber Jackson had not been ugly, he would still have attracted to his house all the beauty of New York; for, as I have said, he was rich as well. Indeed, to dine at his table was the quickest way to become acquainted with the classics of American beauty and wealth.

Yes, he was a remarkable man, but only those who shared his confidence as Winslow now shared it really knew how remarkable. Beneath his somewhat terrible drollery, he hid a purpose that could only flag with achievement. Generally known as the funniest man in New York; he was, actually, the divinest and, some would say, its most dangerous dreamer. What was he rich for? His dream? Why was his life so splendidly hospitable? His dream? Why did he trouble himself about the Rev. Arthur Winslow? His dream. What was his dream? You shall hear.

Dinner at Mulciber Jackson's was apt to be almost too showily symbolic of the power and beauty of America. If one could make any criticism against the taste of his entertainments, it was that his guests were too uniformly remarkable. There was never any one to be met at his dining-table that was not in some way or another illustrious, except possibly, yourself. You almost felt that you had been asked to a dinner of public monuments.

Winslow had certainly felt that till he had grown used to Mulciber Jackson's dinners; and, the first occasion on which he had sat at the great man's table, he had noted, with a certain terror, the way [the guests—for the most part magnates from Wall Street, purposely chosen by a host who realised the clerical interest in rich people—had talked about various gigantic undertakings, as Titans might spin tops together. To hear them talk of fifty millions of dollars—as if the subject wasn't money at all, only 'horse-power,' or so many 'volts,' put Winslow's customary eloquence to silence. To his fancy they were like so many presidents of the Elements. Here was a man talking of owning the Sea, as though he were Neptune; another of electric power, as though he had bought up the bolts of Jupiter; a third discussing rapid transit as though he were Mercury; and there was a woman who talked of corn as though she were Ceres. There, too, sat a new god discussing oil in a loud voice.

How curiously near the fact Winslow's fancy was he had little known. But the occurrences of this last evening recalled and confirmed it.

During dinner he had been vaguely conscious that something unusual was in the air. His beautiful companion had been indiscreet enough to half ask him questions, which, she remembered too late, she had no right to put.

'Was he . . . .?' but 'No! she forgot . . . .'

And he remembered afterwards that the faces of the men wore a curiously uplifted, one might almost say, religious expression.

When the ladies had withdrawn, Mulciber Jackson took the opportunity of a private word with Winslow. He had not, of course, failed to notice the effect on his face, of a sudden strain of music, stealthily escaped and quickly recaptured, as it might be said, from the limits of the world: an apparition of sound strangely coming and going along subterranean corridors of approach.

'Arthur,' he said—for he was on terms of affectionate friendship with the minister—'I have a surprise for you to-night. You will, I know, understand and appreciate; and I know it will startle you at first, but, after the first surprise, well, I have hopes I will talk of later.'

Presently the guests rose and departed to a quarter of the house which was quite new to Winslow. A quiet-looking door opened up a deep passage slanting gently downwards. The walls of the passage were decorated by frescoes of a decidedly religious character but the religion was one that has long since passed away.

FIRST CHURCH OF THE RESTORATION

Mulciber took Winslow's arm, and detained him a little way behind the rest.

'I suppose you never really suspected your friend Mulciber of religion,' he said. 'You will see; I shall be surprised if you are not profoundly stirred—and even changed; or rather decided.'

Mulciber was unwontedly nervous for so rugged and hairy a man; and his limp made his face twitch painfully.

The corridor at length brought them to an exquisite little elevator of painted cedar, in which they were rapidly carried as it seemed into the very centre of the earth. As they glided downwards, strains of the same music Winslow had heard before came up to meet them; and presently, as the elevator finished its journey, Winslow found himself in a hushed world of worship and white marble. As from a small private chapel he was looking out into a beautiful little Greek temple.

The temple was already filled with kneeling worshippers, and white-robed priests moved about the altar in the offices of a ritual which was unfamiliar to the young Anglican priest, but which yet seemed not quite strange to him.

Music and singing of an indescribable mournfulness blent with incense and the piercing fragrance of spring flowers.

Yet, beneath all the terrible sadness, there seemed an undertone as of some lost joy rising from the dead.

It was the Easter-Day of some great old sorrow.

It was impossible for Winslow, with all his susceptibility to beautiful ritual, the æsthetic and the emotional side of religion, not to be profoundly moved.

Presently a great hush fell over the temple, as the high-priest took and held up before the people a strange red flower, with curiously lettered petals. Then in a moment a great sob seemed to break from the very hearts of the adoring worshippers.

'Ai! Ai!' they cried. 'Ai! Ai!'

And again 'Ai! Ai!' as the priest elevated the sacred flower for the third time.

Then Winslow realised that he was in a temple of Apollo, and that this was a solemn fast of mourning for the death of Hyacinthus, the beloved friend of the god.

He looked at his friends. One and all they were bent in an attitude of the profoundest worship.

Then he too bent his head.

.   .   .   .   .   .

Later on, when Winslow was alone with Mulciber Jackson in his little private smoking-room, his host turned to him with some eagerness.

'Well, what do you think of it all?'

RICHARD LE GALLIENNE

'I hardly know,' Winslow replied. 'I am yet too confused, almost intoxicated, with my impressions. Besides, it was so all unexpected, so strange. Tell me what it means?'

'I suppose you think that it was all a mere masquerade, the latest device of a jaded luxurious society, seeking after novelty.'

'At first I did,' the minister answered, 'but there was a note of seriousness in it all that soon led me to think otherwise.'

'I am glad of that, for it was quite serious, and represents a very serious movement which will presently astonish society as it has not been astonished for two thousand years. If I tell you what it means, will you give me your word, without any professional reservation, that you will keep what I shall tell you absolutely secret?'

'I give you my word.'

'You have read Heine's "Gods in Exile"?'

'I have.' (Winslow was a Harvard man.)

'Well—the gods are to be in exile but a very little longer. The old gods are coming back. Two of the most important of them came over on the *Teutonic* last week, and are living here in New York at this moment—of course, under assumed names, awaiting the Event of which I will presently tell you.'

'But you cannot be serious. "Gods in Exile" was merely a fancy . . . a witty imagination.'

'I am perfectly serious, and Heine's fancy was only a fancy in that he represented the gods in a much worse plight than they have ever been in. That was his incorrigible irreverence, to which not even his own profoundest beliefs were sacred. Actually, none knew better than Heine the true status of the eternal gods in a world, and amid a civilisation, from which they had been formally banished, but which they actually control.'

'But, Mulciber, you speak of the gods as if they were actually alive—as if, indeed, they had ever really existed at all, and were not mere myths of the popular imagination. Even supposing them once to have lived, they died at the birth of Christ.'

'Pardon me. So far as I have heard or read, the death of but one god has been ever reported, the death of Pan—and Pan's death was a legend of which Christianity was sorely in need at the time, for the simple purpose of combating the very vigorous existence of the very god the legend declared to be dead. "Great Pan is dead!" Why, even you, as a Christian minister, face to face with the warm instincts of humanity, must know that, of all the gods, Pan is the god likely to survive all the rest.'

'Well, continue,' said Winslow after a pause. 'I confess that I am somewhat bewildered. Let me listen, and I will try not to interrupt.'

'Then, you must first try to realise that all I tell you is not fancy—strange as it may sound—but actual truth. The old gods, as we call them, have never died. They have only been deposed for a short time. They are soon to come back to their thrones. Actually they have never left them; it is only officially that they have been exiles.'

'Go on.' Winslow nodded.

'Let us talk a little theology,' continued Mulciber, smiling, 'I am sure you won't object. I have often seen the race to which I am popularly supposed to belong, praised for a theological concept which is, it seems to me, its one mistake, a concept contrary to all human experience, and perhaps on that very account, so whimsical is humanity, a concept which has enjoyed remarkable success. The Jews have invented most things, but their most illustrious invention is the invention of the One God. The Jews are the most abstract, the least, human, people in the world. They are a nation of idealists, of dreamers, of philosophers, of artists. They are skilled in essences, in sublimations of the fact—rather than the fact itself. And, if you consider the real significance of the industry with which they are most popularly associated, you will see how that alone, and best of all, proves my contention. The industry of the Jew is money-making. Money-making is the essence of all industries. Thus the Jew, unwillingly enough compelled to touch earth at some point, touches it where all its various concrete activities concentrate into an abstract synthesis, or distillation, hopelessly, I know, to mix one's metaphors. Money is the distillation of all human labour. It is a volatile, immaterial thing, the abstract flowering result of all the varied processes of human life. The Jew, the aristocrat of all aristocrats, hating to soil his delicate fingers with the rough and common work of the world, but, realising that some work he must do if he is to continue living upon a pleasant planet, naturally chooses to touch life at its most abstract or immaterial summit. Not for him the coarse and narrowing activities of popular industries. Like some poet who will not soil his hands with the writing of a realistic novel, the depicting of the stock-yards of human life, but will sing only of the moon and the stars and the face of woman, so the Jew will consent only to take hold of that material which has already passed through so many processes of refinement, that no hint of those cleansing processes remains upon it; as one might distil attar of roses for a living, and disown any connection with the revolting processes by which the common gardener rears the rose to its haughty immaculacy.'

'Is it proper for a Greek to be quite so fond of using Latin?' Winslow asked, laughing, interrupting merely that Mulciber Jackson might gain a moment in which to breathe himself.

Taking a draught of White Rock, Mulciber continued:

'I have, as I said, only referred to the most notorious pre-

-occupation of the Jew as an illustration of his abstract habit of mind. A race so mentally constituted would naturally produce a Moses and a Spinoza—as it would naturally produce a Shylock. Above all other races, they are the Mental Race. In spite of their remarkable persistence, they are the least rooted in earth of any people. Their patriotism—is a patriotism of the mind. They will never go back to Palestine. Their idealism is too great. It soars above such mere earthly sentimentalism. They were just the people, therefore, to conceive an abstract One God—a god remote from humanity, understanding nothing of its needs, its joys or its sorrows, a god that indeed felt constrained on that very account to send his own more human son upon the earth, the better to comprehend the strange race of men. Through the humanity of this divine son, the concept of the One God, paradoxically enough, has gained its widest acceptance—though the monotheistic ideal which Christ taught has all along needed the aid of his divine mother and the saints, to make it acceptable to a humanity that instinctively feels the need of many gods—a god for every need. Gods succeed in proportion to their humanity. Jehovah has never been acceptable to the world, and he owes his present position to the endearing humanity of his son. On the other hand, that humanity has been disastrously thinned by the Jewish blood in his veins. Christ, with all his divine humanity, was still the son of a Jewish god. He brought the world a gift of which it stood sorely in need, a gift by virtue of which he must hold his eternal place in any Pantheon—the gift of Pity—but, with it, owing, as I said, to his Jewish ancestry, he brought abstract restrictions upon the kindly instincts and operations of humanity, which have prevailed over the true gift he gave. It was not really necessary that all the other gods should go, for Christ to come. Their banishment was but that inevitable eclipse of other stars which must always accompany the lighting of a new star. Now that the new star has settled down to a normal place in the heavens, we see that the old stars are still burning. That's what I mean when I say that the old gods are coming back—or rather that they have never gone away. Christ will not be banished because they come back. His place will still be his. They merely resume their own.'

Winslow was evidently struck by this reasoning.

Mulciber Jackson continued: 'Yes, humanity is too complex to be satisfied with one god. It is impossible for one god to understand all the needs, all the hopes and aspirations, of humanity. That there is one god greater than all the rest our own Grecian theology has formulated. Zeus is recognised as the Father of the Gods. But his wisdom is so great that he leaves the lesser gods undisputed sway in their own dominions. He would not dream of

FIRST CHURCH OF THE RESTORATION

instructing Neptune in the management of the sea, or of interfering with the purpose of Apollo. But we must not wander too far afield. I shall hope to have many opportunities of discussing with you such mere points of doctrine. To-night it is not theories I wish to talk with you, but facts.

'Now you and I may think as we please about the old gods, their management of the world and so on, but the fact remains, as I have said, that they are coming back—coming back not only to their old power, but to a power far greater than any they have ever wielded before. If you doubt this, consider a moment the condition of the world, and can you sincerely say that it is a Christian condition? Ostensibly, we still live in the Christian era, our churches are externally Christian. Christian ethics are supposed to rule our lives. Officially, the world is Christian—actually, it is what you would call "Pagan." What is the world most interested in to-day? Is it in the Kingdom of Heaven, in the inheritance of the meek, in the amelioration of the poor, in the spiritual life? No, the world is interested in Power and Beauty. War and Women and Wealth are practically all it thinks of. It still professes Christ, but its real divinities are Mars and Venus and Plutus. Of this there can be no doubt at all.

'These three divinities were never seriously disturbed by the Christian heresy. Like some royal family, overthrown awhile by popular sedition, they went into retirement indeed, but into retirement no less splendid and luxurious than the public life to which they had been accustomed. They have never changed the manner of their lives in the smallest particular, nor has the number of their worshippers ever appreciably decreased. The only difference has been that the worship offered to them has been a secret rather than a public devotion, and for that very reason, the more sincere. Actual godship has always been theirs, but, naturally, with the pride of their race, they have dreamed of the time when it should once more be publicly acknowledged. It is not meet that the immortal gods should rule the world in hiding, however superb be their hiding-places.

'Now it has been decided that that time for a public restoration of the old gods has come. Not only do all the signs in the world at large point that way, but those familiar with the inner working of the so-called religious world know that it too is prepared for and sympathetic towards the change. The many new churches which have sprung up of late years, particularly in America, many of them, as you know, with immense wealth and social power behind them, have not only been useful in preparing the way for us, by familiarising men's minds with the idea of a coming change, and the necessity of it, but the majority of them are secretly affiliated to our cause, and ready, at the right moment, to throw off the mask and openly acknowledge allegiance to the old gods, whom they actually worship under Christian names. How nearly related to us the oldest and most powerful Christian church has always been, you need not be told. The change there will be very slight. The saints will but resume their old names, and hardly any appreciable changes in the ceremonial will be found necessary. In regard to the newer churches, you must have noticed the prominence given to love in their doctrines. Mystical phraseology is often used to veil it, and it is sometimes referred to as sisterly love or brotherly love ; but that it is one of the many forms of the worship of our august lady, known variously as Urania and Aphrodite, no one acquainted with its ceremonies can doubt. Enough then to convince you that the world is ready and waiting for the revelation which I have made to you to-night. I am but one humble mouthpiece of a vast organisation which is backed by all the power and wealth and other influence of the world. You may take my word that, on a certain date, which I will confide to you, the world will officially cease to be Christian. Christianity will not be abolished. Actually it has never been more than a small sect. It is too spiritual, too un-earthly, an ideal ever to take hold of great numbers of men. By an accident it became constituted as a powerful hypocrisy. Now it will shrink back to sincerer dimensions. The number of real Christians in the world will be no smaller than before, and they will be free to worship as they choose, without oppression, or the intru-sion upon them of those hypocrites who have vulgarised their beautiful creed. Orders are already given throughout the world that on that day of Restoration the images of Christ are everywhere to be respected. His place among the gods is his for ever—the place of the God of Pity. It is only, as I said, the old gods who resume their places—the Gods of Power. On that day, in every great city of the world, temples of Jupiter and Apollo, of Diana and Venus, will be opened. They are now in course of erection—supposedly as Christian churches. When you give me your decision, I will reveal to you the full extent of our plans ; but first you must give me your answer to this question : Will you consent to be the High Priest of Apollo of the First Church of the Restoration, in New York ? '

After Mulciber Jackson had finished speaking, the friends sat some moments in silence. The minister was visibly moved. A great conflict was going on in his soul.

'You have been chosen for me to speak to, Arthur,' added Mulciber presently, 'not merely because of your popularity and your gifts of eloquence, but because we believe that while you have been a sincere priest of Christianity in its more human aspects, you have also come to see its limitations as a complete formula of human life. It supplements us, but it can never permanently

FIRST CHURCH OF THE RESTORATION

displace us. Man needs all his gods: he cannot afford to lose any of them. And, similarly, some men are born to be priests of one god, and some priests of another. Believe me, you were born less a priest of Christ than a priest of Apollo.'

Such was the proposal that was agitating the mind of the Reverend Arthur Winslow, as he paced Central Park, on the morning of the 14th of May, this present year.

Of his decision I know nothing.

BROOCHES
BY CYRIL DAVENPORT, F.S.A.

ANY of the early ornaments used by our savage ancestors are still among us in forms differing but little from their prototypes.

Probably the first ornament used by primitive mankind consisted of brightly coloured bird's feathers stuck in the hair, and it is likely enough that when communities were first formed under the chieftainship of some powerful savage, his ceremonial mark of authority was either the single feather of some rare bird, or a combination of feathers in some specialised form placed on the head.

This early mark of dignity survives in the richly feathered hats used on full dress occasions by the members of all our great orders of knighthood; in the cocked hats with white or black feather ridges along their tops worn by civil servants; the regulation head-dresses of many of the territorial as well as colonial regiments; and in the plumed hats of our military staff officers. The wearing of feather plumes by ladies at Court has also been the subject of strict regulation for a long time.

Another very early and obvious adornment ready to the hand of primitive man was the necklace, made at first with strings of berries or bird's eggs, then of shells, claws or teeth, and as men became more skilled in the use of tools, beads were artificially made of wood, coral, amber, jet and bone, and, in time, of metal, stones and glass. Although never so important a badge of dignity as a feathered head-dress, the necklace is yet not entirely devoid of official recognition, as the use of the orange cowry in this manner is still a sign of chief-tainship in Fiji, and among ourselves we count the ancient collar of 'S.S.' a valued dignity, formerly the badge of an esquire, but now, I believe, only worn by judges or heralds. As official necklaces also must be ranked the collars of the great orders of knighthood, those of the Golden Fleece and the Garter at the head of them. Of the lesser ornaments, bracelets, armlets, ear-rings, nose-rings, toe-rings and labrets, some are still worn, and others happily discarded, the finger-ring alone being seldom used by savage tribes, but largely worn by civilised man.

All these decorations are worn next the skin, and are usually simple in plan, often consisting of one piece of metal or other sub-stance, except, of course, necklaces, which, apart from the torques, are usually made up of strings of beads or their equivalents. The pin or brooch, however, in all its forms is an accessory to clothing, and consequently appears at a much later date in the history of civilisation. The brooch is also of a more complicated structure, consisting materially of at least two distinct parts, the pin for piercing the material to be fastened, and the ring or arc affixed to it, either

95

BROOCHES

for the purpose of preventing its slipping out, or covering up the sharpened point, or perhaps for both purposes.

As primitive men gradually migrated northwards and southwards from their tropical birthplace, some extra protection against the cold had to be provided beyond that supplied by unaided Nature, and the animal skins or leaves which probably preceded more effective garments, had to be kept together by some means or other. It is very likely that at first materials such as these were roughly sewn together, where necessary, with animal sinews or vegetable fibres, each of which formed ready threads. At the same time these rough sewings had the disadvantage of being practically fixtures, as it would be very inconvenient to be continually unlacing them, so that the need for some fastening which would enable clothing to be easily changed at will must have made itself felt at an early period.

In all probability the first fastening of this kind was found in a fishbone or a large thorn, both of which are obviously well fitted for the purpose of pinning loose edges together, the thickened tops preventing them from running through the material. Pins of wood, bone and metal still exist, which are apparently copied from these natural products.

Ultimately, as the working of metals became gradually better understood, long dress-pins were made of bronze or brass of like patterns, but their tops show in more or less ornamental forms. Pins of this kind belong to what is known as the bronze age, that is to say, the particular time in the history of each nation, at which the elementary working of metal became known. Copper was the first metal to be worked by men, and when melted with tin it forms what we call bronze, a noble material, and one in which some of the finest art productions have been made. After the bronze age came the age of iron, and during this latter period the gold and silver works to which I shall presently refer were made.

The first real change from the simply thickened head of a bronze pin appears to have consisted in a flattening out by hammering. The flattened disc was presently pierced and strung with a piece of wire, the ends of which were brought round and round. This ring was not only valuable as a stop for the pin, but it also had from the beginning a certain decorative value of its own, and has been the ancestor of all the subsequent ornamentation which has appeared on brooches.

The modifications that have taken place in the shape of this ring are very interesting to follow, and for the present ignoring the innumerable variations of small importance that occur in isolated cases, I find that the main changes have taken place in three different ways, which I shall call *annular*, *circular* and *linear*.

In the first case the ring remains small in comparison to the length of the pin. It assumes the form of a single bent wire, the two

1

2

3

The
Hara
Brooch.

The
Hunterston
Brooch.

The Lochan Brooch.

4

5

Scandinavian Brooch
found in Iceland

Anglo Saxon Brooch
found at Sheat Down
Isle of Wight

Brooches.

1

2

The
Lura
Brooch

The
Hunterston
Brooch

3

The Lochbuie Brooch

4

5

Cantivarian Brooch
found in Ireland

Anglo Saxon Brooch
found at Chessel Down
Isle of Wight 1861

Brooches.

loose ends of which are thickened, flattened, and ornamented in various ways, and the ultimate development of this type is to be found in the beautiful Scottish and Irish annular and penannular brooches. Specimens of the ordinary types of these brooches can be found more or less abundantly in all our museums, as they are by no means uncommon, but to see them at their finest a visit will have to be made to the museum of the Royal Irish Academy, and that of the Dublin University. The most decorative brooch of this class is the 'Tara' brooch, made of a white bronze, probably copper, with a large proportion of tin, and some silver, gilded (Plate, Fig. 1). It was found near Drogheda in 1850, and is of an unusually ornate finish throughout. It has the unique peculiarity of having had two chains attached to each side of the ring, which is four inches in diameter. One of these chains is lost, but the other remains ; it is a closely woven chain of 'Trichinopoly' pattern, and the junctions to the brooch are very beautifully designed with scrolls and heads of animals, and two remarkable human heads cast in a deep red glass. The body of the ring is arranged in compartments, the floors of which are filled with minute and exquisite Celtic scrolls and lacertine ornaments. The compartments are divided from one another by jewels, bosses of amber with gold tops, bosses of gold, or of rich translucent enamels in concentric circles. The head of the pin is enlarged and ornamented in a similar way, ending in an animal's head. The pin, which is nearly nine inches in length, is ornamented with Celtic tracery for some distance from its upper end. It is altogether a marvellous piece of jewellers' work, and is, probably, the finest specimen of its kind in existence. Another celebrated brooch, known as the 'Hunterston,' is made of the same white bronze as the Tara brooch, and is of about the same date and also gilded. The design as a whole is not quite so ornate as the Tara brooch, but the strong simplicity of the richly wrought ring with the amber bosses is, nevertheless, most charming (Plate, Fig. 2). Compartments adorned in the same way with Celtic scrolls are divided by amber or jewelled bosses on both brooches, but on the Hunterston are no enamels, chains, or glass cameos. It was found in 1830 on the estate of Mr. Robert Hunter of West Kilbride, Ayrshire. The ring measures nearly five inches in diameter, and the pin, the head of which is decorated with Celtic tracery and amber bosses, is left quite plain, and measures about fourteen inches in length. The reverse side has compartments with lacertine ornamentation, the inner and outer borders being chased or engraved with interlaced patterns and scrolls, ending frequently in monsters' heads. An inscription in Runic characters is engraved on the flat surfaces. The amber which appears largely in Scandinavian and Anglo-Saxon jewellery was plentifully found on the coasts of Denmark and the neighbouring countries. It darkens with age and the surface disintegrates, but still

BROOCHES

it retains a rich dark colour, and bosses of it are often decoratively fastened down with gold studs having ornamental tops.

Another very fine specimen of the Celtic annular brooch is known as the 'Ardagh' brooch. It was found in 1868 on the estate of Mr. Gould of Ardagh near Limerick, and is ornamented with Celtic interlaced designs in silver gilt, with figures of birds, and possesses also some very finely worked bosses of translucent enamels, analogous to, but not so elaborate as those on the 'Ardagh' cup, which was found on the same estate. All these brooches were made about the same period, some time between the ninth and the twelfth centuries;

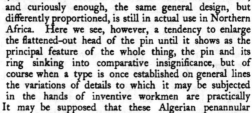

and curiously enough, the same general design, but differently proportioned, is still in actual use in Northern Africa. Here we see, however, a tendency to enlarge the flattened-out head of the pin until it shows as the principal feature of the whole thing, the pin and its ring sinking into comparative insignificance, but of course when a type is once established on general lines the variations of details to which it may be subjected in the hands of inventive workmen are practically endless. It may be supposed that these Algerian penannular brooches have arrived at their present form by a similar development from the primitive ring as that followed by their Celtic brethren.

In the second of my large divisions the ring enlarges until its diameter is equal in length to that of the pin; and to this division belong the immense majority of brooches, because when the circle of the ring is filled up and becomes therefore a solid disc, we get at once the prototype of all brooches that are circular, oval, oblong, or square. To this class belong brooches set with large stones, as the Koh-i-Noor, and cameo, coin and miniature brooches. Although these extraneous objects are in themselves only ornamental, they practically take the place of the structural metal disc itself, which is, moreover, often directly represented by a narrow setting of metal.

At the same time the early Lombardic and Scandinavian jewellers produced much beautiful work in metal on circular brooches, the disc of which was left open. These are often charmingly ornamented with quaint animal and bird forms, the ring being broadened and bossed out as required. The same kind of open-ring brooch was much used in England about the fourteenth century, but richly jewelled as well as beautifully worked by the goldsmith. The open ring with a pin about the same length as its diameter is also the direct ancestor of the buckle, the essential difference between which and a true brooch being that the pin of a buckle goes only once through the material to be fastened, while that of a brooch pierces it twice. The peculiarity of a double piercing was noticed by the ancient Greeks, one of whose names for a brooch was Διβολος, meaning twice-pointed. At the same time it must not be forgotten that in the case of a buckle, one side of the ring is fastened to the material, thereby possessing a substitute for the second piercing. The discovery that the blunted pin of a buckle would work better if set on a central bar is a modern innovation, as is also the reduplication of the pin on the bar. The Merovingian, Scandinavian, and Anglo-Saxon jewellers also ornamented the head or upper part of their buckles very elaborately. On many of these 'buckle-plates' the ancient workmen have lavished their utmost skill : they are not only freely inlaid with garnets and other inlays, but they also have upon them most exquisite gold tracery of hammered or pressed work.

In Merovingian, Lombardic, German, Scandinavian, and Anglo-Saxon work, circular brooches are very numerous, and as a rule they have a strong family likeness. Among them all none are more beautiful than the Hamilton brooch, and another with the portrait of a queen in enamels, both of which are Anglo-Saxon work of the ninth century or thereabouts, and both of which have already been figured and described in the ANGLO-SAXON REVIEW. Besides these exquisite examples there are others of more acknowledged Anglo-Saxon styles and commoner, possessing a refined beauty, which, although it closely resembles Continental work, still appears to me to excel in delicacy of execution and finish. These brooches have been most plentifully found in the south-western parts of our island. They are usually made of bronze, silver gilt, or gold, and are cleverly set with *cloisons* in geometric patterns, into which are set flat-shaped garnets, pieces of green and blue composition, bosses of shell or bone, and spaces of thin gold impressed with delicate filigree designs.

There is yet another kind of circular brooch which is very ornamental, and, although highly favoured here, was not indigenous; it is a circular disc of bronze set with a slice of glass in which are designs in colour. These slices are cut of a rod of sticks of coloured glass arranged in set patterns, just the same manner as Tunbridge Wells ware is, or the millefiori glass of Murano, and the art of making these rods was brought over here by the Romans, who were skilled glass-workers. A glass rod made in this way can be softened by heat and drawn out to almost any extent, the pattern, however small, always remaining consistently arranged as it was at first. The Roman and Anglo-Roman designs used in this glass-mosaic are generally simple, but at a much earlier date most exquisite work of the same kind was made by the Egyptians, not however applied to brooches.

The Scottish brooches of silver set with native pearls, each on a little tower of its own, are an interesting and specialised form of circular brooches, the 'Brooch of Lorne,' said to have belonged to Robert Bruce, is the best known of this kind, it closely resembles the 'Lochbuy' brooch, of fifteenth-century workmanship: which was found on the estate of the Macleans of Lochbuy in the Island of Mull (Plate, Fig. 3). It remained in that family for a long time and is now in the British Museum. The centre ornament is a crystal cut *en cabochon* set on a raised daïs of silver, ornamented with bosses and circlets of filigree, and edged with ten semicircular projections. At the foot of this central tower is a trench bordered by a low ornamental edging ; and the outer circle ornamented with filigree flowers with six petals, bears ten tall turrets, each decorated on the outer side with two diamond-shaped ornaments, and each bearing at the top a Scottish pearl. A simple outer edge with a moulded pattern encloses the whole.

Another of these curious brooches is also in our national Museum, it has the ring broadened but left open, closely set with pearls on tall stalks, alternating with crystals and pieces of amethyst. It is known as the 'Glenlyon' brooch, and has been preserved in the family of the Campbells of Glenlyon for many generations. It is an amulet brooch and has the names of the three kings of Cologne engraved upon it—'Caspar, Melchior, Balthasar,' and also has the rare peculiarity of an ornamental bar crossing the centre, two pins meeting it coming from opposite sides.

To go back once more to the original pin with a wire ring run through the top, there is yet another manner in which it changed its form, that which I have called the linear direction. Whether the actual ring was at first flattened and drawn out into a wire of the same length as the pin, or whether the ring in the head of the pin was multiplied until it became a chain, which presently coalesced into a wire, cannot be certainly known. But somehow or other it became evident that a turning round of the head of the pin could be effected which could be brought back and made easily into a point-protector. Among the remains of the lake dwellings in the Lake of Neuchatel a pin with the fragments of a short chain was found, and, so far as it goes, this curious discovery supplies a missing link.

A pin of the linear type, now known as a safety-pin, is said to have been found among the ruins of Mycenæ, although I do not find it mentioned by Dr. Schliemann, and no brooch, even of this very early type, has as yet been discovered on the site of Troy, but at both of these places numbers of pins have been found with highly ornamental tops.

The safety-pin may be considered as consisting of two essential parts, the pin itself and the bow or arc above it, joined at the head by a turn or spiral forming a spring, and at the further end turned down and flattened out into a small saucer-like hollow for the safe reception of the point. The pins themselves of brooches at all times have had little ornamentation upon them for obvious reasons, so that it is to the arc we must look as a field for future developments, and indeed these developments have taken place in numberless cases on such definite lines as to have acquired the characteristics of different nationalities clearly enough to be easily recognised.

The ancient Greeks made a short steep arch in the arc near the head, and then prolonged the cup for the point to a considerable extent, ornamenting the arc with most exquisite gold granular work and finishing the projecting socket also with beautifully modelled animal forms, chased and finished with the utmost delicacy. On some of the Etruscan fibulæ of this class there can be found some of the most beautiful goldsmiths' work that has ever been made—such as cannot be made now.

Among the Bœotians the socket for the pin was broadened out into a plaque of considerable size, and this itself became a field for ornamentation, not of the delicate Greek and Etruscan applied kind, but engraved designs of the Swastika or some other of the curious astronomical figures, the real origin of which is perhaps lost.

The Romans liked their fibulæ large, and they used for the arc, very commonly, a thick wire variously bent, and the arc is large, reaching from head to point of the pin, the socket, although often enlarged, never forming the important feature that it does so markedly in Greek work. The wire arc is often decoratively bent into a series of spirals, largest in the centre, and some of the most decorative specimens are closely strung with large beads of amber and rings and beads of metal all along the arc.

In Austria and other places on the Continent, early fibulæ have been found, the arc of which is broadly flattened out, ornamented with small engraved designs, and thickly hung with pendants. In these cases the arc was evidently intended to be worn downwards, and when used, such brooches were very ornamental. The idea of a pendant no doubt began in Rome, but these specimens have not a regular fringe like the Hallstadt specimen I have drawn, but only one or two 'pendeloques.'

To revert once more to what I may call the safety-pin type, it will easily be seen that supposing the brooch to be made of one piece of wire, it would be easier to make the turn, or turns, at the head, if some kind of bar or short stick were used to make the turn upon. Both in early Roman and in the Anglo-Roman work, which nearly resembles it, brooches with a short bar in this position are freely found, and I think that this peculiarity is only a crystallisation of what was originally a temporary expedient. It has been held by many antiquaries that these T-shaped fibulæ are really intended to represent a cross, but I am more inclined to accept the constructive explanation. Possibly, when the origin of the cross-bar had been for a long time forgotten, it may have gradually assumed the significa-tion of a cross, and its form may also have been gradually modified so as to bear out this interpretation more and more.

The T-shaped fibula, in its slow journey from the south of Europe to the north, passed through many changes, but through them all the distinctive bar, or, at all events, the straight top can be traced.

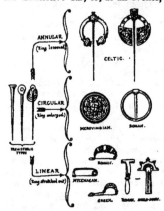

Numbers of brooches that have been found in France, Germany, and the northern countries of Europe generally (Plate, Fig. 4), have actually the rectangular top easily recognisable, while others show it in a modified form, rounded or semicircular. Several of the Anglo-Saxon brooches of this type, num-bers of which have been found in Kent and the south-east of England generally, are beautiful specimens of jewel-lers' work. They are finely wrought in bronze or silver, often gilded, and set with garnets and inlays of coloured composition, and lines of silver with small niello-work patterns upon them (Plate, Fig. 5).

The 'Boar's Head' brooches of Scandinavia are, in all proba-bility, survivals of the T-form, as their tops are straight, the points of the arms of the T being joined to the lower part of the stem, and the whole thing made solid; the designs upon the surface of these brooches are in fact the lines followed by the wire curves and turns in many of the early specimens. The brooches are very heavy and cumbersome, and have assumed a decadent and useless form, as they are so heavy that they would soon pull to pieces any ordinary material into which they might be fixed.

In England we have kept to the lighter form of a little earlier date, and we have never gone beyond it. The Anglo-Saxon type of T brooch is indeed simpler than its immediate Scandinavian ancestor. It is quieter in outline, and not so ornate in surface decoration. It is a very decorative style of brooch, and as a national one might well be revived among us, flat garnets and all.

The diagram (p. 102) will show the three ways in which the prehistoric pin, with a wire ring through its top, has become modified into brooches. The upper line shows the 'Annular' or 'Penannular' development, in which the wire ring becomes the direct inspiration of the ornamental treatment which reached its highest point in the Celtic brooches. In my sketch, as also in the Plate, for reasons of space, the pins of these brooches are not shown as long as they should be, but they actually are about three times as long as the diameter of the ring to which they belong.

The middle line shows the 'Circular' line of development, in which case the wire ring enlarges until its diameter equals the length of the pin, and to this type belong the majority of all modern brooches as well as buckles of all sorts.

The lower line shows the 'Linear' development, in which case the wire ring is stretched out, losing entirely its ring character, and changing into a wire arc, which, in course of time, itself undergoes many changes. The simplest ancient specimen of this early change is said by Daremberg and Saglio to have been found at Mycenæ, and no doubt it was in common use in Greece and Rome. From the Roman pattern, with a top cross-bar, have developed the numerous Merovingian, Scandinavian, and Anglo-Saxon long-shaped fibulæ with enlarged tops, squared or rounded.

THE PARTITION OF SOUTH AMERICA
BY S. PÉREZ TRIANA

ALTHOUGH South America, geographically speaking, only includes the continent which begins at the Isthmus of Panama, both in England and the United States the words are usually applied to the region extending to the south of the United States beginning at Mexico, down to the southernmost end of the continent.

A pertinent question, well deserving the attention of the statesmen of the Old and the New World, is whether the political geography of South America, or, to speak more properly, of Latin America, is likely to be altered within the near future. By an alteration in the political geography I mean a substantial modification of the political *status* of the numerous nationalities which at present exercise sovereignty over that large section of the American continent. This is a problem, the elements of which are complex and possibly not as widely known or appreciated outside of the countries most deeply interested in the course of events as might be desired. There are many signs in Europe and in the United States which seem to point in the direction of an unavoidable partition of Latin America, even as Africa has been divided, or as it is sought to divide China amongst the European powers.

The principal causes leading to that desire for expansion—so powerful and overwhelming that in the endeavour to satisfy it all traditions are set at naught, and laws and international treaties, where they exist, are set aside or moulded to it—may be summed up in the over-production of manufactured wares and of human beings in the older or more powerful nations of the world. Recent statistics show that whilst population in France remains practically at a standstill, England, Germany, Austria, and Italy see their swarming multitudes grow apace year by year; such is also the case in the United States of America. Russia need not be taken here into account, since the accepted and old-established policy of the Czars demands that any addition to the territory of the empire should be continuous and uninterrupted by oceans. The other countries, including France, notwithstanding the drawback of the stagnation of its population, all are seeking new lands beyond the seas wherein their overflow of population may settle, and new markets for the surplus of their manufactured production. The energies thus brought to life, tame or gentle though they may be in their inception, very soon acquire an aggressiveness of which the events recently witnessed in China are an appalling instance : violence and outrage, not only to the established conventionalities of international and civilised life, but also to human nature itself, are in such cases the rule of the day, and the so-called Christian armies of

S. PÉREZ TRIANA

Europe, the pseudo forerunners of western civilisation, behave in a manner which the Tartar conquerors of former centuries might envy, though perhaps even they might consider them barbarous and cruel.

In this little planet of ours, where every inch of ground has been labelled by its owner, it may be asserted, in a general way, that the only prey worthy of notice still remaining in weak hands is the vast, rich, and thinly populated region extending south of the Rio Grande on the continent of America down to Cape Horn.

That vast territory, with the exception of the remaining European colonies, English, French, and Dutch, belonged at one time to the Crowns of Spain and Portugal. The many republics emancipated from the Spanish metropolis during the third decade of the nineteenth century, and the republic of Brazil (a former Portuguese colony) are the sovereign powers holding sway over that large section of the American continent. Their autonomy, independence, and national existence have been recognised for many years both by the European powers and by the United States. That is the existing conventionality. If international law were a reality, a shield to the weak and not a form which the strong can violate and break whenever it suits their convenience, it might be expected that the evolution of national and political life in Latin America would take its course without any fear of intrusion at a given moment of foreign elements coming either from across the seas or from the northern part of the continent. But reality prevails over conventionality; the autonomy and independence of those countries is a conventionality which can last only so long as it is backed by sufficient power to keep it alive, and is bound to be destroyed whenever the necessities of international life may so require.

It is, therefore, from this point of view that the possible, and, in the opinion of many, the probable partition of Latin America has to be studied. A few facts may be here brought to mind which will tend to define the real condition of affairs.

The territorial area of Latin America is large enough to contain a population several times that of Europe. The various climates to be found in that large section of the world include those of the temperate and of the tropical zone; even in the very heart of the tropics large sections of land are fit to be inhabited by Europeans, owing to the fact that the Andes range of mountains are sub-divided into minor ranges, and form a great many plateaus varying in height, and affording all temperatures, from the hottest to the coldest, the highest peaks being capped by perpetual snows. The intercommunication between the healthy plateaus and the hotter and less salubrious regions in the torrid belt is at present, in many cases, slow and difficult. This arises from the scarcity of population;

but when the lands become more settled, modern means of transport will soon be established, and it will be feasible for Europeans to exploit the hotter regions, as they will have without great difficulty access to cooler altitudes, which might be considered as breathing and recuperating places.

Those mountain ranges, therefore, which in the most backward sections of Latin America have thus far constituted a drawback to their progress, acting as obstacles to easy communication, are in reality a source of strength and a basis for the establishment of white populations in days to come. So much for the climatic conditions in a large part of the tropical area where they differ greatly from those of Europe.

The vast plains extending in South America as an immense carpet of verdure at the foot of the mighty Cordilleras towards the east are irrigated by the most wonderful water-systems on the face of the globe. The Orinoco and the Amazon, rivers which flow into the Atlantic from the very heart of the tropical belt, are formed by a veritable network of navigable rivers which penetrate into the heart of the continent in every direction, forming natural waterways, and facilitating the exploitation of those wonderfully rich territories into which civilised man has hardly entered.

The forests teem with natural wealth, and the Andes are certainly, if not the richest deposit of mineral wealth of all kinds in the world, as rich as any region known to man.

The mining records of the old colonial days, when miners busied themselves solely with the search after precious metals, show an output of gold and silver which is a positive revelation to those who are not familiar with the facts. In those days the miner had to pay into the treasury of Spain one-fifteenth of the gold and silver which he extracted; and it is a calculation based on the sums so paid that warrants the preceding assertion. It must be remembered that mining was extremely limited in its scope in those days, when neither pumps nor drills, nor modern methods of blasting, were known. The miner of that period could barely scratch the earth. Gold deposits, consisting in gold-bearing rock, frequently, if not always, grow richer as they grow deeper. Vast regions of the Andes still remain unexplored. It is safe to assume, therefore, that the enormous output of gold and silver which flowed from the colonies both to Spain and to Portugal during the sixteenth, the seventeenth, and the eighteenth centuries is only an indication of the unmeasureable wealth in gold and silver in those countries.

Where the natural wealth of the forests, or the rich deposits of precious metals, or of other sorts of metals, are not so abundant, or are lacking absolutely, the soil is generally most fertile. This consideration applies principally to the land outside the tropics, where the endless pampas of Argentina and Uruguay roll through untold leagues watered by the Parana and its many affluents, and also to the territory forming the republic of Chili, which is not only admirably adapted for the cultivation of all European cereals, but also abundant in coal, copper, iron, and so forth.

All this wealth and this immense territory, with its unlimited potentialities, are under the political sway of the various Latin American nations. The total population of Latin America could easily and comfortably live in any one of several of the larger nations, and there would be space to spare. If we take that population at seventy millions (which is a liberal allowance) it could be established in Mexico or Colombia, or in Venezuela or Argentina, leaving the rest of the continent free to the world at large. Such being the real condition of affairs in that part of the world, is it probable that the swarming multitudes of Europe, where the soil begins to be narrow, and the cities and the country are overcrowded, and life becomes more difficult each day, will not by sheer force of expansion be driven in the direction of those bountiful lands, which lie waste, untilled, and unexploited? It does not seem probable that the mere conventionality of autonomy and national sovereignty, a weak dyke against the powerful current of humanity, should stand for long. It seems natural and inevitable that the stream of mankind will flow thither, and in one form or another occupy and exploit the land.

In one form or another—there is the rub. Is that form to take the aspect of immigration? Are the new-comers to arrive on the Latin American shores as men who leave their homes, their countries, and their nationality behind, and accept the institutions of the land to which they arrive, submitting to its laws, and becoming citizens of the new nation; or are they to arrive as conquerors and invaders eager to extend abroad the dominion of their flag and the tenets of their national laws and institutions? If matters are to shape themselves in the manner first indicated, the road is open and free. The laws of immigration in all the countries of Latin America are most liberal. The foreigner is welcomed with open arms. He can, if he wishes, in all of them, easily acquire the rights of citizenship; or he may retain his nationality and enjoy all the privileges of the natives. For that peaceful invasion, no matter what large proportions it may take, there is no obstacle whatever; and were such an evolution to find no objections and no difficulties arising from other sources, it could be made without violence and without danger to the existing nationalities, since, even if the stream of foreign populations were so great that it would swamp the native element, it is not to be supposed that amid ordinary circumstances it would entail violent modifications. The final result or remodellation would be attained in an easy and natural manner, like the merging of affluent streams into one common bed.

THE PARTITION OF SOUTH AMERICA

But the obstacle and difficulties arising from other sources hinted at are not to be found in the laws and temper of the Latin American nations. The European powers cannot see with favourable eyes a large part of their population going to foreign shores, to form there part of a new nationality, a possible rival of the country of their home in years to come. The great Powers naturally desire that, even as trade follows the flag, the flag should follow the immigrant into foreign lands when the circumstances and condition of those lands are those existing in most cases in Latin America. They aim at having those new countries, which may form the home of millions of their subjects, become a colony and part and parcel of the original Empire; and, as they will omit no effort on the opportunity presenting itself towards obtaining that result, the peaceful migration to, and establishment in, Latin America of millions of Europeans does not appear likely to take place.

There is another consideration that has to be taken into account in this connection. It is the Munroe doctrine, about which every one talks as of something that every one should know, but is seldom defined with precision—only a very few people understand it.

In 1823, when the independence of Spanish America was not yet a fully accomplished fact (the battle of Ayacucho not having come off at that date), and after the continental sovereigns of Europe had publicly avowed their intention to help the King of Spain to bring back the truant colonies of America to the fold of the mother-country, President Munroe proclaimed in a message to Congress that the United States of America would consider the interference of a European Power in American affairs, for the purpose of establishing its sovereignty on any part of the American continent, an unfriendly act to the United States. It has been generally thought ever since that if any European Power were to attempt the conquest by force of arms or the acquisition of territory in America, should such a thing be possible, by purchase or otherwise from any American nation, the United States, reverting to the declaration of President Munroe, would oppose such conquest or acquisition by force of arms if need be. In all probability this belief is correct. Though the reasons to-day may not be exactly the identical ones which prompted President Munroe, the United States of America certainly cannot admit of any European nation gaining a foothold on the American continent—much less since they themselves have frankly adopted the policy of expansion, and quite recently have so interpreted their constitution through their Supreme Court that they may hold colonies—that is to say, sections of territory belonging to the Union, the inhabitants of which are not to be on a par as to civil rights with the citizens of the United States. Here, then, is to be found a formidable obstacle in the way of any European nation, or combination of European nations, seeking to apply to

S. PÉREZ TRIANA

Latin America the methods adopted for the partition of Africa and of such sections of Asia as have been parcelled out amongst European Powers within the last thirty or forty years, or any other methods tending to that end.

Thus far we have considered the question from what might be called the huntsman's point of view. It is pertinent to take into account the fox's view.

Autonomous life and independence from the metropolis in Latin America dates from the third decade of the last century. The political life of the various nationalities, during the period of seventy-five years thus far elapsed, does not, on the whole, present a favourable record. Internal strife has been rampant in all those countries during the greater part of those seventy-five years. Of progress, save in a few instances, there has been but little, and mediæval conditions of life (from a material point of view) still prevail in large sections of those nations. The name republic has been and is in most cases a misnomer. The governments have been and are mostly personal despotisms, more or less tolerable and progressive according to the personality of the respective ruler. It were useless to seek to hide these facts, which are glaring. Of course, as might be expected, they are misjudged and painted blacker than they are as a rule, since generally in each case, when the opportunity arises, the totality of the sins of all the nations and all the epochs is heaped as an overwhelming load of accusation by the average European and North American observer upon the case at issue. Some countries in Latin America have already emerged from the dire epoch of internal revolutions. Mexico in the north, Argentina and Chili in the south, seem to have acquired a degree of consistency which warrants the belief that powerful and permanent nations are in course of evolution in those localities, and that they have already acquired sufficient strength to assure their national life and independence. The degrees of attainment in that direction vary in all the other Latin American nationalities. It were invidious, and would lead to no purpose, to seek to tabulate them in this writing; but undoubtedly, in the present temper of Europe, the continued state of restlessness or ill-disguised civil warfare prevailing in some of the richest South American nations would ere long have led to an attempt at conquest, were it not first and foremost for the obstacle arising from the Munroe doctrine.

Coming back, however, to the fox's point of view, I think that the sentiment of Latin America to the United States should be considered. It is evident that of late years a certain influence has come over that sentiment, and that the feelings towards the United States have been steadily undergoing a radical change.

Latin Americans as a whole during the greater part of the last century were wont to look upon the United States as their

109

THE PARTITION OF SOUTH AMERICA

natural protector. The great men of the American Revolution were held in reverence. The names of Washington, Hamilton, Jefferson, Franklin, and all the other founders of the northern republic were household words. Washington's sway as 'the first in peace, the first in war, and the first in the hearts of his countrymen' extended practically all over the continent. We Spanish-Americans were taught to look upon him, looming before us hatchet in hand, as the embodiment of truthfulness and of patriotism. Franklin's utilitarian philosophy was familiar to every one. The war of the American Revolution seemed a rather tame affair in comparison with the South American War of Independence, and the military achievements of North Americans appeared as child's play in comparison with the feats of daring in that sanguinary struggle which rent the Latin part of the continent for a period of fifteen years. The men who followed in the wake of the founders of the republic—the Maddisons, the Websters, the Henry Clays, the Calhouns, down to Lincoln—came in for their share of sympathy and respect. When the United States seized and kept a huge part of the Mexcican Republic, after a war which American historians themselves have called a great national crime, the various nations in Latin America were so busy with their own internal strife that the echo of that great blow was hardly perceptible. The War of Secession (which in Latin America, as well as nearly all over the world, was wrongly believed at one time to be primarily a war of sentiment, in which the principal motive had been the abolition of slavery) tended greatly to increase the love and sympathy of Latin Americans for the United States.

When the Cuban Revolution for the emancipation of that island from Spain in 1868 broke out, the heart of the great majority of Latin Americans sided with the Cubans, and the support which that patriotic effort found in the United States increased the feeling of sympathy among Latin Americans for the great Republic of the north. During the recent struggle between Cuba and Spain, Latin-American sympathies continued on the Cuban side. Cuba was only seeking to achieve what they themselves had accomplished long before. The support which, in this latter instance, was given from the United States to the Cuban insurgents was taken to be a logical sequence. However, when, in the course of events, the United States declared war against Spain, a feeling of distrust began to make itself felt all over the Spanish-American world. Those who believed that the United States would go to Cuba simply as liberators, and that, after freeing the island from the Spaniards, they would hand it over to its own children, continued to be partisans of Uncle Sam; but among many the idea began to gain ground that the United States were fighting their own battle, not the battle of the Cubans, and that these latter were only exchanging

Spanish masters of their own blood and language for Anglo-Saxon masters, who would treat them even more harshly than the Spaniards. In this case blood told. The events in Cuba and Porto Rico since their severance from Spain have not tended to increase or even to maintain the love of Latin America for the United States. It may be granted that Cuba, as a land, may improve greatly under American sway—that railways will be built, factories erected, forests exploited, and that some Cubans may profit individually; but historical lessons to be gathered from what has come to pass in Texas, in California, and in New Mexico show that all those advantages will hardly benefit the Cubans themselves as a whole. It is no consolation to a man for the destruction of his hut that it may be turned into a palace if the first condition of the change is that he must be driven from the premises. Even as a blister quickens the blood and makes it circulate, or a smarting blow produces the same effect, the conduct of the United States towards Spain, and in Cuba and in Porto Rico since the end of the war, has re-established the current of Spanish-American love and sympathy towards the mother-country. It may be too late for practical results to be obtained, and that new current of sympathy may be unable to achieve aught else than a display of Platonic sentiment; but in their endeavour to obtain the trade and the sympathy of Latin America the United States will find to-day graver obstacles than they had to encounter before the recent Spanish-American War.

Greater familiarity has certainly not begotten contempt for the great nation of the north among Latin Americans; but it has not tended to increase the love or the sympathy of the weaker nations for the more powerful nation.

Mr. Blaine—who, like all American politicians, looked upon politics as a business, but nevertheless had in him the stuff of a statesman—sought to bind the Latin Republics of America intimately and closely to the United States. He may be said to have been the last statesman in the history of the States, where the dollar-making politician has been paramount since the close of the civil war. He convened a Pan-American Congress, in which the United States showed that Olympic ignorance of pertinent detail so often displayed in their dealings with weaker countries. He sought the establishment of treaties of commerce specially favourable to the United States. ' Reciprocity Treaties ' was the name given to the projected conventions. The ignorance consisted in leaving out of the problem the fact that since the early days of their national existence nearly all, if not all, the Latin American nations had entered into commercial treaties with the European nations which contained the most-favoured-nation clause. For these and other reasons, Mr. Blaine's Congress was a failure, and, if we may judge from undeniable signs, it may be prophesied that the new Pan-American Congress convened to meet at Mexico during the present year will achieve no greater success than its predecessor.

Latin Americans cannot be asked to wish to place their countries commercially under the yoke of the gigantic American Trusts; nor is the pattern of Tammany (rightly or wrongly considered as the standard of American municipal administration) attractive. Models should be set as perfect as possible; and the good ones are not so abundant in the United States as one might desire. Furthermore, as a rule, the citizens of the United States in their dealings, political, international, or social, with Latin Americans are either patronising or overbearing. That product of American civilisation which seems to be the highest evolution of American life—the self-made man, who worships only his maker, and in most cases is considered by outsiders as irredeemably self-conscious—is an importation which Latin Americans can hardly desire to make into their country from abroad. They have enough to bear with their own local political despots, and the change would not be desirable.

The idea prevails in Latin America that when the United States proclaim, *urbi et orbe*, that America should be for Americans, they mean America for the citizens of the United States. It is not strange that the exclusion of the rest should find no favour with the excluded.

From the point of view, therefore, of the thinking man of Latin America, the protection of the United States, with or without the Munroe doctrine, is considered dangerous, and similar to the shade of those trees of tropical latitudes, like the Pedro Fernandez, which, though they may afford a shelter from the sun, ultimately kill him who rests under their branches.

The conditions of these countries of Latin America still in the throes of political revolution, or in permanent restlessness, are certainly unfavourable. The native races which the Spaniards found on the continent, though subject for a good many years after the conquest to the cruellest possible treatment, and though in some localities they have never attained real equality of rights with the conquering race, have not been exterminated. The Anglo-Saxons in the north hunted down the American Indian as if he were a wild beast, and to-day hardly any representatives of the aboriginal races are to be found in the United States or in Canada. The Indian population in Mexico, in Central America, in Colombia, Ecuador, Peru, Bolivia, and other states, is most abundant, and in some cases forms a very large percentage of the inhabitants. The races have mixed—not only the white and the Indian, but also the negro race. The ethnical composition of the Latin American population is, therefore, complex. Add to this mixture of races colonial traditions

which remained behind deeply rooted after Spanish supremacy had
been abolished, a republican form of government in theory, advanced
ideas in philosophy scattered broadcast, a desire to imitate the
federal system of the United States, which requires a great degree of
homogeneous education and habits of self-government, without due
preparation, and the efforts of the Catholic clergy in many of those
countries to keep them under absolute control as in a land of
promise where the good old practices of the Inquisition may be
re-instated in full force to the greater glory of God; and one will
understand how it is that revolutions are frequent and restlessness
permanent. True it is, as it is generally said, that a change of
government in many instances can only come about by violent
means; but a change of government in the countries where such
things happen means not a change of administrators of public
affairs, but a radical change in public life, and in many details
affecting the private life of the individual. When the change
reaches the hearth, when it interferes with the private life of the
individual, or the manner in which he is to educate his children,
worship his God, or bury his dead, it is not strange that men in
Latin America should fight and die for their convictions, as they
fought and died for them during centuries in Europe.

On the other hand, such a state of affairs fosters and facilitates
the advent of military despots and speculators, who are enabled by
the circumstances to establish their personal rule for their own
profit and that of their followers.

Notwithstanding the condition of affairs described, an armed
invasion of any part of Spanish America would be a most hazardous
undertaking (even were the United States to stand aloof) for a
foreign Power, and the undertaking would be no less risky for the
United States themselves. The Transvaal War has demonstrated
the possibilities which determined men may develop in defending
their own soil; and even where the most unfavourable circumstances
and conditions enumerated in the preceding paragraphs prevail, in
the weakest and most backward countries of Latin America, when
it comes to the defence of the soil, the utmost degree of resistance is
sure to be found. The most aggressive of observers have been bound
to confess over and over again that the fighting qualities of the children
of Latin America are equal to those of any nation under the sun.
The soil and the climate would be the allies of the natives in defending their country against a war of conquest. The partition of
Latin America, therefore, by violence, would not be an easy task.
Little fear need be entertained on the subject : the rivalry among
the great Powers is the best guarantee of the safety of weak nationalities. The so-called concert of great nations has been recently
shown to be most dangerous when called upon to act for those very
nations themselves : it is not a strong factor in international politics.

THE PARTITION OF SOUTH AMERICA

What the great Powers may obtain in individual sections of Latin America is paramount influence through the channels of trade and of finance; but, by an anomaly, of which probably there is no example in history, the competition among the powerful will prevent the abolition of sovereignties which, in former times, when one or two great nations alone dominated the world, could easily have been eliminated. It has been said that the European settlements or colonies established in various sections of Latin America may be considered as the basis of a possible conquest. This is a fallacy. There are large German colonies in Brazil and in Chile, and a very large Italian colony in Argentina; but the settlers in all these cases, though they may cherish their traditions, and love the home in which they were born, are not likely to become the soldiers of a crusade against the nation in which they have established themselves. Germans and Italians, as a rule, have left the countries of their birth, where the conditions of modern militarism prevail supreme. In the new country neither they nor their children may be called upon at a given moment to fight for the maintenance of dynasties or governments which, from sheer necessity, must daily increase the burden upon the citizens. Most of those settlers spring from the humbler classes. In the new country they find opportunities to better themselves and their children which they can never dream of obtaining at home. It would be unreasonable to expect any readiness on their part to sacrifice all these personal advantages, which appeal directly to every one of them, for the doubtful establishment of conditions of life similar to those prevailing in the mother-country, or of conditions of life which would be affected by the circumstances obtaining in the mother-country.

The partition of Latin America, therefore, is not probable, notwithstanding the many reasons which at first sight seem to point in that direction. The vast wealth of that immense section of the world, its untouched potentialities, will have to be developed without the destruction of the national sovereignties which, weak though they be, are guaranteed to the respective nations more by the rivalries of the powerful than by their own intrinsic strength.

Of all the great Powers of Europe, England is the one whose record inspires the greatest sympathy amongst Latin Americans. England showed herself very favourable to the Spanish American patriots struggling for the independence of their country against Spain early in the beginning of that war. British volunteers, individually or forming regiments, fought under the flags of the struggling young republics, and the memory of the British Legion, which distinguished itself in so many battlefields in Venezuela and in Colombia, is still cherished with gratitude among Spanish Americans. Shortly after the overthrow of Spanish power, England facilitated loans to the newly-established Governments, and entered with them into treaties of commerce. It must not be forgotten that Mr. Canning in 1823 warned off the Holy Alliance from all attempt at helping the King of Spain in his struggle with his colonies. During the whole of last century, British gold and British enterprise have been found all over the Latin American continent in the work of developing its wealth. For a long time English trade was supreme in Latin America; but of late years the Germans have entered the field with such skill and tenacity of purpose that England has lost a great deal of ground.

The other European nation which might exercise a great influence in Spanish America is Spain. In November of last year a Spanish American Congress was convened under the auspices of the Queen Regent of Spain. It met at Madrid, and, whilst no immediate practical results were achieved, one thing was made manifest: the hearts of Spanish-speaking peoples of America turn with sympathy and with love to the mother-country. Whether these sentimental influences can be so combined as to benefit the future of the race on both sides of the Atlantic is an open question, the study of which would require the consideration of numerous elements and circumstances. Action and fact, tangible and effective, must ever be preceded by sentiment. It only needs energy of the right kind exercised at the opportune moment for the sentimental potencies to solidify.

Are we, at the beginning of this twentieth century, about to witness a resurrection of the Spanish race; or is the opportunity to be lost and the numerous elements to drift asunder, each one in a different direction?

It were well, not only for the Latin American peoples and for Spain, but also for the world at large, that the Iberian peninsula and her former colonies, mindful of the lessons of the past and modern requirements, should influence the destinies of the world.

CELEBRATED WOMEN OF RECENT TIMES. BY THE RIGHT HON. SIR ALGERNON WEST

FTER the conversation we had together on the subject, no new one, of the influence and position, social as well as political, of women in the present day, you asked me to put on paper what I had heard and seen and thought of the power of the various illustrious women who had lived in my time. Did you think, when you asked this, that you were calling upon me to solve a problem which all the continuous ages of the world have admitted to be insoluble—a problem which began with Eve's disastrous influence over our first parent, and exists to-day as a mystery, limitless and inscrutable ?

If it is impossible to explain the influence of women in the past with all the accruing advantages of historical retrospect, how much more would the task be Sisyphean when the play which we hopelessly attempt to understand is being enacted before our very eyes ! So it ends in my only being able to tell you a little of some clever women of a past generation that have lived in a day when they did not smoke or speak in public.

To begin with my childish recollections, I should tell you of the Princess de Lieven, who came to this country as French Ambassadress in 1812. She was soon surrounded with flatterers and admirers ; but, Charles Greville tells us, she became neither proud nor conceited. She was full of vivacity, spirit, and good nature ; but the wide range of her sympathies and affections, without any particular sensibility, without any passion or softness, proved that she had a good heart. She almost passionately loved social and political influence over famous men of every country. While often from an attachment to individuals she herself became a partisan, she was clever enough to form a salon in which men of all parties met on common ground, in which political bitternesses became entirely obliterated. She was the intimate friend of all the distinguished men of her day : Castlereagh, Canning, Wellington, Palmerston, Russell, Aberdeen, Talleyrand, Grey, and Guizot. What must have been the influence and charm of a woman who, after the glorious spring-time of youth had passed, was able to retain the friendship of such men as I have mentioned, and won, perhaps, more than the friendship of Guizot and Lord Grey, whose correspondence with her filled three volumes ! Madame de Lieven was as great a political power in Paris as she was in England. She died only in 1857, and was therefore a contemporary and somewhat of a rival of Lady Palmerston, who, of course, is fresh in my memory. The essayist, Abraham Hayward, wrote a description of her salon, her cleverness, and her charm :

SIR ALGERNON WEST

Without aiming [he says] at the fame of a wit like Madame de Staël, or that of a beauty like Madame Récamier, or that of a party idol like Georgiana Duchess of Devonshire, without once overstepping by a hair's breadth the proper province of her sex, by the development of the most exquisite feminine qualities, by grace, refinement, sweetness of disposition, womanly sympathies, instinctive insight into character, tact, temper, and, wonderful to relate, heart. . . .

Lord Lamington, one of the Young England Party, in his interesting book, 'The Days of the Dandies,' pays a lasting compliment to the help she afforded Lord Palmerston through his long career, and tells us of the charm of her frank and genial manner, which, he says, and says truly, I believe, came from the goodness of her heart. Her influence was essentially political, and Lord Palmerston's success was the one thing she lived for and thought of : ostracism from her parties for a time was the penalty of anybody who did not fall in with his views, and so great a man as Lord John Russell fell sometimes under this punishment. One of the greatest of the *Saturday* reviewers told me that if ever his articles did not give satisfaction, he was banished from her parties for at least two Saturdays. When she had bidden her own friends, she would summon the Parliamentary Whip and consult with him as to whom it would be politically advantageous to invite. When Lord Palmerston became Prime Minister, her Society naturally became less exclusive, and I remember hearing of a lady who lost a bracelet at one of her big receptions calling at Cambridge House the following morning, and being told by the porter that after such a party as that it was not likely that the bracelet would be forthcoming. If to be a statesman's wife is a profession, she was, I think, far and away at the top of that profession. She always knew what to say, and what not to say.

Then, I can dimly recollect Gore House—which was soon to be occupied, during the Exhibition of 1851, as a restaurant, by Soyer the famous cook—and the existence of a woman of a totally different position and character from Lady Palmerston, the 'gorgeous Lady Blessington,' who brought under her spell all the literary world and all the dandies of the day, among whom Count D'Orsay, called by Byron the 'Cupidon déchaîné,' shone with meteoric brilliancy. A penniless Irish girl, who, after two unhappy marriages, drew into the intimacy of her salon Bulwer, Disraeli, Landseer, Jekyll, Grant, Mulready, Brougham, Louis Napoleon, Moore, Rogers, Campbell, and Byron, Charles Greville tells us she had no knowledge, genius, imagination, or conversation ; but I think he must, when he penned that paragraph, have felt a fit of the gout coming on him, for imagine what those meetings must have been when Byron, who found all Society vapid and *ennuyante*, and said that he never could get on with literary men, tells of Moore :

The wonder is not that he is *recherché*, but that he wastes himself on those who can so little appreciate him, though they value the *éclat* his reputation gives to their stupid Soirées. I have known a dull man live on a *bon mot* of Moore's for a

117

week, though he was guiltless of the point of it. In Lady Blessington's Salon alone could the epigrammatic repartees and spiritual anecdotes of Jekyll have flourished. Her literary powers were of no mean order.

By her 'Book of Beauty' and other ephemeral publications she helped to keep the ruin she had precipitated by her reckless extravagance from her door for some time. I imagine she might have described herself somewhat as the fascinating Beatrix Esmond did to Harry :

> My face is my fortune, I cannot toil neither can I spin, but I can play twenty-three games on the cards ; I can dance the last dance ; I can hunt the stag, and I think I could shoot flying. I can talk as wicked as any woman of my years ; I have a pretty taste for dress, diamonds and gambling ; I love sugar plums, Malines lace, the Opera, and everything that is useless and costly.

In reading the lives of distinguished women, I am always struck by the exaggeration of the biographers. Their heroines are possessed of all the charms of beauty, with temper, goodness, and charity, and their foibles and frailties are absolutely ignored ; yet they were mortals, not always endowed with intuitions of wisdom and unapproachable felicities of thought and expression.

I recollect an essay bordering on the fulsome, written by Abraham Hayward, in which he exemplifies Lady Palmerston's extraordinary goodness of heart by relating how, after a magnificent dinner she had presided over to some foreign princes, she got into a cab and went round the corner to visit her old friend, Lady Tankerville, who was dangerously ill. The biographer of Lady Blessington gives us an account of a little dinner at Gore House. After a description of gleaming satins, curving breasts, starlight jewels, grey blue eyes, mobile and tender mouth, &c., the author describes the banquet in a sentence worthy of Lothaire :—

> The soothing light of candles fell upon a table set with a service of chased silver and old gold, beautified with the luxuriant colour of mellow fruits and odorous flowers in dishes and bowls of sea-green Sèvre and porcelain. The rich amber and deep ruby of rare and fragrant wines caught the light of taper flames whose reflections in the goblet-shaped glasses gleamed as might sacred lamps on the altar of Epicurus ; servants in powder, wearing magnificent liveries of green and gold, walked silent-footed as if they trod on air, serving ready the pompous procession of dishes whose insinuating flavour wooed the most reluctant appetite—and so on.

Lady Jersey was the high priestess of the Tory Party and a devotee of Disraeli ; only rarely did distinguished Whigs penetrate the doors of her salon in Berkeley Square, where an ex-minister of less party proclivities now lives. Politics and measures were there discussed with an eagerness unknown in these degenerate days ; and among the cynical ladies who were perhaps a trifle jealous of her powers of conversation she was satirically christened 'Le Silence.' Her beautiful daughter, Lady Clementina Villiers, added enormously, no doubt to the fascination of her mother's salon. Her fame spread to Paris, where she was treated as royalty on the occasion of her frequent visits to that capital.

What Lady Jersey provided in the way of intellectual intercourse with the Tories, Lady Grey, the beautiful subject of Sir Thomas Lawrence's pencil, the wife of the great Prime Minister, offered to the Whig oligarchy. All the Whig Reformers of the day met in her house, and the humour of Sydney Smith was ever ready to enliven the political atmosphere—so contagious was it that my wife has told me that if he asked for pepper at dinner people smiled, and if he sneezed they went into convulsions of laughter. A mother of eight children, many of them distinguished, all of them clever, themselves contributed largely to the success of her salon. I see her now with a beauty undimmed by age, her lovely Irish eyes beaming after she had passed the allotted time of life, surrounded by all that should accompany old age—honour, love, obedience, and troops of friends. Lord Byron said :

> Lord Grey and his family were the personification of Madame de Staël's *beau ideal* of perfection and might serve as the finest specimen of the pure English patrician breed. His uncompromising and uncompromised dignity, founded on self-respect and accompanied by that certain proof of superiority, simplicity of manner and freedom from affectation ; with her mild and mature graces, her whole life offering a model to wives and mothers—really they are people to be proud of, and a few such would reconcile one to one's species.

Later Lady Waldegrave opened her doors in Carlton Gardens and Strawberry Hill to a large and less exclusive society. Her object was, particularly after her marriage with Chichester Fortescue, essentially political, and she devoted her talents to the ambition and successful career of her husband. She restored Strawberry Hill, which had been left to her by her second husband, re-collecting what she could of Horace Walpole's treasures which had been sold, and collected pictures of the Walpole family and those of her own, among which was Sir Joshua's famous portrait of the three Ladies Waldegrave. To this collection she added drawings of her intimate friends.

The Duc d'Aumale, Lords Grey and Clarendon, and many famous politicians were constantly her guests — a generation younger was represented by Lords Dufferin, Ampthill, Julian Fane, and William Harcourt—in London and the country, where her hospitality was unbounded. An old friend says that to her might be applied the words of La Bruyère, ' She was a handsome woman with the virtues of an honest man.'

Lady Clanricarde, the daughter of Canning, exercised much social and political influence. She was very beautiful, and was said to have been like her father. She was a student of politics and spoke her mind freely ; indeed, Macaulay thought she showed more political animosity than was quite becoming a pretty woman ; but he admitted that, being the daughter of a statesman who was a martyr to the rage of faction, she might be pardoned for speaking sharply of the enemies of her parent. ' With knitted brow and flashing eyes and a look of feminine vengeance about her beautiful mouth, she gave me such a character of Peel, as he would certainly have no pleasure in hearing.'

Your patience would become exhausted were I to talk of Lady Ashburton at the Grange and Bath House, where she made brilliant conversations with Carlyle, Thackeray, and Kingsley ; or of Lady Granville, who entertained the Whig aristocracy in her house in Bruton Street, once occupied by John Duke of Argyll, where Effie Deans sought for him in vain, and where in my time Charles Greville, as Lady Granville used to say, was 'my lodger'; or of Madame de Flahault, Lady Sydney, or Lady Molesworth; but I must say one word of Lady William Russell, whose parties I used to enter with modesty, of course, added to a feeling of alarm. She seemed to have read everything and known everybody. Her sons, Odo and Arthur (Arthur was a great friend of mine), lived with and almost worshipped her, and added much to the charm of her society. She had an accident, which confined her to her sofa in South Audley Street, and there the lady, with somewhat of an imperious manner, who recollected Madame de Staël and Byron, entertained English and foreign celebrities with her brilliant conversation and her quick repartees.

With the experience of others joined to that of my own, I must endeavour, somewhat feebly I admit, to discover what it was that gave to the clever women of the past that word so dear to Madame de Staël, 'consideration.' It was not only wealth or morality, or the want of it ; neither was it only cleverness or beauty or power of conversation.

A clergyman travelling with some navvies was shocked at their language, and asked them where they learnt it. 'Learnt it, Governor !' said one of them. 'You can't learn it—it is a gift.' And what is the social gift that can form and keep a salon ? I believe it to be the blessed inspiration of graciousness, a surface power of concentration, and a keen but momentary sympathy which loves to give pleasure to others. What is graciousness in a woman is tact in a man, so often designated by foolish persons as humbug. Do we not experience from time to time the invigorating effect of manner which flatters our self-vanity, and adds an inch to our stature ?

There are many women with that gift among us now. If I might venture to allude to one pre-eminently endowed with it, it is our gracious Queen. As she passes, with a beautiful and bewitching smile, there is not one in an assembly, however large, who does not appropriate it to himself individually and does not become a happier man.

SIR ALGERNON WEST

Why, then, are there not salons as they existed in the beginning of the century? I think it is partly because society has grown so largely, and opens her wide embrace to all who wish to be embraced ; and with the growth of society has come a preponderating love of wealth, an increase of amusement in entertainments, restaurants and plays which our forefathers could never have dreamt of or imagined. Besides, the great political questions of a past time which sharply divided society into hostile camps have for the moment become hushed, and the women of to-day are too restless and indifferent to trouble themselves with details which would require thought and study.

A salon, too, requires much trouble and some sacrifices. It demands that the presiding genius should always be at home, and the more active women of to-day would not submit to such curtailment of their independence. And then it requires the merging of individual friendships more or less with a cosmopolitan miscellany, even if that miscellany be composed of the salt of the earth. So the days of salons are over.

The influence, as subtle and as all-pervading, remains, and will remain as long as there are men and women. It may not be directed into the same channel by the same means. The fashionable women of to-day are steeped in hero worship, and neglect measures and cultivate men—you know with what measure of success.

THE TEMPLE GARDENS
BY JOHN HUTCHINSON

AS here I sit, alone—for here 'alone,'
    As on the silent wastes where Arabs spread
Their shadowy tents, or where the billows
      moan
    O'er Austral reefs round isles untenanted,
    A man may be—what time, by Pleasure led,
Or Care, or cares, the human crowds pass by,
Unnoticed as the clouds which cross the summer sky—

Here as I sit alone, my eyes I close,
    And Fancy wanders to a far-off time,
When here no human monument arose,
    But Nature reigned in solitude sublime ;
    And this green sward, still green as in Earth's prime,
A Forest glade, upon the river gave,
Which laved its virgin flowers with unpolluted wave.

Into my ears, above the human hum,
    Which, as an under-song, rolls ceaselessly,
The murmurs of that untamed river come—
    Or flowing from far inland fountains free,
    Or back broad-breasted rolling from the Sea,
With flood imbrined—murmurs which to the mind,
I know not how, bring saddening thoughts of human kind.

But soon that dream is over, and I pass
    To other times, less distant, though remote,
When on these paths and o'er this self-same grass
    Men trod,[1] to holiest purposes devote—
    Men who above the warrior's thick-mailed coat
The priestly mantle threw—God's liegemen, sworn
To double service in a world of help forlorn.

Let those who will at such devotion scoff:
    Not mine such freedom, living in a day
When men to nought th' obsequious bonnet doff
    Or due respect or ordered reverence pay
    Save to the 'golden god,' and those whose sway
Controls his gilded portals, which to pass
Men covet more than honour or good name, alas !

[1] The Knights Templars.

122

JOHN HUTCHINSON

But, who that stands within that sacred 'Round,' [1]
   Where by their knightly forms the Ages sleep,
But feels in presence of a faith profound,
   Which shames our troubled doubtings by the Deep
   Which bounds our Present; which to overleap
Poor Reason strives in vain—checked, baffled still,
By limitations fixed by the Eternal Will.

But turn we from such thoughts to brighter themes
   Befitting happier times, when Law's strong hand,
Supreme o'er all, restrained the wild extremes
   Of tyranny and licence, through the land
   Displacing random justice, henceforth banned,
And here, where warrior knights before held sway,
Great Themis fixed her seat, to reign, and reign alway.

Great Themis, but not She, whose dread decrees,
   In old Olympian days, men's councils swayed;
But She, her milder sister, round whose knees
   The sons of freemen gathered, unaffrayed,
   To learn the ways of Justice, undismayed—
She who her rules from ancient Custom draws,
And guides the steps of men by Law, not Laws.

Here as I sit, where rolls the River by,
   Or where the Fountain, as it falls and springs,
Brings to the vacant mind the memory
   Of streams, and rills, and woodland murmurings,
   And dreams of far-off drowsy Country things,—
Here as I sit, or walk dim paths along,
The shadows of the Past around me flit and throng—

The shadows of the Past, the mighty Dead,
   Whose names are Oracles, whose words were Law;
Whose wisdom lives in tomes, if little read,
   The objects yet of reverence and awe;
   Whence smaller wits, as from a mine, may draw
Material which, skilfully outspread,
May gain them fair renown, and class them with the dead.

Here walks, by shades attended still more grave,
   The reverend form of him [2] whose pregnant pen,

[1] The name given to the more ancient part of the Temple Church.
[2] Coke.

123

THE TEMPLE GARDENS

Dipped deep in Learning's secret fountains, gave,
  By worthiest aims inspired, to English men
The Bible of their Law, unwrit till then,
Or writ, as erst the Oracles divine,
On rolls obscure, with pain deciphered line by line.

Here, too, with stately head bowed down, as 'twere
  With Learning's weight, another form I see [1]—
The form of him who, to endowments rare
  Joining the gift of perfect probity,
  Lived self-contained, in days of faction free;
Pursuing Truth, where'er her footsteps trod,
With philosophic mind, impartial as a god.

But who may those, who, trained to thought severe,
  Judges and Statesmen, Orators and Wits,
In bright succession through the ages, here
  Have won renown and fortune, benefits
  Untold conferring, number? Stately flits
Before my wondering vision the long train,
Guardians of England's Law and Conscience, and her brain.

But not by these alone, or such as these,
  The Sages of the Law, am I beset:
There, in the light he loved, reclined at ease,
  Where the green sward the latticed shadows fret,
  His unmistaken presence lingers yet—
The shade of him,[2] who led the laughing line
Of pilgrims, laughing yet, to Canterbury's shrine.

As there he sits, upon that soul-lit face,
  I watch the mirrored fancies as they pass;
The tear that trembles in the eye I trace
  For 'patient Grisel's' unearned woes, alas!
  The smile that flits, like sunshine on the grass,
Along those lips, as she her story tells,
Bath's much-wed wife, who still triumphant with us dwells.

From him attention wanders to the form
  Of one[3] alike, yet how unlike, who drew
With hand as tender, and with love as warm
  (In lines, if of less vigour, yet as true),
  Presentments of a world he little knew,
Save as a traveller, homeless and apart,
Through eyes suffused and dimmed by tenderness of heart.

[1] Selden.   [2] Chaucer.   [3] Goldsmith.

JOHN HUTCHINSON

Illustrious Shade, pass on thy way beloved—
  Beloved while simple faith and guileless ways
Have power to move, as they have moved,
  All human hearts—pass onward from my gaze
  Where o'er thy grave the moonbeam haply strays—
Thy grave, a shrine to gentle spirits dear,
A shrine which hallows Law's too worldly atmosphere.

     *   *   *   *   *

But who may all the tender thoughts, which throng
  Within the pensive mind unbid, recall ?
The memories which to those 'Courts' belong?
  The ancient glories of that storied Hall,
  Where kings and knights have held high festival?
'Twould need a Muse with stronger wing than mine,
To rise to such a theme, nor from the height decline.

O much-loved spot, be far removed the time,
  When thoughtless change, named Progress, shall presume
To invade unbashed, thy quietude sublime,
  And all the quaintness of thy Past entomb ;
  Long may the freshness of thy verdure bloom,
Long may thy Fountain into sunlight spring,
And long thy sacred birds beneath it splash the wing !

Long may the horn [1] at eventide repeat,
  With echoes weird, its hospitable call ;
Nor ever thy young diners cease to eat
  Their way to fortune in their cherished Hall,
  Nor fail to keep their 'Grand Night' festival,
Linked in the kindly bonds of 'Brotherhood,'
Their only 'rule of Law,' based on the 'Common Good.'

[1] The Temple substitute for the modern dinner-bell or gong, supposed to be a survival from the Knights Templars.

PIERRE RONSARD: A FORGOTTEN LAUREATE. BY J. C. BAILEY

HERE is no triter theme than that of the uncertainty of fame. A man is the delight and admiration of his contemporaries, graced with every mark of royal favour, honoured alike by the applause of the many, and by the sober judgment of the few; and in the next age he is a shadow or a jest. Another dies, and only a few friends have any sense of serious loss; but let twenty or fifty years go by, and the ' perfect witness of all-judging' Time grants to Hobbema or Corot honours of which they had never dared to dream, and admits Collins and Chénier to that high company in which no place is found for Gay or for the Abbé Delisle. There is a third class, not very numerous, who have experienced another stage of these vicissitudes, and whose fame has known not only life and death, but a resurrection as well. Of these, none has been, in turn, more universally famous, more entirely forgotten, and, at last, more honourably restored to a just measure of his ancient glory, than Pierre Ronsard, captain of the Pléiade and prince of poets at the courts of the Valois kings. Born in 1524, and dying in 1585, he enjoyed the favour of Francis I., Henry II., Francis II., Charles IX. and Henry III., especially of Charles IX., who delighted in his society, and loaded him with pensions and preferments. But the mention of five French sovereigns by no means exhausts the list of honours and distinctions he received from the great. Catharine de Médicis defended him from the jealousy of rivals; Margaret of Savoy was his unfailing friend; Elizabeth of England gave him a diamond; Mary of Scotland, even from her prison, found means to send him a magnificent sideboard; Tasso sought his judgment on the Jerusalem Delivered; Chastelard, on the scaffold, preferred his Hymn of Death to the consolations of Church or confessor; and the poet himself accepted the universal verdict, and proclaimed his acceptance again and again with serene self-assurance. And yet, before he had been dead sixty years, Jean de Balzac was asking Chapelain whether he was serious in speaking of Ronsard as a great poet; and he had scarcely been dead a hundred years before it was allowable for the lawgivers of French poetry to sneer at him without reading him. And now his turn has come again, and the editor of the final edition of his works, completed in 1895, by an additional volume containing a glossary, can dedicate it gratefully to the greatest of French critics, who laid the first stone of this restoration, and can preface the life of his poet, in true sixteenth-century fashion, with laudatory verses from such men as Théodore de Banville, François Coppée and Sully Prudhomme, as well as from Ste. Beuve himself.

J. C. BAILEY

Such revulsions of taste appear strange at first sight, but in reality they are the most natural thing in the world. There is truth and reason in each; the final truth, we may hope, in what must surely be the final revulsion. The mind of Europe, at the moment of Ronsard's birth, was in the condition of a youthful king just come into possession of his kingdom. All the voices round him cry in chorus, speaking only of the splendour and riches and delights that await him, and, without a single word of warning, call to him to make haste and 'enter in and possess the good land.' The promised land of the age of Francis I. was the New World of Greece and Rome. All things were to become new: the 'vieux temps,' always thought of with half contempt in logical France, was to be altogether put away and forgotten; a new era in art and literature and learning was to dawn forthwith. There is nothing in which Ronsard is more characteristic of his time than in his utter disregard of all that came before him in his native tongue, in his perpetual reiteration of the most daring of themes, *Magnus ab integro saeculorum nascitur ordo.*

The literature of the ancients was indeed only half understood, but the half-understanding was enough to give men some true, if faint, perception of the qualities that go to make a classic. Filled with an enthusiasm for the new-found masterworks of Greece and Rome, which if not wholly intelligent was still not wholly ignorant, they were resolved to equal them in their native French, the infant, as it seemed to them, still in its cradle, born but yesterday of the royal edict which ordered its public and official use. At least they felt that if France was to have a classical literature she must strike out a new path for herself. They were conscious of something in the ancients which could never be reached on the old lines. And in truth the literature, like the life, of the middle ages, was always in danger of losing itself, at one moment in the subtleties of the schools, at another in the inanities of the court, at another in the obscenities of the tavern. To produce a classic it was necessary to quit these bypaths: to walk in the main road of human life, and offer an interpretation of it which could satisfy an intelligence free at last and learning to think and judge with all its powers. The Frenchman of Ronsard's day, coming from his own old literature to the great writers, could not but recognise a humanity, a sanity, a note of good sense and civilisation which was strange to him: more easily still he recognised a largeness of utterance, unheard before, except in a special field and an unknown tongue, through the majestic medium of the Catholic Church. Feeling instinctively that literature of this sort satisfied the demands of the awakened human intellect in a way no mediæval literature could satisfy it, he desired that his own country, too, should possess men of letters who could offer him, in his own language, the same free and rational criticism of life, and the same elevation of style.

Revolutions are seldom quite conscious of themselves, but this one was as nearly so as such things can be. The demand for change, and the definition of the direction it was to take, were clearer than usual, and Ronsard, Du Bellay, and their friends set themselves to meet it consciously and deliberately.

Unfortunately the will is not everything in these high matters. It is indeed a thing of the first importance. The man who begins with the determination to do some great thing for the literature of his country, has taken the first step towards doing it. When we hear Ronsard proclaiming that 'there is as much difference between a poet and a versifier, as between a hack pony and a high-bred Neapolitan charger, or, to make a better comparison, between a venerable prophet and a travelling quack,' we feel that we are deal-ing with a man who has the great ambition which must go before great achievement, and in whose voice the trumpet note at least will not be wanting. Style is largely a matter of character, and a man who had so much of the heroic strain in him as Ronsard, was sure to find for himself a language by the side of which that of Marot would appear mean. The need of a new largeness of utter-ance, then, which was one of the two things men felt in the ancients and desired in French, was genuinely, if not completely, satisfied by Ronsard. It was the note which he struck even more than anything he said that secured for him immediately the enthusiastic admiration of his contemporaries. And who will doubt that they were right when he has before him such verse as:

> Car elle m'a de l'eau de ses fontaines
> Pour prêtre bien baptisé de sa main,
> Me faisant part du haut honneur d'Athènes
> Et du savoir de l'antique Romain.

There is style here especially in that magnificent last line, not the style of Pindar or Milton, but still something for which it would be vain to search in Marot, or, one may safely add, in any of Marot's predecessors. His contemporaries were in this way not so altogether wrong in saluting Ronsard as the Virgil, even the Homer, of their age: for it was plain from the first that he possessed, what none of his countrymen had possessed before him, a real touch of the *os magna sonaturum* of the great poets.

Even in this matter of style he could only approach his model from one side. His uncritical verbosity is as unlike as possible to the 'curiosa felicitas' of Horace, or to the reserve and dignity which is always felt behind the tenderness and sympathy of Virgil; and there is too much crackling of sparks in his flame for it to be compared with the white glow of Pindar. But if he falls below the ancients in style, he falls below them still further in his mastery of his theme. Indeed, the truth is that it was possible for the men of the Renaissance to envy the sanity and humanity of the great Greeks and Romans; yes, and even to think they could attain to something like it; it was not possible for them really to attain to it. The child is not made a man by the reading of a few books, though they be the best. The swaddling-clothes of the middle ages could not be thrown off in a moment, and the childishness of verbosity, the childishness of self-importance, the childishness of a servile literalism remain the witness, in Ronsard's own pages that the age of manhood was not yet. What can be more completely in the manner of a monastic chronicler than the rebuke administered with perfect seriousness to Virgil in the preface to the 'Franciade' for his untruthfulness in making Dido contemporary with Æneas? One cannot but feel there the remorseless literalism of an intellectual child, as one feels the child's passion for exact imitation in his instruction to his epic poet to clothe his heroes occasionally in skins of lions or bears, and to fortify their courage with oracles and signs.

After all, ripeness is a necessary part of sanity, and that brilliant and delightful world of the Renaissance pays the inevitable penalty for its youthful high spirits and bright colours and adventurous enthusiasms, the penalty of crudity. And if there is, in this way, a lack of perfect sanity in the treatment which Ronsard and his contemporaries give to their theme, there is also a lack of humanity, of the power to see human nature as a whole and from all sides, by which the theme itself is necessarily narrowed. We get youthful hopes and youthful fears, love and sorrow and death, and we are touched with sympathy as well as admiration: but a serious interpretation of life, or even a serious conception of what life means at all, such as we do get in different ways from Voltaire and Bossuet, Pope and Johnson, of this there is scarcely a trace. Poetry is, as yet, at school: and the poets are schoolboys writing exercises on the successes and disappointments that make up their lives. It is exactly the same with our own Elizabethans, if we leave out the dramatists. Their lyrics are often beautiful, sometimes exquisite, occasionally perfect; but any one who comes to them with any acquaintance with the great literature of the world as a whole finds them extremely limited and monotonous. The eternal complaints about the stony-hearted mistress, with their probable insincerity and certain exaggeration, are as tiresome in Surrey and Watson as they are in Ronsard: and the transitoriness of youth and the spring, and nearly all that is most delightful in the world, though a true and beautiful theme for poetry, is, after all, not an inexhaustible one. We turn with relief from a literature which can only give us a thousand more or less pretty variations on one or two charming airs to Molière's wide acquaintance with

PIERRE RONSARD

human life and sane and lucid judgment of it, to the wisdom and knowledge of Goethe, to the wisdom and strength of Wordsworth.

Yet, within his own limits and dealing with his own themes, Ronsard is admirable. In his hands French poetry attains a dignity it had never known before. He is, in the first place, almost always a scholar and a gentleman, and rarely descends either to the ribaldry or to the pedantry which had so often disgraced his predecessors. His conception of life, narrow as it seems to us, was large and satisfying to the men of his day, and he wields his weapon with an ease and dignity which have not even now lost their charm. He has neither passion nor originality but he handles his themes from time to time with a sureness and lightness of touch in the presence of which all defects are forgotten. He himself complains, in a rare moment of modesty or depression, that he was only a half-poet; and, though he is much more than that, there is some reason for what he says; for he is by temper and ambition far above the versifiers, and yet, in his whole moral and intellectual stature, far below the supreme poets. He has not, like Dante or Wordsworth, any key to offer, either to the speculative mysteries or the practical difficulties of life; but he has, what the mere makers of verses have not, the poet's imagination which sees ordinary things in a light in which they are not seen by ordinary men. There is more of the craftsman than of the *vates sacer* in him; but his craftsmanship is of that generous and enthusiastic order of which the very highest need not disdain to be companions.

For all these reasons, and not merely for the interest of his historical position, he deserves to be much better known than he is. Half the prejudice which exists in England against French poetry is due to the belief that the stilted rhetoric which fills so much of it fills the whole. A good selection from the work of Ronsard and his friends would do much to dispel this mistake. There is, indeed, rhetoric enough in the men of the Pléiade; but it is the rhetoric of poetry, not like the other, that of prose. And how much else there would be in such a selection of what we value most in poetry! There the lover of our own Elizabethans would find something of the quaint charm which secures forgiveness for their conceits, something of their power of rich and splendid utterance, much of their fine enthusiasm for knowledge, and of that love of beauty, in all its forms, in man and art and nature, whose genuineness shines clear through all the mist of affectation which surrounds it. This is not the place to make such a selection, but one may quote freely of a poet so little read; and hope that those who care at all for these things may go farther, and make a larger selection for themselves.

And, first of all, there are two things which no one who ever wrote about Ronsard could refrain from quoting. They would bear being quoted again even if English lovers of poetry knew him better than they do. Both are on the eternal Renaissance theme—'Gather ye rosebuds while ye may,' 'Golden lads and girls all must Like chimney-sweepers come to dust.'

> Mignonne, allons voir si la rose
> Qui ce matin avoit déclose
>   Sa robe de pourpre au soleil,
> A point perdu ceste vesprée,
> Les plis de sa robe pourprée,
>   Et son teint au vostre pareil.
>
> Las ! voyez comme en peu d'espace
> Mignonne, elle a dessus la place
>   Las ! las ! ses beautez laissé cheoir !
> O vrayment marastre Nature,
> Puis qu'une telle fleur ne dure
>   Que du matin jusques au soir !
>
> Donc, si vous me croyez, mignonne,
> Tandis que votre âge fleuronne
>   En sa plus verte nouveauté,
> Cueillez, cueillez votre jeunesse :
> Comme à ceste fleur, la vieillesse
>   Fera ternir votre beauté.

Was ever more grace of movement, charm of fancy, simple felicity of expression, crowded into eighteen lines ? I am by no means one of those who cannot read Boileau, but I suppose that most English readers of this delightful piece will think with me that it has more poetry in it than is to be found in all the works of the Historiographer Royal.

The other is the famous sonnet. If what I have just quoted shows with what lightness and grace Ronsard could throw off a sketch, this is proof of the grand outline and gorgeous colour he had also at command when he chose :

> Quand vous serez bien vieille, au soir, à la chandelle,
>   Assise auprès du feu, devidant et filant,
>   Direz, chantant mes vers, et vous esmerveillant :
> Ronsard me célébroit du temps que j'estois belle.
>
> Lors vous n'aurez servante oyant telle nouvelle
>   Desja sous le labeur à demy sommeillant,
>   Qui, au bruit de Ronsard, ne s'aille réveillant,
> Benissant votre nom de louange immortelle.
>
> Je seray vous la terre, et, fantosme sans os
> Par les ombres myrteux je prendrai mon repos :
>   Vous serez au fouyer une vieille accroupie,
>
> Regrettant mon amour et vostre fier desdain.
> Vivez, si m'en croyez, n'attendez à demain :
>   Cueillez dès aujourd'huy les roses de la vie.

This splendid Renaissance pride, which makes us smile even

while we agree in Benvenuto Cellini, compels assent here by sheer magnificence of serene self-assurance. It is its own justification, for it has lifted the poet into such an atmosphere of inspiration that his work still glows, as if fresh from the fire, with a light and heat which can never be quenched.

There are few finer sonnets in any language. The slight pause after the fourth line, the fuller pause after that magnificent eighth line, the admirable opening of the sestet, all mark the perfect crafts-man; and but for the break in sense, which almost makes a separate couplet of the last two lines, though the poet has done what he can to avoid it by not rhyming them together, it would be as splendidly perfect in technical excellence as it is in ideal conception.

But Ronsard is far more than the poet of two exquisite pieces. His first-rate work is indeed not much in bulk when compared with the whole amount of verse he left behind him; but that amount is enormous; and it remains true that, when all poor and mediocre matter has been removed, there is still left a larger volume of verse than has sufficed for many poetic reputations. If we admit that his Amours are, in the main, intolerably tedious, his Pindaric Odes, in the main, intolerably artificial, and his famous ' Hymnes ' for the most part sonorous commonplace long drawn out, we not only leave a great deal untouched by our criticism, but we have to make exceptions even here. Nothing can alter the fact that the great Ode to Michel de l'Hôpital as the protector of the Muses is a magnificently imagined attempt to revive Pindar's method of build-ing up a great poem on a merely personal and occasional basis. The enthusiasm of Ronsard's contemporaries for this Ode is a proof of finer appreciation than one might expect, for his poetic imagina-tion never rises so high as it does in its general scheme, and especially in its splendid pictures of the Palace of Ocean, the Hall of the Fates, and in the great speech of Jupiter when he grants their sphere to the Muses his daughters.

> Mais par sur tout prenez bien garde
>   Gardez vous bien de n'employer
> Mes presens en un cœur qui garde
>   Son peché, sans le nettoyer :
> Ains, devant que de luy respandre,
>   Purgez le de vostre saincte eau,
> Afin que net il puisse prendre
>   Un beau don dans un beau vaisseau ;
> Et, lui, purgé, à l'heure à l'heure
>   Divinement il chantera
> Je ne sai quel vers qui fera
> Au cœur des hommes sa demeure.

And if the ' Hymnes ' have plenty of commonplace in them, one can understand the admiration felt for the Hymn to Death by that age to which splendid rhetoric of stately movement was a new thing, and which could not be expected to distinguish fully between fine words and great poetry. And the Hymn to Night, with its true Renaissance richness of effect, retains its charm even for us to-day.

> Nuit, des amours ministre, et ministre fidelle
> Des arrests de Vénus, et des sainctes loix d'elle
> Qui secrette accompagnes
> L'impatient amy de l'heure accoustumée,
> O mignonne des Dieux, mais plus encore aymée
> Des estoiles compagnes.
>
> .   .   .
>
> C'est toy qui les soucis et les gennes mordantes,
> Et tout le soin enclos en nos âmes ardantes
> Par ton present arraches.
> C'est toy qui rends la vie aux vergiers qui languissent,
> Aux jardins la rousée, et aux cieux qui noircissent
> Les estoiles attaches.

Poetry pleases by a combination of the artificial and the natural. Both elements are always present in it, but now one and now the other appears to be dominant. Here we see the craftsman deliberately producing his effect by phrase and fancy carefully combined and worked up; elsewhere, as in the elegy on the felling of his favourite wood, the genuine feeling of the man makes itself felt so directly and so simply through the thin covering of art that we almost forget that art has had any hand at all in the result. Poets have in all ages pleaded against the encroachments of the plough: but it would be difficult to find in all literature a lament over fallen trees more beautiful or more evidently sincere than that of Ronsard over the forest of Gastine. After a vigorous denunciation of their destroyer, he goes on:

> Forest, haute maison des oiseaux bocagers !
> Plus le Cerf solitaire et les Chevreuls legers
> Ne paistront sous ton ombre, et ta verte crinière
> Plus du Soleil d'Esté ne rompra la lumière.
> Plus l'amoureux Pasteur sus un tronq adossé,
> Enflant son flageolet à quatre trous persé,
> Son mastin à ses pieds, à son flanc la houlette,
> Ne dira plus l'ardeur de sa belle Janette ;
> Tout deviendra muet, Echo sera sans vois :
> Tu deviendras campagne, et en lieu de tes bois,
> Dont l'ombrage incertain lentement se remue,
> Tu sentiras le soc, le coutre, et la charrue :
> Tu perdras et silence et haletans d'effroy
> Ny satyres ny Pans ne viendront plus chez toy.

Then comes the personal note:

> Adieu, vieille Forest, le jouet de zephyre,
> Où premier j'accorday les langues de ma Lyre,
> Où premier j'entendi les flèches résonner
> D'Apollon, qui me vint tout le cœur estonner.

133

PIERRE RONSARD

The whole Elegy would well bear quotation. 'All Magnanimous men love trees,' said Edward Fitzgerald; and certainly it is not always that the poets of the sixteenth century have a subject with which modern lovers of poetry can so fully sympathise, as they can with Ronsard here.

In fact, it is from the side of Nature that it is easiest for us to approach Renaissance poetry. We are not nearly so interested in the woes of lovers as they were; nor is rhetoric adapted from the Greek or the Latin on the fallacies of hope, the folly of avarice, or the shortness of life nearly so new to us as it was to them. But there is no old age for the 'daffodils that come before the swallow dares,' or 'the bank where the wild thyme grows'; and in that field the Pléiade in France and our own Elizabethans are at once original and immortal. Nothing, indeed, is ever quite new in life or in literature; but it is in the main true that the men of the Renaissance saw Nature from a new point of view and rendered her charm in a new manner. That manner had its defects and its exaggerations and they were amply visited upon it. It was, indeed, less simple and less serious than the highest poetic treatment of Nature. It rarely saw far below the surface of things, and it coloured that surface with tints borrowed from literature and art. Woods and streams were, for it, not simply beautiful things, still less the sources of a philosophy of life; they were, above all, things charged with literary associations. Still, with all its defects, this manner was the outcome of a genuine delight in the new-found beauty of the world, and the poets of our century were not mistaken in feeling that their first need a hundred years ago was to go back to this naïve and charming method. For in it, most undoubtedly, lay dormant for two centuries the living germ of the Romantic movement. And so one passes back, with a feeling of difference indeed, but not at all of strangeness, from Keats to Spenser, and from Heredia, or Hugo, to Ronsard.

These comparative considerations help to explain why we more easily find ourselves at home in the literature of the Renaissance than the men of the eighteenth century did. They had lost the old key: we have made a new one. But such arguments do not and cannot affect the absolute value of that literature in itself, and the thing that really needs explanation is not why we can enjoy it, but why any one ever failed to do so. It is said that in the reign of Louis XIV. a man of taste would have been ashamed to confess that he read Ronsard. The revolutions of literary opinion have occasionally been amazing: but one refuses to believe that any further wave of carelessness or ignorance can again overwhelm the poet who wrote, for instance, so exquisite a thing as this in which he prays to his beloved fountain of Bellerie that he may be delivered in his fever from the torturing thought of its delicious cool waters.

J. C. BAILEY

Escoute un peu, fontaine vive,
    En qui j'ay rebeu si souvent,
Couché tout plat dessus ta rive,
    Oisif à la fraischeur du vent.

Quand l'esté mesnager moissonne
    Le sein de Cérès dévestu,
Et l'aire par compas ressonne
    Dessous l'épi du blé batu.

Ainsi tousjours puisses-tu estre
    En dévote religion
Au bœuf et au bouvier champestre
    De ta voisine région ;

Ainsi tousjours la lune claire
    Voye à mi-nuict, au fond d'un val
Les nymphes près de ton repaire
    A mille bonds mener le bal.

Comme je désire, fontaine,
    De plus ne songer boire en toy
L'esté, lors que la fièvre ameine
    La mort despite contre moy.

Poetry of this sort need not ask to be tried by any mere comparative or historical standard. If it be indeed still in its childhood,
it is a childhood of that wonderful kind whose productions disdain
to be compared with any but the works of full-grown men. Two
hundred and fifty years later Keats would have been proud to sign
it for his own.

The charm of Ronsard lies, I think, principally in two things,
the effect as of ' something rich and strange' which the best of his
more elaborate work produces, and the graceful play of fancy, which
is all the more delightful now that it is grown so rare in a serious
world. We had the former in the prayer to the fountain: here it
is again, in a prayer to the evening star :

Chère Vesper, lumière dorée
De la belle Vénus Cytherée,
Vesper, dont la belle clarté luit
Autant sur les astres de la nuit
Que reluit par dessus toy la lune ;
O claire image de la nuict brune,
En lieu du beau croissant tout ce soir
Donne lumiere, et te laisse choir
Bien tard dedans ta marine source.

Je ne veux, larron, oster la bourse
A quelque amant, ou comme un meschant
Voleur, dévaliser un marchant ;
Je veux aller outre la rivière
Voir m'amie : mais sans ta lumière
Je ne puis mon voyage achever.
Sors doncques de l'eau pour te lever,
Et de ta belle nuitale flame
Esclaire au feu d'amour qui m'enflame.

135

PIERRE RONSARD

The last rhyme is one of those which set Malherbe's red pencil
to work : but for all that, no one now will deny that this charming
piece satisfies the demands of the imagination as few French poems
did between Ronsard's day and Hugo's.

One might quote a hundred examples of his lightness and grace.
What can be prettier, for instance, than this welcome of the spring
and the butterflies ?

> Dieu vous gard, troupe diaprée
> De papillons qui par la prée
> Les douces herbes suçotez :
> Et vous, nouvel essaim d'abeilles,
> Qui les fleurs jaunes et vermeilles
> Indifféremment baisotez.
>
> Cent mille fois je resalue
> Vostre belle et douce venue :
> O que j'aime ceste saison
> Et ce doux caquet des rivages,
> Au prix des vents et des orages
> Qui m'enfermoient en la maison.

or, again, his farewell to his own 'Pays de Vendomois,' when he is
starting for Italy :

> Terre, adieu, qui première
> En tes bras m'a reçeu,
> Quand la belle lumière
> Du monde j'apperçeu !

or the address to the Hawthorn which begins so charmingly :

> Bel aubespin verdissant,
> Fleurissant,
> Le long de ce beau rivage,
> Tu es vestu jusqu'au bas
> Des longs bras
> D'une lambrunche sauvage.

and ends, perhaps, still better :

> Or vy, gentil aubespin,
> Vy sans fin,
> Vy sans que jamais tonnerre,
> Ou la coignée, ou les vents,
> Ou les temps,
> Te puissent ruer par terre.

or the praise of the Rose and the Violet, which must be the last of
my quotations :

> Sur toute fleurette déclose
> J'aime la senteur de la rose
> Et l'odeur de la belle fleur
> Qui de sa première couleur
> Pare la terre, quand la glace
> Et l'hyver au soleil font place.

136

J. C. BAILEY

Les autres boutons vermeillets,
La giroflée et les oeillets,
Et le bel esmail qui varie
L'honneur gemmé d'une prairie
En mille lustres s'esclatant,
Ensemble ne me plaisent tant
Que fait la rose pourperette,
Et de Mars la blanche fleurette.

Que puis-je, pour le passe-temps
Que vous me donnez le printemps,
Prier pour vous deux autre chose,
Sinon que toy, pourprine rose,
Puisses toujours avoir le sein
En mai de rosée tout plein,
Et que jamais le chaut qui dure
En juin ne te fasse laidure.

Ny à toy, fleurette de mars,
Jamais l'hyver, lorsque tu pars
Hors de la terre, ne te fasse
Pancher morte dessus la place ;
Ainsi toujours, maugré la froideur,
Puisses-tu de ta soefre odeur
Nous annoncer que l'an se vive
Plus doux vers nous, et que Zephyre
Après le tour du fascheux temps
Nous ramene le beau printemps.

I might go on quoting for ever, if it were not for considerations of space. The astonishing thing, as I said, is that, as men have never altogether given up caring for the spring and the flowers, they should have ever lost the taste for such poetry as this. The fact seems to be that in the sixteenth century, when every one was young, there was an overflow of enthusiasm and colour and ornament. The poets were, in a sense, children delighting in the prettiness of a world of new toys, and asking for no more. The making of verses was a new game, and it was an unfailing amusement to see how many combinations could be got out of a very small pack of cards. But that could not last for ever : and the next century found the pack too small and the pictures on their faces insipid. The sentiments and the imagination, most of all perhaps the fancy, had outrun the mind in the poetry of the Renaissance : and the inevitable result was a reaction to a state of things in which poetry no longer decorates life or plays with it, but criticises it, educates it, forms it. And this was the main effort of literature both in France and in England for nearly two hundred years. It became the first duty of the poet to talk common sense. He was no longer to be a dreamer, or a wanderer, consorting with nymphs and shepherds, but a plain man mixing with his neighbours and using the language of 'the town,' meaning what he said and saying what he meant. And no doubt the change had many good

137

results. There was a most necessary pruning of the youthful exuberance, which had been far too conspicuous in both the language and sentiment of the poets of the Renaissance. And literature, in becoming more matter-of-fact, became at first more sincere. It is not fair to ask too strict a consistency of poets : for poetry is the outcome of a mood of inspiration, which will not always come upon a man in the same way, and, besides, the imaginative temper is specially inclined to see things from different sides at different moments. But the exaggeration and inconsistency of many of the men of the Renaissance is such as to make it impossible to believe in their seriousness. Not only is the whole of their treatment of the subject of love profoundly tainted with affectation and obvious insincerity, but also they are Epicurean at one moment, Stoic at another, now the loosest of Pagans, now the most orthodox of Christians and Catholics. Death is sometimes treated as sleep or extinction; at another moment as the gate of heaven or hell. The result is that an impression of entire want of seriousness is left on the mind. Half the interest of Wordsworth or Shelley or Goethe lies in the consciousness of profound conviction behind all the poet says. It may not all be quite consistent; but it has all been lived through, deeply felt, and made a part of the poet's nature. No one could feel that about Ronsard : on serious subjects he is a rhetorician, not a thinker : and his rhetoric is at the service of all opinions and all causes. It would be impossible to go to such a man for inspiration as to the higher parts of life and conduct. He has, indeed, little to say about them, and that little is not his own.

One reaction produces another. We pass in the seventeenth century, from a literature whose high qualities are almost exclusively of the imagination, to one whose high qualities are almost exclusively of the intelligence. Poetry, which had in the previous period been content simply to see and to feel, made it its special function to think. It was the beginning of the great era of critical activity, which has continued down to the present day. But in the special field of poetry it led to exaggerations which produced the inevitable reaction at the beginning of our own century. In their desire to be certain of building upon a foundation of common sense, poets forgot to proceed to the superstructure which could only be reared by the help of the imagination. Poetry, rejoicing in the energy of the intellect, did not feel the need of anything more, and delivered itself up to a reign of didacticism in which it was made the vehicle for expounding theories on any and every subject, from the constitution of the universe to the 'art of preserving health' and the science of the chase. Such subjects may be possible poetic themes, under certain conditions of treatment; but here the treatment became that of the intelligence alone. The result was that a new reaction, this time in favour of a new birth of the imagination, was inevitable : and we are familiar with it in the nearly contemporary movements headed by the Lake poets in England and by Victor Hugo in France.

A revival of interest in Ronsard, as I have said, naturally followed. For the romantic protest was especially directed against the absence of colour, and liberty, and variety, as well as of the true poetic imagination, in the verse of the eighteenth century. And as the men of seventy years ago travelled back in search of these qualities, they found La Fontaine, indeed, half consciously in possession of some of the best of them ; but to find them in full and conscious perfection it was necessary to go behind Malherbe—to go, in fact, to Ronsard and to the Pléiade. It was Malherbe who taught French poetry the Alexandrine drill and clothed it in the tight-fitting drab uniform which so long impeded its free movement. Ronsard could use the great twelve-syllable metre with splendid effect ; but the quotations I have given show that he did not confine himself to it. In fact, he is the inventor of a great many of the best French measures which lay unused for two centuries, to be re-discovered and revived in our own. Even so late as at the reception of Leconte de Lisle into the Academy, Alexandre Dumas could still maintain the extraordinary traditional theory that all poetic subjects could be successfully handled in Alexandrines, and that no other metre was required. Ronsard knew better. He has an infinite variety of metre and movement, and it is to that that he owes a large part of his revived popularity. But he owes even more to his quality of imagination, to what may fairly be called his qualities of soul, than he does to any technical excellences. His editor justly calls him 'créateur du style noble dans la poésie française.' Other critics have spoken of his rich harmonies, of his creative instinct, of his 'élans sublimes.' Ste.-Beuve praises his 'fibre héroïque et mâle.' It is in such things as this that his special distinction lies, as his special charm lies perhaps in the ease and grace of his delightful lyrics. He was wanting in the sense of order, in patience, in that watchful self-criticism which gives the crown of perfection to the thought and utterance of poets. And the very language he had to use was as yet unformed. But his unconquerable ardour and enthusiasm forced a way through all obstacles, and gave France, as has been said, a poetry, before she had a language, of her own. Throughout his life he was buoyed up by the conviction that he had been born to accomplish a great task, that through him, more than any other man, French poetry was to acquire a new greatness of conception, a higher dignity of speech. And that, in spite of all defects and all difficulties, he did, in large measure, accomplish this task, not merely for his own age, but for all time, is proved by the fact that even to-day the words that rise readiest to the lips, when the critic is speaking of Ronsard, are such as I have quoted—'noble,' 'heroic,' 'sublime.'

THE WAYS OF AN OLD WORLD
BY AMELIA YOUNG

N New Year's Day, 1787, was published the first number of *The World, or Fashionable Advertiser*, a daily paper started by a certain Captain Edward Topham, late of the First Life Guards, best known to the London of that time as the 'Tip-top Adjutant,' a sobriquet that had been bestowed upon him by no less a personage than George III. in recognition of many and valuable regimental services.

If notoriety could satisfy, Edward Topham would have had ample reason for contentment. His name was in every mouth, and his portrait in every print-shop. He had been caricatured by Rowlandson and Gillray. His epilogues, spoken by eminent actresses, had elicited the rapturous applause of crowded houses. And to his sartorial triumphs, an account of which would fill a volume, the homage of a servile imitation had been duly paid. He had revolutionised the (masculine) dress of the period. The short coat that was indeed but little more than a jacket, the very short waistcoat, and the breeches so long in their upper quarters as almost to reach to the chin—the costume in which Rowlandson had immortalised this model adjutant—had been adopted with flattering unanimity by all the fine gentlemen of the Town.

But it is with the journalist, and not the man of fashion, that this article would treat, and we have only referred to the triumphs of the dandy to account for the intense excitement created by the appearance of his paper. He had taken good care, we should add, to make it widely known that his journal would appeal to every class—'to the statesman in his study, the fine lady in her boudoir, the gossip in the clubs and the coffee-shops, the actors and actresses in the green-room, and last, but not least, to the sporting fraternity, of which he was proud to proclaim himself a member.' Expectation, therefore, was on tip-toe, and we are not surprised to learn that three thousand copies of the *World* were sold on the morning of its first appearance, and that 'further demands made it imperative to issue more to accommodate the Court at Windsor.' Next day the proprietor deemed it advisable to apologise to the public, 'having heard that vendors had had the audacity to ask sixpence and fourpence a copy in consequence of the uncommon avidity for the *World*.' That apology was a good stroke of business, combining courtesy with advertisement. And, after all, sixpence was not much to ask for so very amusing a production !

Let us begin at the beginning, with the opening address from the pen of the proprietor :

AMELIA YOUNG

Like many other great men coming into office, we might promise a great number of fine things, which you might believe, and we never intended to perform. But as we are not Prime Ministers, and as you do not yet know us, perhaps you might be right in not trusting to what we advanced. In the affirmative, therefore, little shall be said, and we will indulge only a faint hope that we shall not be behind in Fidelity and Fashion, though we much fear that if we should be dull our printing will discover it. Finding it, however, difficult to promise like some other people what we will do, we will attempt the more easy task of saying what we will not. We will not cover our paper top to bottom with Parliamentary debates. We will not gently sport away the character of women of fashion, and if any gentleman should happen to walk down St. James's Street in a dress somewhat the worse for wear, we will not immediately suppose the colour to be buff and blue. We will not affirm that Mr. Pitt is an angel, nor can we deny that Mr. Dundas is a Scotchman. Such are the things we shall not do. What we shall, time only can bring forth. Some small deviations of character, however, we fear may be imputable to our paper. Yet have we some reason to think, though we have rejected the ton, yet it will rest with us, and that many a fair face and amiable character will take in the *World*.

Following this somewhat eccentric and ambiguous opening address is a leader upon the Prince of Wales's expenditure, advocating 'a larger allowance for the patriotic Prince who spends his money so royally and lavishly among his own subjects.' The perusal of this article leaves us where it found us. It is *vieux jeu*. We have read much upon this well-worn subject. We expect more amusing things from Captain Topham—side-lights thrown upon less familiar ground, a peep behind the social scenes of the day.

And we are not disappointed. The ex-guardsman was certainly an admirable caterer, collecting news from here, there, and everywhere. No trait or type of the age escaped his piercing vision. But before turning to ' news,' properly so-called, let us glance at the advertisements, which, more than any other part of the paper, hold the mirror to the manners of the period. The first that meets our eye is in the form of a letter, and is addressed to Mr. J. Dubourg, Notary Public, 5 Grocers' Alley, Poultry:

Sir,—Stupidity is but a misfortune, but impudence and calumny are vices which betray the baseness of the heart. I am told that you spread a rumour in town of my not having been admitted a notary public. And what are *your* motives I leave every honest man to determine.—(Signed) Peter Guedon, James Street, Golden Square.

Mr. Guedon's indignant protest against the conduct of J. Dubourg is followed by an announcement from Misses Stuart, milliners, of 8 Gerard Street, Soho, to the effect that they have 'lately received from Paris the Nina cap, now so universally admired there.' Mr. Love, of 10 Haymarket, next begs to inform the ladies that they can obtain at his warehouse, at reduced rates, all the fashionable powders of the season—violet, pink, orris, and maréchale—at the reduced price of 12s. a pound (from which we are led to infer that the ' ton' of 1787 was in the habit of investing largely in these little facial aids to success), also the celebrated

141

orange pomatum, the price of which is not mentioned. Was this celebrated pomatum a 'restorer,' we wonder? If so, we think the receipt must have been handed down to some of Mr. Love's descendants, judging by the orange hue of many of the dyed heads of to-day. That blonde tresses were as much admired then as they are now we gather from the frequent mention of Mr. Dowling, whose flaxen-hair powder is advertised daily in the *World* throughout the summer months of 1787. It was, it seems, 'an extremely delicate preparation, warranted not to soil the finest pocket-handkerchief, and in constant demand of the most respectable people in the metropolis.'

The well-known firm of Justerini advertises the names of liqueurs which are unknown to the present Crême-de-menthe consuming generation: Cedrata, Huile de Vénus, and Giroflé. Surely this last named must have been confectioned to revive the drooping energies of the tired chaperon or the old young lady whom no partner came to claim. Dancing was a serious matter in those good old days, and the advertisements of Mr. Welch, who offered to teach 'the Cotillon, the Devonshire, the Minuet de la Cour, and every essential requisite to accomplish either sex for the most genteel assemblies,' appear constantly in the columns of Captain Topham's journal. Mr. Welch's rival, Mr. Hopkins, 'goes one better,' and promises not only to teach every fashionable dance, but also to render his pupils 'capable of appearing in society with that particular satisfaction to their friends and pleasure to themselves which is ever the attendant on true politeness and good breeding.' An academy where the secret of social success was taught with the 'Devonshire' step, and where self-confidence and the minuet were simultaneously acquired, should scarcely have needed to advertise, we think. Possibly, however, Mr. Hopkins agreed with a vendor of raisin wines, whose name figures in the same column, who introduces himself and his wares with the announcement that 'Puffing seems at present to be very much the *ton*.'

Another frequent advertiser is Mr. Wright, of the well-known Lottery Office, who is perpetually leading the youth of the period into temptation by announcing 'a tempting list of prizes.' No wonder, then, that we find in close proximity to his insertions the information that 'a young gentleman of great respectability and fine prospects desires on a particular occasion to be immediately accommodated with from one pound to two thousand by the mode of *post obit*'; also that another gentleman (possibly somewhat older and possessed of less fine prospects, but) 'well made and of genteel family wishes to devote his remaining years to the services and felicity of an amiable companion for life of independent fortune *or* £400 a year. The most inviolable secrecy of course.'

AMELIA YOUNG

A third specimen of the impecunious class, a gentleman of liberal education and good connections, goes straight to the point and informs those who are desirous of contracting with him an honourable hymeneal alliance that no one with less than twenty thousand pounds need apply. Would-be candidates for the honour must possess, moreover, 'a dignity of mind and sentiments superior to those prejudices which prudish dispositions are too apt to entertain against an acquaintance formed through the medium of advertisement.'

Sometimes it is the lady who woos through this same medium of advertisement—but, of course, in a less direct fashion.

'A gentlewoman turned thirty, but of amiable and pleasing character, desires to assist in the domestic management of his house an elderly gentleman of fortune whose sentiments are not contracted, and who would treat a dependant as a friend. It is to be hoped,' adds this large-minded lady, 'that none will answer this but those whose character and situation in life command respect, as this advertisement is not inserted by a titler.' We do not quite know what a 'titler' meant; but we think it possible that Mrs. Fabula may have answered to the title. She certainly does not suggest one whose character and situation in life command respect. On August 15 there appeared in the *World* the following paragraph:

A card to Mrs. Fabula.—M. P. presents his compliments to the lady who was pleased to answer his advertisement in the *World*, of the 7th instant, from a certain water-drinking place in Kent. He is very sorry to labour under the apprehension that his appearance must have been despicable in her eyes, as she did not take the smallest notice of him when he appeared at the place of her own appointment. Should the lady out of delicacy have neglected the opportunity of making herself known to him, he will esteem it as a favour if she will oblige him with a few lines in answer to this, directed as before to 33, Wells Street, Oxford Street, and if she should think proper to propose an epistolary correspondence, or an interview as before mentioned, he will endeavour to comply with her demands. The strictest secrecy observed.

But a truce to frivolity! Let us turn now to the publishers' column and see what the men and women of 1787 were reading. In the first number of the *World* are advertised: 'The Poems of Mr. Gray' and 'The Ears of Lord Chesterfield and Parson Goodman,' besides three novels, 'The History of Charles Falkland and Miss Savile—in a series of letters,' 'The Happy Release, or the History of Charles Wharton and Sophie Harley,' also in a series of letters, and 'Amoranda, or the Reformed Coquette.' The epistolary form of narrative was apparently as much in vogue then as it is just now, for every other novel published during that year of our Lord 1787 was 'told in a series of letters,' mostly love-letters. Here and there we come across an autobiography, such as 'The Memoirs of a well-known Woman of Intrigue, written by Herself and embellished with a beautiful Likeness of the Author';

THE WAYS OF AN OLD WORLD

but whatever the method of narrative—epistolary, biographical, or autobiographical—the theme is always love. 'A Narrative of the Life and Death of John Elliott, M.D., containing an Account of the rise, progress and catastrophe of his unhappy Passion for Miss Mary Boydell, together with an Apology written by Himself under the pressure of expected condemnation for attempting to assassinate Miss B.,' is a work that was advertised repeatedly during the autumn season. So is 'The History of Miss Greville,' in three volumes, a book which, we think, must have been brought out at the writer's own expense, as it is sold for him or her (the latter, we should say) at Mr. Carruthers' lace warehouse. To each advertisement of this 'History' is appended an extract from the *Monthly Review*, assuring us that 'it is beyond the power of any one with the smallest share of divine sensibility to rise from the perusal of these volumes without feeling his heart meliorated, his affections expanded and directed to their proper objects, and his virtuous inclinations confirmed.' Could the author of 'The Pilgrim's Progress' have asked for more?

'An account of the Russian Discoveries between Asia and America,' to which are added the history of the transactions and commerce between Russia and China, by W. Coxe, Chaplain to his Grace the Duke of Marlborough, and a member of the Imperial Œconomical Society of St. Petersburg, might surely afford interesting reading to-day, whilst the mercenary spirit of the present age stands rebuked by the author of 'Letters which passed between an illustrious Personage and a Lady of Honour at Brighton,' who announces that 'these documents are not published to gratify impertinent curiosity or for the mere purpose of pecuniary advantage. There are nobler ends in view, as there will be found in them principles and sentiments breathing a spirit of honour and philanthropy which cannot but improve every sensible mind.' To judge by the publishers' column of the *World* in 1787, we should say that the moral and mental improvement of their fellow-creatures was all that the writers of that period cared for. An exception to this rule, however, is furnished by Mrs. Steele, the authoress of 'Memoirs of Sophia Baddeley,' every copy of which (she announces) is signed by herself 'to prevent piracy, which she has good reason to apprehend.' In some of the advertisements she gives the pirate a name, John Trussler, and we live in expectation of an action for libel; but there is no record of any such proceeding.

But to return from books to their readers—and there is more to be learnt from the gossip of the day than from many folios—let us hear what men and women were *doing* just then. At Bath they were card-playing, of course. '*Rouge et noir*' has been introduced, and is considered equal to sudden death. Amongst the distinguished hosts and hostesses are Colonel Campion, who has had little readings at his house on Sundays, "Books of Kings and Histories of Aces," and Mrs. Macartney, who has given a buff and blue dance.' Party spirit ran high at that time, and neither Mr. Welch nor Mr. Hopkins could have made Whig and Tory keep step together. Cork bustles were in vogue at Bath that season; but the *élégantes* who affected Paris fashions were wearing 'muslin robes over pale Pekin petticoats drawn up *à l'Anglaise*, yellow gloves and shoes, the latter trimmed with rose pink, and earrings of blue beads.' Quite a riot and blaze of colour !

A story from Brighthelmstone can scarcely have furnished pleasant reading for the Court at Windsor, which had shown such avidity for the *World*. An amateur theatrical performance had been lately given, it appears, in aid of the families of some poor seamen or fishermen, drowned in a recent gale off the Queen of Watering Places. At a public dinner the following evening, at which the Prince was present, a very nervous young gentleman had to propose a toast. 'As his Royal Highness patronised the performance, you must couple his name with the unfortunate families,' whispered a friend ; whereupon the nervous young man rose and proposed the health of ' His Royal Highness and his unfortunate family.'

The early numbers of Captain Topham's paper abound in curiosities of journalism. A letter picked up at an inn in Norfolk and forwarded anonymously to the editor of the *World* is well worth giving in full :

DEAR BROTHER,—Having shipped off all my little theatrical matters to our races, having nothing by me to work upon at present of any consequence, but a good Queen Catherine and an old Doyley, have heard you have got a nice Desdemona, and as I expect to pick up a capital Othello at Hull, what think you of a meeting betwixt them the week after next at Leeds ?

If your properties are good, and you can bring over a neatish bed to smother her in I shall be obliged to you.

Have you a delicate male singer you can lend me, as I have just engaged a young thing in the singing way ? If I can contrive to put a new part into his hands it may do our business for the races. I hear there is a good pretty Alexander at Wakefield. Get him for me if you can at 16s. a week. If he can touch Falstaff or Sir Charles. Easy you may offer a guinea, as I love to do the thing handsome.

I am, brother, much yours.

We wonder whether it was in mind or body that the young singer was required to be delicate, and we sincerely hope that ' good pretty Alexander' was not delicate in any way if he had to tour upon 16s. a week.

For the delectation of the *beau monde*, the *World* constantly gives ' news from the Court of Versailles, and therefore for our own Court and premier *ton*.' English fashions, it tells us,

more and more prevail, and tea-drinking parties are becoming as general at Versailles as in London. Of these tea-parties the most brilliant is at the apartments of the Comtesse de Polignac. Of English gentlemen who have the honour to be-

THE WAYS OF AN OLD WORLD

admitted, the Duke of Dorset, Lord Pembroke and Mr. Conway are at present in most acceptance.

Our Brussels correspondent writes that

> Lord Torrington's dinners are not as formerly of such rarity, but they are not spoilt by diplomatic ostentation, and there is enough, which is as good as any proverb upon earth.

From Aix la Chapelle comes the information that

> Mrs. Robinson (of both dramatic and romantic fame) is of the little convalescent beauty remaining here, and she is, in spite of painful indisposition, in first order of fine forms. The personalities also remain, as well as *the* person in the first order— showy equipage, a premier hotel, a little *gros jeu* and deep play, and among other Perditaisms as of yore a little literature.

There were gay doings in Herts during the early part of 1787, when the Salisburys' name stands first and foremost on the list of entertainers. They gave a grand party at Hatfield soon after the New Year—'A ball and supper,' one paper terms it: a phrase to which the *World* takes exception, voting it un-English. The hostess received her guests 'in blue sattin.' Many of the ladies wore richly figured brocades; but some were attired in simple muslin —beauty unadorned, &c.! A few affected Spanish hats with handsome buttons and loops; but to the coiffure Nina was awarded the palm of success, at which we are scarcely surprised, when we recall the advertisement daily inserted by the Misses Stuart, of 8, Gerrard Street, Soho! The gentlemen on this auspicious occasion wore plain dark full suits of velvet and cloth. To judge by the list of the company that appears in the *World* of January 8, we should imagine that the sterner sex greatly preponderated at the Hatfield *fête*; but this is accounted for when we learn a little later that 'only the gentlemen gave their names to be announced.' Some of the fair sex, however, took care to let their approach be duly heralded, for on the very short list appended to the long string of men's names we read that the Ladies Sefton, Sebright, Forrester, Essex, and Anne Cecil were present, besides the Misses Hamilton (who both wore the Nina cap), Mrs. Wynne, and Mrs. Dorrien.

The Tripolin Ambassador seems to have caused some inconvenience by arriving an hour before he was expected; and he might really almost as well have stayed away, for he never left the card-room, remaining there the whole evening, sipping *café noir* with his interpreter and his secretary, even when the other guests went in to supper. Perhaps he preferred the semi-darkness, for we are furthermore informed that 'the lighting arrangements in the card-room were very bad, and such lamps as they had arrived as much too late as the Tripolin came too early.'

The Salisburys' party was followed by others in the neighbourhood.

AMELIA YOUNG

Mr. Deleat and Mr. Brown, aided by his accomplished sisters, are amongst the entertainers [says the *World*]. At Hatfield, of course, the entertainment was on a larger scale, but more full of good appointment and voluptuous accommodation, it could not be than at Mr. Deleat's and Mr. Brown's. Lord and Lady Melbourne were both absent from these entertainments. The loss of so much loveliness as her ladyship's cannot be endured without cause. *Lord Carmarthen was not well enough to be among the dancers.*

Are we to infer that Lord Carmarthen's absence accounted for Lady Melbourne's? I take it that we are. The *World* correspondent is of opinion that her ladyship missed much. He waxes enthusiastic over the Deleat party. 'How bright the treat, how long the dance, how well they ate!' he exclaims in an outburst of frank animalism.

The amateur actor was as energetic then as now; but he evidently played to a far more patient and long-suffering audience. We hear of a very grand house party at Blenheim, when the guests were invited for a week, and a dramatic performance was given every night.

At Hinchinbrook the amateurs were ambitious enough to attempt O'Keefe's 'Agreeable Surprise,' a criticism of which was sent to the *World* by an onlooker (probably a rival amateur), who politely alludes to the lady who took the part of Cowslip as a 'Fusty Thing.' They were acting also at Alnwick Castle, at Hall Place, and at Shanes. Miss Hamilton, the owner of the Nina cap, meets with much success, and Lord C. FitzGerald and a certain Mr. Fector of Dover also come in for their share of praise.

But the receipts of the Bath Theatre suffered greatly in consequence of these entertainments, it appears. And no wonder! After that week at Blenheim, who would have cared to see a play again for a year?

No chronicle of the *World* of 1787 can be considered complete that omits to mention the verses that filled so conspicuous a place in its columns. On June 29 there appeared a short poem entitled 'The Adieu and Recall to Love,' signed 'Della Crusca,' a pseudonym adopted by one Robert Merry, an ex-lifeguardsman and a well-known member of the English colony then residing in Florence—a little mutual admiration society that included, amongst other small celebrities, Mrs. Piozzi of Johnsonian fame. 'The Adieu and Recall' made a decided sensation in London. 'I read the beautiful lines,' writes Mrs. Hannah Cowley in her 'Memoirs,' 'and without rising from the table at which I was sitting answered them.' This answer, entitled 'The Pen,' and signed 'Anna Matilda,' appeared in the *World* on July 12. Thereupon began a long amateur correspondence in verse that attracted, alas! hosts of imitators—writers who copied all Merry's worst faults, his ridiculous affectations and tiresome tricks of style, without showing a symptom of his undeniable talent. The paper was soon flooded with trashy rhymes

147

that were devoured by the ladies of the *haut ton*, but evoked the bitter scorn and indignation of William Giffard, who dips his pen in gall and wormwood when he writes of the Della Cruscans and their easily pleased admirers.

> Bedridden old women and girls at their samplers rave of the rubbish. The rage for amatory verses rises to a frenzy. Every day appear absurd effusions signed 'Della Crusca,' 'Anna Matilda,' 'Orlando,' 'Delia,' or 'Carlos.' A thousand nameless names catch the infection, and from one end of the kingdom to another all is nonsense and Della Crusca.

Nevertheless, the profits of the paper were increasing by leaps and bounds.

Before taking leave of this subject we should mention that the newspaper correspondence between Della Crusca and his Anna Matilda continued for two whole years without any knowledge of each other's identity. Then at last these two lovers upon paper met face to face, when disenchantment, disillusion, was the result. He was thirty-four and she was forty-six: and forty-six in those days was equivalent to—shall we say?—sixty now. So they met to write no more! One more poem by him, 'The Interview,' and a few vague, foolish lines in reply by her, and there was an end of the correspondence, to the sore grief and disappointment of the world of fashion. Mrs. Robinson (formerly the Prince's own Mrs. Robinson) was in despair; she had been among the number of Della Crusca's warmest admirers, and in the early autumn of 1787, determining not to be outdone by all the Anna Matildas and Lauras of the day, had rushed into verse herself, and contributed 'as of yore a little literature' to the organ of her old friend and champion, Captain Topham.

> Where amidst ethereal fire
> Thou strik'st the Della Cruscan lyre,
> Round to catch the heavenly song,
> Myriads of wondering seraphs throng.

Poor Perdita! She at all events was resolved to be 'Della Cruscan ere it was too late.'

The end of the year furnishes us with rather less lively reading. The winter season had set in again; but Herts was dull, for Lord Salisbury was ill and could not recover, and although the Melbournes, Mr. George Byng, and Mr. Brown, gave parties, we have no very bright or amusing account of them. We grow tired of the amateurs who seem to be always acting, with (of course) occasional intervals of quarrelling. The weather was very cold that Christmas. The Hackney, Highgate, and Hounslow stages were delayed by heavy falls of snow, and news travelled slowly. Let us conclude our chronicle of the year with the article in which the proprietor of the *World* took leave of his readers for 1787.

AMELIA YOUNG

The *World* is now one year old, and amazingly big for its age. When it started our very good-natured friends shook their heads. Our enemies having none, tried what they could do without them. Our object to try whether our print could not fix itself upon higher ground, on illustration and better manners, should mix information of what is doing everywhere with what ought to be done. When Junius wrote there were but four morning prints. The *World* has risen upon eight. When Dr. Johnson commended the *Morning Chronicle* there were seven or eight morning and evening papers in London. When this came out there were twenty. Some extraneous assistance we have had—who would not be grateful and proud for the assistance of Della Crusca, Anna Matilda, and Arley? Their poetry would never have appeared if the *World* had not produced it. If the serious continue to say we talk like those in earnest, while men of pleasantry are not baulked in their laugh, women of delicacy may join it without a blush.

Self praise, moreover, we know, is no recommendation, and good old Hannah More tells a different tale. She had often blushed over the *World's* gossip, and she has taken great pains to assure us that not even 'the elegance of Captain Topham's style' justified the existence of such a journal.

NELSON
BY JUDGE O'CONNOR MORRIS

MODERN research, and the genius of Captain Mahan, have conclusively shown that the ultimate result of the great strife between Revolutionary France and Europe was determined by belligerent force at sea. This was hardly perceived until our own day; superficially the war had a different aspect. France, invaded on all her borders in 1793-94, defeated the hosts of the old order of things; led by Napoleon from triumph to triumph, she dictated the Peace of Campo Formio, at the point of his sword. She was wellnigh brought to ruin in 1799; but the situation was transformed by the young master of war; Marengo and Hohenlinden struck Austria down; she became Queen of the Continent at the Peace of Amiens, and the position of England seemed to be much inferior. When the war was renewed in 1803, Napoleon failed in his project of the descent; but the rout of Austerlitz broke the third Coalition up and half of Germany was made a dependency of France. Prussia madly rushed to arms in 1806; but her power was annihilated on the day of Jena; her ally Russia succumbed on the plains of Friedland after an arduous and protracted conflict. After Tilsit the domination of Napoleon appeared established; his empire extended over three-fourths of the Continent; Alexander was but his crowned vassal for a time; he was supreme from the Niemen to the Straits of Messina. The change suddenly came to the amazement of mankind; but the fall of Napoleon and the prostration of France were apparently due to military results secured on the theatres of war in Europe. The rising in Spain marked the first turn in events; the Tricolor indeed waved over Madrid for years; but the flower of the Imperial armies perished in a disastrous contest; the 'Spanish ulcer' consumed their strength; the sword of Wellington threw a heavy weight into the scales of fortune. In 1812, Napoleon directed the armed strength of the West of Europe against the Czar; his eagles flew over the domes of Moscow; but the Grand Army was destroyed in the frozen steppes of Russia; the ruin was the most appalling ever beheld in war. The Continent now rose against its master; France made a convulsive effort to retain her military power; Napoleon did wonders with rude levies; but after a long and dubious struggle, he was overwhelmed at Leipzig and driven out of Germany. The invasion of France in 1814 followed; Wellington advanced from the Pyrenees to the Garonne. Despite a resistance worthy of the great master, the Allies ultimately made their way to Paris, peace being signed within the precincts of the vanquished capital on the Seine. The end, however, had not yet come. Napoleon made his marvellous escape from Elba, and, having overthrown the tottering throne of the Bourbons, for a moment re-established his fallen empire. But the League of Europe again declared against him; he was finally crushed on the field of Waterloo. The old order of the world was partly restored after a frightful conflict of nearly a fourth of a century.

These gigantic events occurred on land, from the Pillars of Hercules to the central wastes of Muscovy; the land seemed to be the scene of the world-wide contest; its issues, accordingly, were long deemed to have been decided by the shock of hostile armies, opposed to each other in different parts of the Continent. Yet nothing is more certain than that maritime power, and the manifold influences this involves, were the forces which, in the long run, caused the defeat of France and the fall of Napoleon; secured the triumph of the League of Europe, and brought the war to its final conclusion. The ascendency which England had acquired at sea, and which gained for her the resources of an unrivalled commerce, not only enabled her to continue the war herself, despite of reverses to her own and the allied armies, but also gave her the means of supporting the Continental armies, which maintained the conflict with Revolutionary and Napoleonic France, and which, notwithstanding repeated defeats, at last triumphed through the sheer force of overwhelming numbers. Had England, like Prussia, withdrawn from the contest in 1795, Republican France would easily have overrun the Continent, have established a supremacy nothing could have shaken, have made the Revolution the master of Europe. During the tremendous struggle of 1803–14, had not England become the ruler of the seas, had she not gathered into her lap the spoils of the resulting trade, had she not made herself the emporium of an almost universal traffic, she would not improbably have herself succumbed; unquestionably she would have found it impossible to be the paymaster of the Coalition, which, owing to her lavish subsidies, was able to keep the armed forces on foot which ultimately overthrew Napoleon's power; and the Coalition, had she fallen, must have succumbed. The maritime power of England thus made her the mainstay of a Grand Alliance more memorable than that of 1702–15; it sent her army into Spain and Portugal, the scenes of the first reverses that befell Napoleon; it kept her secure within her island fortress, presenting to mankind the ennobling spectacle of a single state defying a despot who seemed omnipotent, a beacon of hope to an enslaved and terrified world. But this mighty force even more directly contributed to the final result of the war. The naval victories of England over and over again discomfited Napoleon's deep-laid designs against her; they swept the flag of France from the seas, and deprived her of a colonial Empire; they crippled and almost ruined her commerce, and more than once reduced her to financial distress, which would

NELSON

have been bankruptcy but for the precarious gains of her conquests. This, however, was not all, or nearly all: the annihilation of the power of France on the seas compelled Napoleon to adopt the fatal policy of endeavouring to exclude England from trade with the Continent, and to force her to submission by destroying her foreign commerce. But the Continental system recoiled on its author; it provoked the indignation of the civilised world; above all, from the very nature of the case, it compelled him to aim at the universal conquests which, in the long run, necessarily caused his tremendous fall. The Nile, Copenhagen, and notably Trafalgar, in this way led to Moscow, Vittoria, Leipzig, and Waterloo.

The war, therefore, in its truest and broadest aspect, was the contest of a Great Power of the land with a Great Power of the sea, in which the Power of the sea emerged the victor. It was something like the gladiatorial duel of Rome; the retiarius, with his far-reaching but scarcely visible net, usually meshed the armed secutor in its deadly fold. Two figures stood out supreme in this mighty conflict. The superiority of England over France at sea had been proved in the early years of the war; her well-appointed and disciplined fleets had prevailed over the bad and ill-found fleets of her ancient enemy. But these operations had not been decisive; the victory of the First of June had had little result; the action of Bridport did him no credit; Hotham, in the Mediterranean, was feeble in the extreme. Napoleon suddenly appeared on the scene; the war, whether on land or on the seas, soon assumed a grander and more formidable shape. The great master did not completely understand the full effects of maritime power; nor did he thoroughly comprehend the problems that are necessarily involved in naval warfare. But from the first moment when he held a command to the last scenes of his career of wonders, he satisfied himself that England was by many degrees the most dangerous enemy of France; and his effort to weaken and destroy her superiority at sea were marked by a perseverance and energy all his own. In 1796–97 he succeeded in forcing or inducing Spain to add her navy to that of France; his ambitious project was, no doubt, frustrated; but the flag of England disappeared from the Mediterranean for a time. In 1798 he made his famous descent on Egypt; good judges have declared that had he preserved the French fleet he might have dealt a mortal blow to our Indian Empire. Three years afterwards he left nothing undone to array against us the navies of the North; although the cannon of Copenhagen made the attempt abortive, it was a grave menace in the existing state of the Continent. When the war was renewed after the peace of Amiens, Napoleon made plans and preparations to invade our shores stamped with extraordinary skill and resource; and if Trafalgar scattered them to the winds, and the chances of success were on the whole against him, not a few chances concurred

152

in his favour. This consummate warrior would not improbably have gravely imperilled our maritime power, had not England had a champion worthy of his steel, and more than his match on an element that was not his own. At every point in the operations at sea, from 1796 to 1805, Nelson confronted and defeated his great antagonist; in this sense he was by many degrees the foremost of British commanders in the Revolutionary War. He crippled the fleet of Spain at St. Vincent and made it of little avail to France; he annihilated the fleet of Brueys at the Nile and ruined Napoleon's projects of conquest in Hindustan; he broke up at Copenhagen the League ot the North; after a long and doubtful game of manœuvres, he brought the hope of invading England to a close at Trafalgar. And as Nelson, by these great exploits, made the supremacy of England at sea absolute, so he was the author in the last resort of the immense results which that supremacy at last assured; far more than the Archduke Charles, or Blucher, or Wellington, he compassed the fall of England's great enemy.

Nelson was born in 1758, near the beginning of the Seven Years War, the most fruitful, for England, of wars of conquest; he had, probably, the old Viking blood in his veins. It is always instructive to study the youth of great men; the materials of information abound in this instance. Anecdotes of his early boyhood give proof of the chivalrous sense of honour and of the fearlessness which were parts of his nature; but these may be passed by without special notice. He owed much to the care of his Uncle Maurice Suckling; the youthful training he had in the craft of a pilot stood him in good stead at Copenhagen and the Nile; his long voyages made him a consummate seaman. It was fortunate, too, that he was promoted soon after he had passed his teens; he became a post-captain at twenty-one; unlike his friend Collingwood, he was not kept in an obscure station. He gained distinction in the American War, if several of his companions-in-arms saw more actual fighting; but he was soon recognised by his superiors as a rising man of mark. One of the best features in his career as a warrior, readiness to seize the occasion when it presented itself and admirable skill in taking advantage of it, was seen in his attack on the fort of San Juan; his resource as a seaman was made conspicuous in his successful escape in one from four French frigates. The most striking proof of the estimation in which he was held in these years, a characteristic that belongs to genius, was the confidence which officers in higher command had in him; this, as long as he was a subordinate, was always manifest. The strong moral courage, which was one of his best qualities, appeared very plainly in his determined efforts to destroy the contraband trade in the West Indies, and to expose the frauds of civil navy officials; this was a thankless, nay a hazardous, but most useful service; his willingness to assume responsibility, sometimes carried to the excess of disobeying superior orders, was exhibited in his relations with at least one admiral. On the whole, when the Revolutionary French war broke out, though unknown outside the sphere of his calling, he was acknowledged to be an officer of great promise, not faultless indeed, but possessing no ordinary gifts. The first part of his splendid career in command begins when he was made captain of the *Agamemnon*, a ship associated with many glorious and happy memories. Nelson soon attracted the notice of Hood; he was the master spirit of the siege of Bastia; he contributed largely to the fall of Corsica. His pursuit of the *Ca Ira* is sufficiently known; it was a fine example of a British seaman's skill; and every one has heard how practically he rebuked Hotham for not having followed up an imperfect victory. That timid chief, however, fell under his lieutenant's spell; Hotham employed Nelson in an independent command, in operations on the Riviera coast; and had Nelson been seconded as he ought to have been, he would have checked Napoleon on his path of conquest in Italy. As it was, he almost stopped one of the movements that led to Montenotte; the two great adversaries had there unconsciously crossed each other.

Hotham, after a short interval of time, was succeeded by Jervis in the Mediterranean command. Jervis, if not a man of genius, was a great admiral. He was the author of the celebrated blockades which discomfited Napoleon's plans of invading England; he had powers of organisation of the highest order; he prepared the fleets that triumphed at the Nile and Trafalgar. He was, however, a stern and unbending martinet. Yet if his nature was very different from that of Nelson, he reposed the fullest trust in his proved subordinate. In the beginning of 1797 the occasion came that brought Nelson's capacity out in full relief. He had been despatched by Jervis to cover our retreat from Mediterranean waters, and had fought a very brilliant frigate action. He had rejoined his chief, who, with only fifteen sail of the line, was on the look-out, off Cape St. Vincent, for a Spanish fleet of not less than twenty-seven. On the morning of February 14, 1797, this great armament was descried, running before a fair wind, on its way to Cadiz; but owing to the carelessness of its leader, Cordova, it was divided into two distinct portions, one of twenty-one, the other of six, ships. The interval between the two was seven or eight miles. Jervis steered to take possession of the gap, in the hope of beating his adversary in detail. The Spanish admiral made an attempt to unite his forces; but only three of his ships crossed the bows of the British columns. His fleet remained broken into two parts, the windward composed of eighteen ships, the leeward of eight, one of the six Spanish ships having simply run away. The British fleet had now mastered the intervening space. Jervis ordered his ships to tack in succession, and in this way to assail the windward squadron; that is, each rearward ship was not to turn against the immediate foe until it had reached the position taken by the first, by these means fending off the foe to the leeward. This was a resolution of caution, perhaps of wisdom; but it gave Cordova an opportunity to escape, at least, to avoid a decisive action; and as the British columns, led by Troubridge in the renowned *Culloden*, sailed, one ship after the other, to bear down on the enemy, the Spanish admiral made an effort to bring together his still divided squadrons, and so to make good his intended course to Cadiz. The Spanish ships were the faster sailers; and the well-conceived manœuvre might have been successful, had not Nelson perceived how it could be baffled. Disregarding the order to tack in succession, he wore his ship, the *Captain*, out of the advancing column, and boldly attacked the head of the windward Spanish squadron. The *Culloden* and the *Captain* were now engaged almost alone for a time; but Nelson's daring move checkmated Cordova's project; British ships came up to support their hard-pressed consorts. The *Excellent*, under Collingwood, wrought great havoc; the *San Isidor* and the *Salvador del Mondo* were made prizes; and every one knows how the *San Nicolas* and the *San Josef* were stormed and taken by Nelson after a marvellous feat of boarding. The two Spanish squadrons made off in rapid flight: they had been completely defeated, with the loss of four ships.

The manœuvre of Nelson won St. Vincent; the battle would otherwise have been almost fruitless; the sudden and bold wearing of the *Captain* out of line strikingly illustrates Nelson's admirable *coup d'œil*, and especially his grand moral courage; he saw and seized the occasion at the risk of disobeying his chief. Jervis, stern disciplinarian as he was, felt what he owed to his great lieutenant; his remark to Calder, an inferior man, is well known: 'I will forgive you, if you do likewise.' It has been a matter of dispute from that day to this, whether the order of Jervis to tack in succession can be justified as affairs stood; it certainly kept back the leeward Spanish squadron, but it gave the windward a good chance of escape. All that can be positively said is that, from what we know of Nelson, he would, in the place of Jervis, have played the bolder game; would have directed the British ships to tack or to wear together, and thus to bear down at once on the windward squadron; and leaving the leeward squadron to its own devices, would probably, at some risk, have won a decisive victory. As it was, however, St. Vincent was a glorious day; the triumph of our arms had come in the very nick of time. The genius of Napoleon had made Spain an ally of France, and had thrown the weight of her navy into the scale against us; our only ally, Austria, was being struck down; Pitt's overtures for peace had been rejected with contempt; a great French fleet had reached the coasts of an Ireland eager to rebel; the nation was threatened with scarcely veiled bankruptcy. The victory of Jervis raised a heavy load from the heart of England; the weakness of Spain at sea had been proved, and France had really little to expect from her fleets; and if the Mediterranean was still closed to us, and the great mutinies in our fleets were at hand, a danger far worse than that of foreign hostile arms, still England had triumphed on her own element, and the maritime power of her chief enemy had been hardly increased. The battle of Camperdown ere long relieved the nation from all fears of invasion; it girded up its loins to continue the war. The blow which Nelson had really struck had baffled Napoleon's first effort to destroy our ascendency on the seas.[1]

As was the case almost throughout his career, Nelson was not adequately rewarded for what he had achieved at St. Vincent. We may pass over his attack on Teneriffe; it was a daring enterprise, one of the two failures of his life. In 1798 he was engaged in an arduous service crowned by the most brilliant and scientific of his splendid exploits. After Campo Formio, England was without an ally on the Continent; Napoleon was sent by the Directory to prepare the means of effecting a successful descent on our coasts. With admirable insight, the young conqueror had perceived that England was the most deadly enemy of France; 'we must destroy those active islanders,' he had written with emphasis, 'or we may expect to be destroyed by them.'[2] His correspondence of this time proves that he contemplated the invasion he planned afterwards;[3] but careful in execution, as grand in conception, he satisfied himself that France did not possess the means. He devised another scheme to strike a weighty blow at our power. Egypt had long been a tempting prize to the ambition of France; Napoleon proposed to make it a French colony; from there he would make his way to the Indies, overthrow our empire in India, and on his return 'take Constantinople in reverse.' This gigantic project has been called an idle dream; but its author declared, many years afterwards, that it was possible, and big with the promise of success[4]; excellent judges have concurred in this view.[5] Napoleon's arrange-

---

[1] For a full account of the campaign and the battle of St. Vincent, see Mahan's 'Influence of Sea Power,' i. 215–231; Mahan's 'Life of Nelson,' 259–284; Clowes's 'History of the British Navy,' iv. 305–316; and De la Gravière's 'Guerres Maritimes,' i. 144–164; I may be allowed to mention my little work, 'The Great Campaigns of Nelson,' 23–42. As to the order of Jervis to tack in succession and the movement of Nelson, reference may be made to Mahan's 'Influence of Sea Power,' i. 225, and to a very able article in the *Edinburgh Review* for October 1886.
[2] Napoleon Corr. iii. 392.   [3] *Ibid.* iv. 56–57.
[4] Napoleon Comment. v. 377.
[5] Mahan's 'Influence of Sea Power,' i. 299.

ments were masked with characteristic art; the soldiery of 'the army of England' were assembled at different points of Italy and France; and hundreds of transports were collected to ferry them over to the promised land of Egypt. The expedition set sail from Toulon on May 12, 1798; the French fleet was composed of thirteen sail of the line, one the *Orient*, the finest three-decker afloat; the army was about 30,000 strong; nor was the enterprise so rash as has been said, for the British flag had long disappeared from Mediterranean waters. Napoleon's project had at first conspicuous success; having seized Malta, long marked down as his prey, he landed in Egypt on July 1, and, having struck down the Mameluke horsemen in a decisive battle, he advanced from the Pyramids, and made himself master of Cairo. But a tempest of war was being gathered against him: England's great seaman was again to baffle his designs. Nelson had been despatched, with three sail of the line only, to reconnoitre the French armament; but his flagship—he had attained the rank of Rear-Admiral —had been disabled by a fierce storm, which had also deprived him of 'his eyes,' his frigates; for a time he had no news of his enemy. He was, however, joined ere long by ten sail of the line; at the head of thirteen, and of one fifty-gun ship, he pursued the hostile fleet with indefatigable haste; for a short time he was almost within its reach; but he was kept in the dark by the want of his frigates; he missed his quarry, and was off Alexandria two days before the French had landed in Egypt. He set off in vain to the Caramanian coast, then made Candia on a bootless errand; and having turned to Syracuse in search of his prey, once more sailed for Egypt in the belief that he would find it there. His energy and perseverance were at last rewarded; on August 1 he was off Alexandria again. He had soon learned that the French fleet lay at a few miles distance in Aboukir Bay.

The French admiral Brueys, a gallant but unskilful seaman, had disregarded Napoleon's orders. The position in which he had placed his fleet was insecure. His thirteen ships were moored in a far-spreading line, at distances too great from each other; the headmost ships were brought near a little islet, on which, however, there were no heavy batteries; the rearward ships stretched at sea along the shore, but they were not at an angle to their consorts, and could not, therefore, cover them with an enfilading fire. It was evening when the British fleet was descried. Brueys and his chief officers believed that an attack would not be risked, but they did not understand the man they had to deal with. Nelson had marked down the French fleet for destruction. He had at the moment but twelve ships in hand, for he had detached the *Alexander* and the *Swiftsure* to observe the enemy; but he bore down at once against the headmost ships of the French, which, he rightly judged, were the weakest and most exposed. The *Culloden* went aground as the British column advanced, but ten ships reached the doomed French line. The *Goliath*, followed by four ships, passed between the islet and the hostile van, and fell in force on it from the inshore side, while the *Vanguard*, led by Nelson and two other ships, assailed it from the side of the open sea. Five of the fleet of Brueys were thus brought under the cross fire of eight British ships. The effects of this grand stroke of tactics were at once decisive; the French van was annihilated in about an hour and a half. The enemy's centre however, made a stout resistance. The great *Orient*, the *Franklin*, and the *Tonnant*, much superior to the British seventy-fours, fought heroically and for a time with success. The *Bellerophon* was driven out of the fray dismasted. But the *Alexander* and the *Swiftsure* had rejoined Nelson; the fifty-gun *Leander*—she had been engaged in an attempt to get the *Culloden* off—appeared on the scene. These three ships, breaking through the intervals in the French line, and admirably seconded by other consorts, swept the enemy's centre with a raking and most destructive fire. As the night advanced the *Orient* blew up; Brueys died, as became him, on her burning deck; but though the *Franklin* and the *Tonnant* continued the fight, they were overpowered, and the French centre succumbed. The rear of Brueys made but a feeble resistance; three of his ships were run aground by their captains. By the early afternoon of August 2, two ships only of the great fleet of thirteen crawled hopelessly away with a few frigates. Villeneuve, the commander of this part of the line, who had succeeded Brueys when that chief had perished, had made no attempt to support his colleagues, though the French rear contained some of the best ships of the fleet. A subordinate was to mete out the same measure to him on the great and terrible day of Trafalgar.[1]

The dispositions of Brueys, before this great battle, as has been pointed out, were faulty in the extreme; the conduct of some of his captains was bad; Villeneuve was a timid and feeble lieutenant. But this does not detract, in the slightest degree, from the admiration due to Nelson for an achievement he alone has rivalled. The attack with his weak fleet was very hazardous; but Nelson saw his advantage, and seized it at once. The masterly manœuvre by which he directed an irresistible force on the French van; the precautions he took to ensure the safety of his ships, in the inevitable

[1] For an account of the battle of the Nile the reader may consult Mahan, 'Influence of Sea Power,' i. 266–272; Mahan's 'Life of Nelson,' i. 320–356; Clowes's 'History of the British Navy,' iv. 351, 372; De la Gravière, 'Guerres Maritimes,' i. 213–236; and Napoleon Comment. ii. 393–398. As to the conduct of Villeneuve, reference may be made to Mahan's 'Influence of Sea Power,' i. 272; De la Gravière, 'Guerres Maritimes,' i. 228; and Napoleon Comment. ii. 397. The best contemporaneous accounts of the battle will be found in Nelson's Despatches and in Captain Berry's narrative.

perils of an action at night; and his skill in averting risk, as far as was possible, are alike worthy of the very highest eulogy. The Nile ranks with Ramillies, Leuthen and Austerlitz as a marvellous exhibition of the art of war. Every one of Nelson's captains, it should be added, supported his great chief with insight and energy. This victory, rightly called by its author a conquest, imprisoned the French army within Egypt; and though Napoleon afterwards invaded Syria, his design of assailing our Empire in Hindustan was completely frustrated by the great English admiral. The results, however, were much more than these. The conqueror of the Nile once more aroused the coalition of Europe against France; the hordes of Suvórof overran Italy; an Austrian army reached the edge of Provence; the Archduke Charles approached Alsace; the feeble Directory was utterly unable to cope with dangers that gathered on every side around. France seemed about to succumb at the close of 1799; and though Massénas' victory at Zürich gained her a respite, the success of her enemies in 1800 was deemed to be certain. The situation was transformed by commanding genius. Napoleon, hastening from Egypt, overthrew the tottering French Government; and seizing the reins of the State in his master hands, had soon made preparations to continue the war. Italy was regained at Marengo, by a march and a battle; the strength of Austria was broken at Hohenlinden; Paul, subdued by the spells of the First Consul, withdrew from the contest, and became an ally of France; the Peace of Luneville brought the Coalition to an end, and made France more than before supreme on the Continent. England, as in 1797, was her only remaining enemy. Napoleon, as before, strove with all his might to assail England, and to destroy her maritime power. He had arrayed against her the fleets of France and of Spain; he now sought to array against her the fleets of the North, and to strike a weighty blow at her foreign commerce. With infinite dexterity, perseverance, and craft, he revived the Armed Neutrality of 1780; the navies of Russia, Sweden, and Denmark were to combine with his own and those of Spain and Holland in operations against the great Power of the Sea; the ports of Northern Germany were to be closed against British exports; Prussia, her satellite, since the Peace of Bâsle, was to throw in her lot with the ruler of France.

The peril was very real and grave; but England was willing and able to face it. In March 1801, eighteen sail of the line, with a considerable number of small vessels, were despatched against the hostile League of the North; but the command of the expedition was not bestowed on Nelson. The Admiralty had been somewhat estranged by his disregard in the Mediterranean of Keith's order, a chief who ought not to have been raised over his head, and by his unhappy passion for Emma Hamilton. The fleet was placed in the

hands of Sir Hyde Parker, a veteran of the inferior type of
Hotham. The operations that followed showed the immense
difference between a man of routine and a man of genius; they
have been described as the most signal instance of Nelson's powers.
After many hesitations, due to the misgivings of Parker, the
British fleet was off Copenhagen by the end of March; Nelson was
for entering the Baltic and destroying the Russian fleet, for Russia,
he rightly judged, was the soul of the Alliance of the North, but
his superior refused to leave an enemy in his rear; it was resolved
to make an attack on the Danish capital. A fleet can reach
Copenhagen by two passes, the 'King's Channel,' to the west and
northwest, and another channel between the Saltholm and Middle
Ground banks; for cogent reasons, which we cannot explain here,
Nelson persuaded his chief to advance by the second. Parker gave
his lieutenant twelve sail of the line and several frigates, and promised
to support him by demonstrations at least; the attack began on
April 2; Nelson's ships moved in imposing array by the passage he had
selected. The *Agamemnon*, however, was unable to get round the
shoal of the Middle Ground, and the *Bellona* and the *Russell* went
ashore; only nine sail of the line were left to join in the offensive
movement. The Danes had covered the front of Copenhagen by a
line of armed hulks and of heavy batteries; a tremendous fire was
maintained for some hours between the assailants and the forces of
the defence. Nelson, however, had selected the most vulnerable
point for the attack; by degrees the guns of the Danes were silenced
along the part of the line where he had first effected his entrance.
But at the part of the line leading from the 'King's Channel,'
and covered by the Trekroner, a formidable work, the resistance
of the enemy was stern and prolonged; the British ships suffered
heavy loss; the Danish batteries, if being gradually overpowered,
heroically kept up a desperate struggle. In the very heat of the
action, Parker, in alarm, made the signal to Nelson to recall his
ships; Nelson characteristically refused to obey an order that might
have caused the loss of his squadron; with admirable judgment,
he continued the fight; and then, when the defence had been well-
nigh spent, he proposed an armistice, on the acceptance of which
he successfully withdrew his crippled ships through the 'King's
Channel.' This skilful conduct probably saved more than one
British ship, for the Trekroner was still all but intact; but the
battle had not the less been won; Copenhagen was at the mercy of
the British fleet.[2]

[1] De la Gravière, 'Guerres Maritimes,' ii. 43, significantly remarks : ' Aux yeux
des hommes de mer la Campagne de la Baltique sera toujours, son plus beau titre
de gloire. Lui seul était capable de déployer cette audace et cette persévérance.'
[2] For the campaign and battle of Copenhagen reference may be made to Mahan,
'Influence of Sea Power,' ii. 44–51 ; Mahan, 'Life of Nelson,' ii. 60–98 ; Clowes's
'History of the British Navy,' iv. 427–493 ; De la Gravière, 'Guerres Maritimes,'

JUDGE O'CONNOR MORRIS

The Battle of Copenhagen was not decisive. It has even been described as a drawn battle; but it gave proof, in the highest degree, of the capacity of Nelson as a consummate warrior at sea. The true point of attack was seen and chosen; the British fleet fell on the weakest point of the Danish defences; the Trekroner was avoided as much as possible. Nelson, too, most judiciously refused to conform to Parker's order; and his presence of mind and resource are seen in proposing the armistice which saved some of his ships at least. He properly succeeded to Parker's command. The armistice with Denmark having been prolonged, he set sail to destroy the Russian fleet at Revel, the trunk of which the rest were only the branches. His quarry, however, had made its escape; the death of Paul brought the Northern League to an end; Russia practically submitted to nearly all the conditions, which preserved the maritime rights of England at sea. Nelson had thus baffled England's great enemy again; his services in the Sound and the Baltic had been immense, if they have not been sufficiently noticed by history. The war between England and France dragged on for a time; Napoleon made great efforts to extricate the army in Egypt; squadron after squadron was despatched for the purpose. These attempts, nevertheless, altogether failed; Nelson took no part in operations in the Mediterranean, but the memory of the Nile paralysed the French chiefs at sea; the army only returned to France after a capitulation and the loss of a well-contested battle. During these months Napoleon made demonstrations along the coasts of France, and gave out that he intended to invade England; but these, it is known, were mere threats; his only object was to divert attention from Egypt. Nelson, however, was given a command in the Channel, and directed to prepare a plan for the defence of our shores. Writers who loudly assert that the fleet must, in all events, be an impenetrable shield to protect England, may be surprised to learn that Nelson held an opposite view, and believed that a descent was possible, if not probable.[1] His plans, however, to repel invasion were not good, and are in marked contrast with Napoleon's offensive projects; as a strategist, indeed, he is not to be compared with Napoleon.[2] While engaged in the service he met the second reverse he experienced in his glorious career. He was beaten off in a boat attack at

ii. 12–38; Thiers, 'Histoire du Consulat et de l'Empire,' i. 283–287, ed. 1895; Nelson's Despatches, *in loco;* and Napoleon's Comment. iv. 376–381. Some of Napoleon's remarks are of much value. I may refer to my 'Great Campaigns of Nelson,' 71–97.

[1] See Mahan's 'Life of Nelson,' ii. 123–126. It is remarkable that Nelson in 1795–6 suggested operations which he thought might be undertaken by the French against Italy, strongly resembling Napoleon's famous project to invade England (Mahan, 'Life of Nelson,' i. 218).

[2] See some valuable observations: Mahan's 'Life of Nelson,' i. 239–5.

Boulogne by La Touche Tréville, much the ablest of the French admirals.

The Peace of Amiens was but a precarious truce; the great Power of the land and the great Power of the sea were ere long engaged in a deadly conflict, the Continent (as it were) looking tremblingly on. The passions of both nations had been thoroughly aroused; English cruisers had seized French merchantmen before the declaration of war; the First Consul had sent peaceful English travellers into French prisons. Napoleon resolved to attempt to make the descent on our shores, on which he had meditated for several years, to 'force,' as he said, 'the wet ditch of the Channel'; and to strike down the great enemy of France in his capital. He had measured the difficulties of the enterprise to some extent at least; but he had boasted to Lord Whitworth that he would run the risk; this was enough to daunt even his audacious genius. The maritime power of England, when the war was renewed, was infinitely superior to that of France, and appeared to render an invasion hopeless. The reforms, indeed, of St. Vincent had somewhat impaired the navy; our fleets were less efficient than in 1801; as always had happened at the beginning of a war, we suffered from the want of thousands of trained seamen. The navy of France, on the other hand, had been increased and improved; France had complete control over the navy of Holland, and could almost reckon on the assistance of that of Spain. The disproportion, nevertheless, was enormous in the resources and the strength of the belligerents at sea. England had about a hundred and twenty warships afloat, and an immense number of smaller vessels; she could bring round her flag more than a hundred thousand disciplined seamen. France had not more than fifty sail of the line, and was weak in frigates and lesser craft; she could not array fifty thousand sailors to man her fleets, and her sailors were not of the best quality. Nor was this all, or even nearly all: unlike what had been the case in 1793-94, the British ships, as a rule, were better than the French; the organisation of our naval service was much superior to that of France, which the Revolution had well-nigh destroyed, and which had never since been nearly restored. The British officers and crews, trained to the work of the sea, had a decisive advantage over their foes, confined, for the most part, within their ports; and the gunnery of our fleets was much more effective than that of the French, which was feeble, unscientific, and based upon false principles. The greatest difference, however, between the two navies was seen in the difference between the men who had been placed at their heads. Nelson was a tower of strength in himself; many of his colleagues were very able men; the British captains were capable and experienced seamen—all were inspired by the confidence of many years of victory. France, on the contrary, did not possess one great chief at sea, with the possible exception of La Touche Tréville; her admirals and captains were inferior men, the last often taken from the merchant service, and the memories of a long succession of defeats hung heavily on them. In Napoleon, indeed, France had a supreme strategist: his strategic combinations in the contest that followed were, we shall see, not unworthy of him. But Napoleon was not versed in naval warfare; he was by no means free from the false theories which the Revolution had spread through the French navy; the extraordinary success he had achieved on the land misled him as to what could be achieved at sea; in the existing situation, matchless warrior as he was, he could not turn the scales of Fortune in favour of France.

In spite, however, of the preponderating odds against him, Napoleon had determined to make the descent; and though the chances of his success were on the whole adverse, he had more chances than mere naval experts will admit. In the arduous and long doubtful struggle that ensued, Nelson was by far his greatest adversary on the seas, and for a time was directly pitted against him; but for Nelson, indeed, he might perhaps have compassed his ends, though Trafalgar brought the hopes of invasion for ever to a close. The strategic position of affairs on the theatre of war must be considered if we would comprehend our great enemy's projects. England, he knew, was far superior to France at sea, if the extent of this superiority was not fully realised; and, apart from this, England had a marked advantage in the situation of the belligerents on what may be called the field of manœuvre. St. Vincent had made the system of our blockades well-nigh perfect; Napoleon was aware that British squadrons could keep French squadrons within their ports for months; they would, therefore, possess a central position and interior lines, and all this favourable condition secures, should their enemy evade their watch and attempt to reach our shores. But the fleets of England were scattered over many seas and could not be everywhere in imposing force. Experience had shown that, despite the most stringent blockades, French fleets could elude the grasp of their foes, and could even make long cruises at sea; and it was possible by skilful demonstrations and feints, combined with operations of real importance, to nullify the advantages which a central position and interior lines give; to deceive and to baffle the British admirals, and to bring a French fleet in superior strength to the decisive point at least for a time. These were the facts and principles on which Napoleon founded his scheme; varied and modified as it was more than once, they inspired and directed his general purpose. It is most improbable that at any time he contemplated crossing the Channel with a flotilla alone, with no other means to effect the descent; the enterprise would be too perilous, and would be unworthy of such a

NELSON

master of war. The project of Napoleon was different. He would construct an immense flotilla; he would assemble it in force within the narrow seas and would ferry over his army in it; but he would cover the descent with a great fleet, to be brought into the Channel by well-combined manœuvres, and for a few days at least, to be in overwhelming force. In this way the invading army would be comparatively secure, and were the landing once effected Napoleon was convinced that London would fall and England would yield. Strategically the plan was very fine, if it did not exactly correspond to the facts of the case; in the words of a distinguished French seaman, 'we see it shine out in portentous lustre before it disappears in eclipse.'

The first care of Napoleon was to strengthen his fleets; he had made Antwerp a great port of construction; he disposed of the naval resources of Holland; French patriotism made him a gift of several warships; his squadrons were soon in respectable numbers. His next care was to form and prepare the flotilla, which was to be the bridge for his soldiery over the Channel, and to convey it to the point selected for the descent; his success in this part of his scheme was remarkable. Light craft were built on most of the great rivers of France, and carried from their mouths to the narrow seas; they crawled along the coast, protected by well-placed batteries, and secure from the efforts of British cruisers; about fifteen hundred reached Boulogne and the small adjoining harbours, which had been deepened and widened to receive them. To these should be added some seven hundred transports to carry the impedimenta of the army of the descent; the flotilla formed a great armament, capable of being propelled by oars and sails, and bristling with about three thousand guns. Meanwhile the forces which were to invade England were drawn together and encamped around the centre of Boulogne. The great stroke was to be made by 132,000 men; but the 'army of England' had the support of two wings, arrayed near the Texel and beside Brest, this being intended to perplex the enemy, and to draw his attention from the principal attack. Extraordinary precautions had been taken to enable the army at Boulogne to embark quickly; these operations became so perfect that the whole armament could be at sea within twenty-four hours; and under the usual conditions of wind and weather, the Channel could be crossed in thirty or forty. The danger to England was, therefore, grave, especially as repeated attempts to assail and destroy the flotilla had failed; and Napoleon's army was the finest he had ever in his command; it was the grand army of Austerlitz, Jena, and Friedland. England, however, was not unequal to herself; and when it had become evident that the descent was at least possible, though there was no suspicion of Napoleon's deep-laid designs, the nation rushed to arms, and hundreds of thousands of men were arrayed to resist the intended invasion. These levies, of course, were very inferior to the trained soldiery of France led by skilful officers; but Napoleon was in error in supposing they were of no value; they would certainly have made a stubborn defence even if a successful landing had been accomplished. The belligerents, in fact, were each too confident of their superiority within their respective domains. The Admiralty were convinced that the British fleets would either keep the enemy within his ports, or would overcome them in the open sea; they never imagined, or they deemed it impossible, that a great hostile fleet could be assembled within reach of our shores, and could gain for the flotilla an opportunity to cross; and whatever has been said by a few experts, they left the Channel much too weakly guarded. Napoleon, on the other hand, believed that once the descent was made, the forces in his path would be scattered like chaff, and that England would lie at the proud foot of a conqueror.

The forecast of the Admiralty proved to be correct, but it failed to take in important facts of the case; but for Nelson, indeed, it might have been falsified. In the winter of 1803, Napoleon addressed himself to the difficult task of bringing a great fleet into the Channel to cover the descent. The fleets of England at this time were engaged in many seas; Cornwallis with some twenty ships of the line was blockading Ganteaume at Brest with about an equal force; Nelson was holding La Touche Tréville, at Toulon, in check, each having from ten to eleven sail of the line; Pellew was blockading a small French squadron in Ferrol; and five French warships were shut up at Rochefort. Napoleon directed La Touche to make his escape from Toulon, eluding Nelson in thick and tempestuous weather; La Touche was then to rally a ship of the line at Cadiz; and, having raised the blockade of Rochefort, was to rally the five French ships at that port; he was then, at the head of sixteen ships of the line, to make for the Channel and second the great invasion. This plan, therefore, like all Napoleon's plans at the time, depended on evading and deceiving the enemy, and Napoleon made great efforts to accomplish his purpose by feints and menaces marked by his characteristic craft. It was given out that Ireland was to be invaded; Ganteaume was to make false attacks on Cornwallis; above all elaborate attempts were made to draw Nelson away from the blockade of Toulon and to induce him to think Egypt to be the destination of La Touche. The principal attack was thus to be masked and assisted by demonstrations on either flank of the whole theatre of war; and the plan was comparatively simple and easy, though we may well doubt if sixteen French sail of the line would have been a sufficient force to master the Channel. La Touche, however, was unable to get out of

NELSON

Toulon, though Nelson, who disliked the system of close blockades endeavoured to induce his adversary to set sail and to fight; and La Touche, much the best of the French admirals, ere long died. The enterprise was now delayed many months, owing to the conspiracy of George Cadoudal and Moreau, and to the creation of the French Empire; Napoleon did not recur to it until the autumn of 1804. By this time Villeneuve had taken the place of La Touche at Toulon; but the Emperor, as he is now to be called, entrusted the principal effort that was to be made, to Ganteaume. That admiral was to break out from Brest and give Cornwallis the slip, as was possible in the heavy gales of winter; he was to make a descent on Ireland and a false attack; then he was to press onwards to Boulogne and cover the flotilla with twenty ships of the line at least. The main operation, however, was to be seconded as before by diversions on other parts of the theatre. Villeneuve was to escape from Toulon and Missiessy from Rochefort; both admirals were to cross the Atlantic to menace our possessions in the West Indies, at this time of supreme importance, and—strange irony of fate—to seize St. Helena, a station of value to our East Indian commerce. The attention of the Admiralty was thus be drawn away from the decisive points, the Channel and Boulogne.

This plan had a beginning of success; Missiessy effected his escape from Rochefort; Villeneuve got out of Toulon, with his whole fleet; Nelson, deceived by Napoleon's profound wiles, at first directed his fleet to Egypt. But Villeneuve, a skilful but irresolute man, with a squadron not inured to the sea, put back to Toulon, crippled by a heavy storm; Nelson had soon resumed his watch off Toulon; Ganteaume was unable to make his way out of Brest. The Emperor's plan had, therefore, again failed; but, by the end of 1804, he had secured the active aid of an ally, who, he hoped, would turn the scale in his favour. Spain had been compelled to declare war with England; all the resources of the Spanish marine were placed at the disposal of the ruler of France. The fleets of the Allies now outnumbered those opposed to them in European waters; but if the navy of France was very inferior to that of England, the navy of Spain was immeasurably worse. Napoleon, indeed, partly understood this; he reckoned two Spanish warships as only a match for one Frenchman; but he never understood how immensely superior were the fleets of England—leaders, crews, seamanship, gunnery, in fact all that constitutes a really efficient force; and this baffled and marred his well-designed strategy. Nevertheless, he now formed his third plan, the boldest, the grandest, the most masterly—but to lead to Trafalgar. Villeneuve was again to take his departure from Toulon with eleven ships of the line; he was to rally the French warship still at Cadiz and a squadron of six Spanish ships of the line; with this

large fleet he was to make for the West Indies, where Missiessy, it
was hoped, would meet him. Meanwhile Ganteaume was to break
the blockade of Brest—Cornwallis, at this time, was inferior in
force; Ganteaume was then to break the blockade of Ferrol, where
there were to be fifteen French and Spanish warships; he was to
cross the Atlantic with thirty-six sail of the line, to join Villeneuve
and Missiessy, who would have twenty-three, and to assume the
supreme command. Should these operations succeed Ganteaume
would be at the head of an armada of more than fifty sail of the line;
and with this immense force he was to recross the Atlantic, to
enter the Channel, and to cover the descent. This was a strategic
combination of the first order; Villeneuve was to draw the attention of the Admiralty to the West Indies; Ganteaume, should he
get out of Brest, was to threaten the enemy along the European
Atlantic seaboard; a huge concentration of naval forces was to be
effected thousands of miles away from our shores; and the united
allied fleets were to reach the narrow seas, where England certainly
had nothing that could cope with them. The value of the central
position and of the interior lines, possessed by our squadrons,
would thus be rendered fruitless; Napoleon truly said that this
deep design was equal to any he had formed in his extraordinary
career.

The operations planned by the Emperor were, for a time,
successful, nay, big with the promise of real success. Villeneuve
had escaped from Toulon with his eleven ships by the end of
March; he did not meet the enemy he already feared; he was joined
by the French ship at Cadiz and the six Spaniards; he was at
Martinique by the middle of May. He had so far accomplished
his mission. But Missiessy had disregarded his orders and returned
to Europe; Villeneuve's mind was already full of foreboding; some
of the French ships had proved to be bad sailers; the Spanish ships,
he wrote, were almost worse than useless. Meanwhile, Nelson,
who, as was his wont, had rather observed than blockaded Toulon,
and had had his station, in a roadstead in the North of Sardinia,
had been straining every nerve to pursue and to pounce on his
enemy; but Fortune, at first, was strangely adverse. He had not
been well served by his look-out frigates; he had not ascertained
whether Villeneuve had gone; he had taken a position between
Sardinia and the southern coast of Africa, in order to be able to
reach the enemy, whether making for Egypt or for Gibraltar and
the Straits. It was not until after the middle of April that he
learned that Villeneuve was in the Atlantic; Nelson's resolution
was at once taken with the energy and decision of a great chief;
under existing conditions it was truly worthy of him. His squadron,
eleven ships of the line, had been in the Mediterranean for two
years; some of the ships had suffered much and were in need of

repairs; but officers and crews were in the highest heart, for the admiral had kept up their health as well as their courage; Nelson decided on making for the West Indies, and bringing the French admiral, if there, to bay, though Villeneuve had now eighteen sail of the line. Nelson, however, was long detained by adverse winds; it was not until near the middle of May, when the allied fleet was close to Martinique, that he set off on his arduous chase, and then with ten sail of the line only. He had not penetrated Napoleon's design; but he was acting upon the true principle that you should close with, and, if possible, defeat your enemy; and, great as was his inferiority in numerical force, he had no doubt that he would be able to cripple Villeneuve at least, and thus baffle the Emperor, whatever might be his projects. He gained ten days on his slow moving enemy; was at Barbadoes by the first week of June, where he was joined by two British ships of the line; and it may be asserted that had Nelson come up with Villeneuve, who at this moment was not distant, the Frenchman, if not worsted, would have suffered such loss, that he could have been hardly able to recross the Atlantic, and to have carried out his master's purpose. Nelson's bold movement was, therefore, perfectly conceived; a battle in the West Indian waters would probably have defeated Napoleon's plan, and even have made the descent impossible, so utterly inferior were the allied fleets. But Nelson, singularly unfortunate in these days, was led astray by a false report, to search for Villeneuve in the Gulf of Paria; he steered far southwards and missed his quarry; no battle was fought, and a great opportunity was lost.

Villeneuve, unlike Nelson, treacherously caressed by Fortune, had, during this time, been awaiting Ganteaume. He had undertaken petty operations from his station at Martinique. Meanwhile, Napoleon's great project had received a check; partly owing to the continuance of long calms, but chiefly to the stringency of the blockade: Ganteaume had been unable to get out of Brest. The Emperor was, accordingly, compelled to modify his plan. He sent Admiral Magon to Martinique with two sail of the line, and ordered Villeneuve, should his colleague Ganteaume not effect his junction with him by an appointed day, to recross the Atlantic with a fleet, now of twenty warships; to raise the blockade of Ferrol, where he would find fourteen ships of the line; and then, having rallied the Rochefort squadron, to make for Brest with this great armament, to raise the blockade there, to unite with Ganteaume, and with a combined force of more than fifty sail of the line, to steer for Boulogne, and protect the invading army. This, combination, forced on Napoleon by the discomfiture of Ganteaume, was, in every respect, inferior to the first; the concentration of the fleets, which was to cover the descent, was to be effected not in the West Indian Seas, but in European waters, within reach of the enemy; it was, therefore, by many degrees more hazardous. Villeneuve, terrified by the idea of Nelson on his track, set sail before the day named in his master's orders. This did not, as was possible, interfere with the plan; but the direction he took was not the best. He made very slowly his way towards Ferrol. Nelson left the West Indies in pursuit, but he did not discover Villeneuve's whereabouts. He had still no inkling of Napoleon's design. He made for the Straits with eleven sail of the line, believing that his adversary was bound for Toulon. But, with rare sagacity, he took care to despatch a light vessel to let the Admiralty know that Villeneuve was on his way to Europe. This admirable precaution may not impossibly have averted from England a tremendous peril. Meantime Napoleon, perfectly aware of the risk his second project involved, was sparing no pains to mask it by different means. He set off to Italy to conceal his purpose; spread reports of French expeditions of various kinds; in short, did what in him lay to draw off our squadrons from the points where his armada was to be assembled. The Admiralty, however, rightly clung to the central position and the interior lines they held; and Nelson enabled them to act, at this critical moment, with effect. When the light vessel he had sent forward had reached England, orders were at once given to Calder to raise the blockades of Ferrol and Rochefort, to search for and to attack Villeneuve. Calder was in the Atlantic in a very short time. He encountered Villeneuve on July 22. It deserves notice that had Villeneuve made better progress he might not improbably have eluded his foe; and Calder had but fifteen sail of the line against twenty, a dangerous disproportion in an emergency of this kind. Villeneuve lost two ships in an indecisive combat; but Calder avoided another action. Villeneuve, having left three of his worst ships at Vigo, had, in a short time, made good his way to Ferrol. If tactically beaten, he had so far successfully attained Napoleon's strategic object.

The first week of August had now come; Villeneuve was at the head of twenty-nine warships; the Rochefort squadron, of five, was at sea. Had the French admiral made at once for Brest, he might possibly have joined Ganteaume, and have overpowered Cornwallis, who had only sixteen sail of the line; the two, in that event, might, perhaps, have arrived off Boulogne. But the move of Nelson, which had placed Calder in Villeneuve's path, had demoralised him, in a scarcely conceivable degree; he declared in weak, nay pusillanimous letters, that his fleet was 'the laughing stock of Europe'; the praises his master gave him did not cheer his heart. He remained shut up in Ferrol, and dreaded approaching Brest. Nelson, meanwhile had done much to checkmate Napoleon; he had reached the Straits near the middle of July, and, when he had ascertained that Villeneuve had not gone to Toulon, he pushed forward at once to Brest, effected his junction with Cornwallis, and left with that admiral nine ships of the line, he himself returning with two to England, after a magnificent service of upwards of two years. It was now the beginning of the third week in August, Calder had rejoined Cornwallis with a fleet of nine warships. Cornwallis had thus thirty-four in hand. Any chances Villeneuve may have had were largely diminished. The positions of the belligerents became interesting in the extreme, as the drama was tending to the final scene. Villeneuve and Ganteaume, if we take in the Rochefort squadron, would, if they were once united at Brest, have nearly sixty sail of the line; but the French admirals were on double exterior lines. Cornwallis stood between them with his now powerful fleet, better by many degrees than those of his enemies. The chances were faint that Villeneuve and Ganteaume could defeat him, join hands, and enter the Channel. Nevertheless, at the supreme moment, Cornwallis made a grave strategic mistake —*insigne bêtise* the Emperor called it—which unquestionably imperilled the whole defence of England. He detached Calder with eighteen sail of the line to observe Villeneuve, reported to be at sea. Villeneuve was thus given a fair chance of eluding Calder, of reaching Cornwallis in overwhelming force, of beating him, and of joining Ganteaume. The French admiral, however, could not shake off his fears; he had put out from Ferrol on August 13 and 14, and made a few leagues on his course northwards; but he met hard weather, and lost spars and masts. He feared that a British fleet was at hand, and, in an evil hour for his renown he took refuge in Cadiz, abandoning all hope of meeting his colleague. Napoleon's great project was thus scattered to the winds; when he received the news he instantly changed his purpose. In a few days his army was in full march for the Danube, to shut up Mack in Ulm, and to achieve Austerlitz.

Villeneuve, at Cadiz, was in command of thirty-six warships; but quarrels had broken out between the Spanish and French officers; he was blockaded by Collingwood with a force much inferior in numbers. Nelson had been received in England with enthusiastic acclaim; the nation had not learned the whole truth, but it felt that his services had been above price; he was sent, an Achilles of the sea, to finish the contest. He was at the head at Cadiz, of thirty-three sail of the line; but he was compelled to detach six to obtain supplies; he was unequal numerically to his adversary up to the last moment. Meanwhile Napoleon, incensed with his unhappy lieutenant—'a poor creature, thinking only of his skin '—had commanded Villeneuve to leave Cadiz, and to risk a battle, he had soon appointed a successor to replace the Admiral. Villeneuve, stung to the quick, made up his mind to fight; it is only just to remark that all his colleagues declared at a council of war, that the inferiority of the Allied fleet was so great in every thing that makes real naval force, that a disaster was certain. Villeneuve was out of Cadiz by October 20, with thirty-three sail of the line. Nelson, who, like an eagle, was watching his prey from a distance had but twenty-seven; but he looked confidently forward to the annihilation of his foe. On the morning of October 21, 1805, a great day in history, the two fleets were within sight of each other off Cape Trafalgar; Villeneuve had turned the heads of his ships towards Cadiz, a confession of weakness, to secure a retreat. His fleet presented the appearance of a great concave front, the ships, in an irregular line with large intervals between. Nelson in order to close with his enemy quickly, changed the memorable plan of attack he had formed; he advanced against the Allied line in two columns, a mode of attack that would have been reckless had he not known what adversaries he had to deal with, but an inspiration of genius as affairs stood. The southern British column, with Collingwood at its head, had come into action about noon; the *Royal Sovereign* almost destroyed the *Santa Anna* with a single broadside, and though the ship was surrounded by a host of enemies, the allied gunnery was so bad that it did little mischief. Some forty minutes later the northern column was engaged; the *Victory*, led by Nelson, broke the Allied line; she shattered Villeneuve's flagship the *Bucentaure* and then fell on the *Redoubtable*, commanded by a really brilliant captain. The great admiral received his death-wound soon after one, struck by a shot from the *Redoubtable's* tops; but he lived to know that the victory of England was complete. The advancing ships of the British columns gradually removed the pressure from their more forward consorts. The Allied ships, crippled and ruined, fell off to leeward; prize after prize was won by the victors. At about five in the afternoon, eleven ships of the line, disabled wrecks of the great armament, crept away to seek a refuge in Cadiz; the *Achille* like the *Orient* at the Nile had perished in flames. Villeneuve had fought the *Bucentaure* bravely to the last; but he was all but abandoned by his lieutenant Dumanoir, who, with ten ships of the Allied force, had given little or no assistance to his chief. He made off with four ships which were soon after captured.[1]

---

[1] For fuller information on the Campaign and the Battle of Trafalgar, reference may be made to Mahan's 'Influence of Sea Power,' ii. 101–197, and 'Life of Nelson,' ii., 179–398. Captain Mahan's narratives are much the best. Clowes's 'The History of the British Navy,' v. 87–166; and De la Gravière's 'Guerres Maritimes," ii. 101–235. The Despatches of Nelson and the Correspondence of Napoleon ix. x. should be carefully studied. De la Gravière's work contains valuable extracts from the diary of Villeneuve, which strikingly illustrate his feeble and irresolute character. Valuable remarks on the strategy of the Campaign and the tactics of the latter will be found in Clowes's 'History of the British Navy,' v., Introduction.

NELSON

Trafalgar swept the flag of France from the ocean; the supremacy of England at sea has never since been challenged. Napoleon indeed, constructed fleets until the last year of his reign; but he had no chance of 'fighting his Battle of Actium.' To annihilate the commerce of England by shutting it out from the Continent became thenceforward the great aim of his policy; but this chimera combined all Europe against him, and ultimately led to his tremendous ruin. Trafalgar and the genius of Nelson were the real causes of this; yet the magnificence of the triumph ought not to blind us to the peril which threatened England from 1803 to 1805. The chances, indeed, were against the success of the descent; the strategy of Napoleon was baffled by the inferiority of his fleets and the superiority of our own. Cornwallis held Ganteaume fast at Brest; had not Nelson missed Villeneuve in the West Indies he certainly would have crippled his foe; the project of assembling an Armada thousands of miles from our coast would in that case have in all probability failed. Nevertheless the Emperor had not a few chances; Ganteaume might have eluded Cornwallis; Villeneuve, as a matter of fact, was not reached by Nelson. Had more than fifty sail of the line been collected at Martinique they would, it is likely, have got into the Channel in overwhelming force, and in that event have covered the invasion from Boulogne. It was not probable that a great hostile fleet could be concentrated against us in European waters. Still had Villeneuve made quickly his way from Ferrol, nay, had he turned the mistake of Cornwallis to account he might have joined Ganteaume, and the two might have mastered the Channel. Captain Mahan has declared that the plans of Napoleon were far from hopeless, and that no seaman can deny they might have been successful, especially as they were not seen through by the enemy. It may be said, indeed, that it was due mainly perhaps to Nelson that they were as completely frustrated as they were. What would have happened had Nelson not pursued Villeneuve; had he not warned the Admiralty by despatching a light vessel; nay, had he not joined Cornwallis at a critical moment? Nelson was the real antagonist of Napoleon in this great passage of arms, as he had been in the Mediterranean and in the Baltic; the consummate strategist, with his imperfect means, was discomfited by the consummate seaman. The conditions of naval warfare |have so changed that it is impracticable to decide exactly what the Campaign of Trafalgar teaches as to the possibilities of invading England. But we may learn from it that our maritime power should be supreme, and that it should further be supported by an efficient army on land. Napoleon, Wellington, and Moltke, concurred in the view that, notwithstanding the superiority of our fleets, a descent on our shores might be accomplished; Lord Wolseley has emphatically added that a madman alone could doubt it.

THE ROMANCE OF THE ADAPTED COPPERPLATE[1]
BY G. S. LAYARD

God bless the King, I mean the faith's defender,
God bless—no harm in blessing—the Pretender.
Who that Pretender is, and who is King—
God bless us all !—that's quite another thing.

SO sang the old Jacobite John Byrom, and, taking my cue from him, I do not propose to enter here into the vexed question of James Francis Edward Stuart's claim to this or that title.[2] It is merely a happy accident that lends me so picturesque a figure round which to group certain pictorial rarities, of which little is known, and of which the *petit-maître* will be therefore grateful for some particulars.

The history of the engraved copperplate is full of that kind of romance which peculiarly commends itself to the lover of what is quaint and curious in the byways of art, and perhaps the most romantic phase of its history is that with which I am about to deal in these papers. It is the sort of romance which was inseparable from what may be called the pre-machinery days, and is as foreign to the spirit of this age as are the slashed doublets of our forefathers or the starched irrelevances of their wives.

It may be, of course, that the Process block of to-day will be found to be full of romance to-morrow. Indeed, the most virile or modern writers is never tired of insisting that romance is as all-pervading in the mental as ether is in the physical world, and that it is only lack of the proper intellectual re-agent that makes the discovery of it difficult.

However that may be, one thing is certain, that most of us find it easier to come at the 'poetry of circumstance' when centuries or decades have left it behind than when it is at our immediate threshold.

In these days of lightning pictorial satire, when Monday's political move is on Tuesday served up in genial topsy-turvy by 'F.C.G.' in the *Westminster* or 'G.R.H.' in the *Pall Mall*, and when *Punch's* weekly cartoon is voted seven days late by the Man in the Street, it is difficult for us to realise the shifts to which political satire was put when the laborious engraved or etched broadside was the quickest method of getting at the picture-loving masses. Just imagine the agony of impatience of the political satirist who had designed his broadside and had to await the tardy engraving of the copperplate, to be followed by the deliberate hand-

[2] It may be mentioned that Jesse, in his 'Memoirs of the Pretenders,' always calls him James *Frederick*.

173

ROMANCE OF THE COPPERPLATE

printing and hand-painting of the impressions before they could be published, perhaps only to find in the end that the nine-days wonder was past, or that events had blunted his most telling points.

So, too, when satirist was employed against satirist, how hopeless it seemed for retaliation to follow swiftly enough upon the occasion to make any retort in kind worth while at all.

Then it was that the wit of man, quickened by necessity, conceived, the clever stratagem of the *adapted* copperplate, of which it is here my purpose to give some remarkable examples.

I fancy I see the victim of some shrewder libel than usual, with which the town has been flooded, pricking off in hot haste to the pictorial satirist in his pay, and demanding the production of a trenchant and immediate reply, so that the retort may be in the printsellers' windows before the attack has had time to do its deadly work.

The satirist names a month as the earliest possible date. His employer curses him for a blundering slowcoach. Before a month is out the mischief will be done beyond repairing. And he is flinging himself out of the workshop when a happy thought comes with a flash into his head.

How about the copperplate of that old broadside which fell so flat a year ago because of its tardiness ? It was meant to be a counter-thrust to just such another attack as this, but it was a month too late. Is there no way of fitting a new barb on to the old arrow ? Is there no way of adapting the year-old weapon to the present necessity ?

And then there follows anxious discussion and careful examination. The head of A. burnished out here can be re-engraved in the similitude of B. C. will stand as he is and do duty, with a new index number and altered footnote, for D. Here an inappropriate object can be replaced by a panel of appropriate verse. The inscriptions on the banderoles issuing from the characters' mouths must be altered, and, hey presto ! in the twinkling of a bedpost we have our answer ready for a not too critical public.

The original lampooner, who counted on a good month's start, will be confronted with a retort before he has time to turn round. The whole town will be set buzzing about the successful ruse, and the laugh will be turned upon the aggressor.

Of course it would be comparatively rarely that the adapted plate could be wholly *apropos*, but such capital ingenuity was exercised, once the stratagem had been imagined, that the practice was not so uncommon nor so unsuccessful as might be naturally expected. In this article I am only treating of those dealing with one particular episode, but I have in my possession at least thirty of these remarkable productions.

From them we find that it was not always the engraver of a plate

174

G. S. LAYARD

who re-adjusted his own handiwork, but piratical hands were sometimes laid upon the work of a master by mere journeymen engravers who did not scruple to leave the original artist's name for the better selling of the plate, although it had ceased to represent even in the remotest degree his sentiments or intentions.

Indeed, I could tell of at least one remarkable plate originally prepared in honour of a certain great personage, which, being thievishly appropriated by his opponents, was by them so judiciously metamorphosed as to cover him with as much confusion as it had originally panoplied him with honour.[1]

This is, I believe, the first time that any attempt has been made to bring this fascinating subject before the public. Incidentally it has been touched upon once or twice in publications of my own as it affected other byways in art, and has been alluded to in the Introductions to the 'Catalogue of Prints and Drawings in the British Museum (Satires),' prepared under the direction of the late Keeper of the Prints and Drawings, George William Reid, by Mr. F. G. Stephens, to which monumental work all students of such subjects are profoundly indebted But it has never been treated with anything approaching the completeness that it deserves. It is practically an unworked phase of print-collecting—a new craze in which the dilettante may specialise.

As I have said, we are fortunate in having in this place so picturesque a figure as that of The Old Pretender, or The Chevalier de St. George, as some like to call him, round whom to group our first batch of these pictorial palimpsests.

James Francis Edward Stuart was, as all who know their history will remember, the son of James II. by his second wife, Mary of Modena. He was born on June 10, 1688, at St. James's Palace.

James II. was then in his fifty-fifth year. By his cruelties after Monmouth's rebellion, by his attack on the Universities, by the Trial of the Seven Bishops, by his Court of Commissioners of Ecclesiastical Causes, and by his misuse of the Dispensing Power he had alienated the whole nation, with the exception of a few Roman Catholics and hangers-on of the Court, and his throne was tottering.

The only element of strength in his position was the certainty that sooner or later the crown was bound to pass to one of the

---

[1] Mozley, in his entertaining 'Reminiscences,' tells the following story of the latter days of the Oxford Movement, which is somewhat parallel : 'Isaac Williams published a volume of poetry called the "Baptistry," upon a series of curious and very beautiful engravings, by Boetius a Bolswert, in an old Latin work, entitled *Via Vitæ Æternæ*. In these pictures, besides other things peculiar to the Roman Church, there frequently occurs the figure of the Virgin Mother, crowned and in glory, the object of worship, and distributing the gifts of Heaven. For this figure Williams substituted the Church, and thereby incurred a protest from Newman for adapting a Roman Catholic work just so far as suited his own purpose, without caring for the further responsibilities.'

ROMANCE OF THE COPPERPLATE

Protestant daughters of his first marriage; for though the present
Queen had borne him four or five children they had all died young.
It was now six years since there had been any hint of a royal birth.
What were probably grossly exaggerated accounts of the King's
early irregularities were matter of common gossip, and the Queen's
health was far from robust. Suddenly, at a most opportune moment
for the Roman Catholics—so opportune a moment indeed that
intrigue at once suggested itself—it was announced to the world that
Mary was with child, and a day of thanksgiving was appointed five
months before the Queen's delivery.

Now was the occasion for reviving a report which had been
sedulously spread by the enemies of the Court from the very
earliest days of the Queen's marriage—*that the King, in order
to transmit his dominions and his bigotry to a Roman Catholic heir,
had determined to impose a surreptitious offspring on his Protestant
subjects.*

In due course came her Majesty's lying-in at St. James's and,
although the King took every precaution, by the solemn depositions
of forty-two persons of rank who were present, against questions
arising as to the child's identity, the celebrated ' warming-pan ' story
was hatched, which continued to gain credence for more than half a
century. Nor were circumstantial details of the most intimate nature
in support of the lie wanting. During the labour, it was maintained,
the curtains of the bed were drawn more closely than usual on such
occasions; neither the Princess of Orange, the nearest Protestant
heir to the throne, nor her immediate adherents were asked to be in
attendance; an apartment had been selected for the Queen's accommodation in which there was a door near the head of the bed which
opened on a back staircase. Though the weather was hot, and the
room heated by the great crowd of persons present, a warming-pan
was introduced into the bed; and finally the pan contained a new-
born child, which was immediately afterwards presented to the
bystanders as the offspring of the Queen.

The following song, sung by two gentlemen at the Maypole in
the Strand, is sufficiently explanatory:

> As I went by St. James's I heard a bird sing,
> That the Queen had for certain a boy for a King;
> But one of the soldiers did laugh and did say,
> *It was born overnight and brought forth the next day.*
> This bantling was heard at St. James's to squall,
> Which made the Queen make so much haste from Whitehall.

The last line referred to the fact that the Queen had played at
cards at Whitehall Palace till eleven o'clock on Saturday, June 9,
whence she was carried in a chair to St. James's Palace, and on
Sunday, June 10, between the hours of nine and ten in the morning,
' was brought to bed of a prince.'

176

"L'Europe Allarmée pour le fils d'un Meunier"
The plate in its first state

The plate in its second state

FIGURE 1

G. S. LAYARD

It is a remarkable fact [says Jesse] that as early as 1682 (six years before this), when the Queen, then Duchess of York, was declared to be pregnant, the same rumours were propagated as on the present occasion—that an imposture was intended to be obtruded upon the nation. Fortunately on that occasion the infant proved to be a female, or doubtless some improbable fiction would have been invented similar to that which obtained credit in 1688.

Undoubtedly the whole thing was a lie, but it did its deadly work.[1] The whole nation was prepared to accept the flimsiest evidence, and within six months father, mother, and child had fled to France.

So much for the story that inspired the remarkable broadsides with which it is here our purpose to deal. It will be noticed that these broadsides are all Dutch in their origin, a fact that is not surprising when we remember that they form part of the propagandum which was soon to land William of Orange, the husband of James's eldest daughter, on the throne of England.

The first that we reproduce is entitled ' L'Europe Allarmée pour le fils d'un Meunier.'

The artist is that remarkably clever Dutchman, Romeyn de Hooghe, whose delicate and facile handling of the point is well exemplified in the seascape at the back of the picture.

Let us examine in detail the most important features of this elaborate broadside.

The centre of attraction is, of course, the surreptitious infant, Prince of Wales, who lies in his cradle to the left of the picture. Those assembled about him are discussing the possibility of the plot having been discovered. On his coverlet are various playthings, amongst which is conspicuous a toy mill, emphasising, of course, the generally accepted belief that he was the son of a miller, for, in their lying, James's enemies were nothing if not circumstantial. This allusive toy figures in almost all the satiric prints dealing with the Old Pretender.

At the foot of the cradle, which is decorated with an owl, an owlet, and a snake (emblems of evil), is a pap-bowl and spoon, half concealed by the arm of ' the first mother '[2] (1), who seems to be

---

[1] Certain imprudent Roman Catholics gave colour to the popular belief by loudly expressing their opinion that a miracle had been wrought. One fanatic had even gone so far as to prophesy that the Queen would give birth to twins, of whom the elder would be King of England and the younger Pope of Rome !

[2] It is not easy to decide which of the female figures is intended to represent Mary of Modena and which the miller's wife. At first sight one would expect the Queen to be represented by the central figure 3, but, on the other hand, I have in my possession a very rare mezzotint of the period which represents Father Petre and the Queen in almost identical attitudes as figures 1 and 2 in the present plate. This view of the matter is supported by the following scandalous verses of the day :

> Some priest, they say, crept nigh her honour,
> And sprinkled some good holy water upon her,
> Which made her conceive of what has undone her.

pointing out to Father Petre (2), the instigator of the plot, that the child has been *born too old*. The Father, whose intimacy with the lady is suggested by a tender fondling of her right hand with his left, fingers his rosary with the other, and gazes fixedly into her eyes.

Edward Petre was one of the best-hated men in the country, and was popularly looked upon as James's evil genius. The King would have made him Archbishop of York, but the Pope refused his dispensation. In the year preceding the production of this satire he had been made a Privy Councillor.

In the middle of the picture sits the 'second mother' (3) in a highly-wrought chair, round the legs of which twine carved serpents. Tears course down her cheeks. With her right hand she points to the cradle as she listens to the councils of the papal nuncio Count Ferdinand d'Adda (4), who, with armour peeping from under his robes and with his armoured foot treading on his naked weapon, recommends submission of the whole matter to the arbitrament of the sword.

Immediately beyond the Cardinal stands (5) Louis XIV., James's faithful ally. In one hand he carries a bag of money, referring, doubtless, to his offer of five hundred thousand livres for the equipment of an English fleet to oppose the Prince of Orange's threatened invasion ; with the other he exposes to view a list of his army.

Behind, and to the right of Cardinal d'Adda, Louis' son, the Dauphin of France, makes as though he would draw his sword, whilst the Pope (Innocent XI.), in shadow at the extreme right of the picture (7, the number is very indistinctly seen on the dark clothing), grasps the keys of St. Peter, and would seem to be sarcastically doubtful of the whole affair. 'The Pope,' says Voltaire, 'founded very little hopes on the proceedings of James, and constantly refused Petre a cardinal's hat.'

Beyond the Pope is seen the armoured figure of Leopold I. (8), with the German eagle on his helmet. With his right hand he grasps his sword-hilt ; with his left he gesticulates as though reminding the war party that he also has to be reckoned with. No. 9 I cannot identify.

Behind Mary of Modena's chair stands (13, the figure is on her breast) Catharine of Braganza, the childless wife of Charles II. She is doubtless lamenting that, when residing at Whitehall, she had not herself manufactured a prince on the Modena plan. Next to her (11, the figure is on the pillar) a doctor of the Sorbonne promises them all dispensations—a hit at James's well known misuse of the dispensing powers. Next to him, with his right hand convulsively grasping a roll of charters, stands James himself (10). In his left he carries parliamentary and corporation papers. With despairing eyes he gazes at the baby who, so far from giving, as he had fondly hoped, the finishing touch to the Roman Catholic triumph in England, is likely to prove the most damning count in the country's indictment of his iniquities and treasons. To the left the midwife (12) encourages him to proceed with the imposture. Below her two monks (14 and 15), greatly alarmed, pray aloud at the head of the cradle.

Immediately behind them two heralds, one mounted on an ass, blow on trumpets to call attention to the Dutch fleet, which is seen approaching through the right-hand arch, whilst through the left a fort is seen belching forth smoke and resisting the landing of the longboats.

In the left corner of the picture certain Quakers (17, 18, 19), whose curious friendship with James must not be forgotten, deprecate the priests' blasphemies, whilst beyond them a crowd of Irish papists is suggested by their waving symbols and torn flag, embroidered with the sacred monogram. Behind the quakers an oriental-looking person scans the heavens through a telescope.

The colonnade beneath which all this takes place has its pillars surmounted by owls and a demoniacal bat. The arches are inscribed with the words ' Het word hier nacht,' and other inscriptions are seen on the walls. On the extreme right of the picture is reared a banner bearing what appear to be the words ' In utrumque Turgam,' of which it is difficult to imagine the meaning. ' In utramque Furcam,' which would be intelligible, has been suggested to me as an alternative reading, but cannot, I think, be accepted. Another friend hazards ' in utrumque (modum) resurgam,' which may be freely translated, ' I shall be ' dormy' either way,' and would certainly make sense. Further than that I cannot go with him.

So much for the first state of this elaborate copperplate which did its part in propagating the lie which went far to lose for James II. the crown of England.

After having served this purpose the plate was laid aside for nearly a quarter of a century. During this period the throne of England had been occupied by James II.'s two daughters, Mary and Anne, to the exclusion of their father, who died in exile in 1701, and of the Chevalier de St. George, whose proclamation by Louis of France as James III. of England [1] had been followed by the war of the Spanish Succession.

In 1713, just twenty-four years after the plate had been engraved, the peace of Utrecht, so vitally important as marking the beginning of England's commercial prosperity, was signed between England and France. Amongst other things it secured the Protestant Succession to the throne of England through the House of Hanover, and the dismissal of the Chevalier from France. The suspension of arms between the English and the French which preceded the signing of

---

[1] In the Stuart Room at Madresfield Court, Lord Beauchamp lately showed me a portrait of the Chevalier, labelled ' James III.' !

the treaty was seized upon as the opportunity for resuscitating the plate and adapting it to the altered circumstances. Now did some pictorial vandal wrench and twist the figures to new and undreamt-of uses and turn the Council of War of 1688 into the Court of Peace between the Roses and Lilies of 1712 ? The plate now professes to be published in London, although from the fact that the publication line runs, ' A Londres chez Turner,' and from sundry misspellings, it would appear certain that the alterations on the plate were effected abroad.

In this second state the plate has been reduced at the top as far as the capitals of the pillars, and at the bottom as far as the left foot of the figure which represented Father Petre in the original. The index figures have also been changed.

The explanation of the design as it now stands is contained in eighty-three lines of doggerel French verse. Taking the alterations one by one we find in the first place that the infant and cradle have been bodily removed, and (1) the ' Plan de Paix' substituted. It bears the legend ' Vrede tussen het Lelien en Roosen hof. Paix entre les Lis et les Roses picantes.'

The central figure (2) of the picture is now changed into an allegorical personage labelled ' Pax,' who holds in her left hand a paper inscribed ' Juste Protestation des Allies,' whilst with her right she indicates the ' Plan de Paix.' In this way the new artist, with some ingenuity, suggests that the spirit of peace is in sympathy with the dissatisfaction of the Allies at the negotiations which are proceeding between England and France. Her remonstrances are addressed to the figure on her left (3), which formerly represented Cardinal d'Adda, but is now labelled ' Polc.' (the Abbé Melchior de Polignac), who tries to allay her forebodings. The difficulty of the Cardinal's hat, which is of course out of place on an Abbé, is ingeniously got over by the writer of the French libretto, who refers to him as a Cardinal *in petto*. As a matter of fact the writer proved a good prophet, for, on the conclusion of the peace, for which Polignac was largely responsible, he *was*, on the nomination of the Chevalier de St. George, created and appointed Cardinal Maître de la Chapelle du Roi. He was at the time of the publication of the altered plate plenipotentiary in Holland for the French. It will be noticed that the *pince-nez* and moustache have now been dispensed with.

The figure behind Polignac (4), which originally stood for the Dauphin, who, by the way, was but lately dead, is now labelled at the foot ' Mont-or ' (the Duke of Ormond's name reversed), and at the head ' Tori.' By an ingenious turn of thought, the Dauphin's warlike action of *drawing* his sword is now metamorphosed into the Duke's conciliatory action of *sheathing* his. This refers, of course, to the instructions which he had received from the English Government, on taking over the command of the troops in the Low Countries from the Duke of Marlborough, to do all in his power to bring about a peaceful issue.

Beyond Polignac the figure (5) which formerly represented Louis XIV., is now put to humbler uses, and merely represents a French herald. The paper in his left hand, which originally enumerated Louis' forces, now bears the gratifying legend :

> Bonne Paix
> De l'Anglois
> Me rend guai.

The lady in front of him (6), who formerly stood for Catharine of Braganza, now represents Maria Louisa of Savoy, the first wife of Philip V. of Spain (fortunately for him not such a firebrand as his second wife proved to be). She turns to her handsome young husband (7) (here somewhat libellously represented by the whilom 'Old Hatchet Face') who has just renounced for himself and descendants all claims of succession to the crown of France. His right hand rests on the scroll of 'charters' as before, but the document in his left now bears the legend : 'Leli afstand onder Conditie' (The lily to surrender under conditions).

Passing almost to the extreme right of the picture, the eagle-helmeted figure (8) which before represented the Emperor Leopold I. now represents his son Charles VI., 'Le Seigneur juste de la Cour d'Orient et Occident.' Clutching his huge sword, he expresses the anger of the Imperialists at the project for peace between England and France. In the end he refused to concur in the peace of Utrecht, and continued at war with France until 1714.

On either side of him are two figures numbered alike (9, 9). That on his right, which bears the word 'Wigh' engraved on his hat, represents the Duke of Marlborough, the deposed military leader of the Whigs. That on his left is one of the Duke's followers, who, by his drawn sword, points the allusion of the librettist to the 'Pacificateur par.le fer.'

To the extreme right of the picture (10) the Pope, now Clement XI. in place of Innocent XI., encourages Polignac in his efforts for peace, and promises him 'La Pourpre' as his reward.

Returning to the middle background of the crowd we find (11,11) two Jesuits. The one who looks over the left shoulder of No. 7 was in the first state of the plate a doctor of the Sorbonne. The index number of this figure is now on his hat. Originally it was on the pillar above him. This the adapter has apparently attempted to turn into a rough ornamentation by the addition of parallel strokes. Becoming dissatisfied, he has crossed out the whole by irregular horizontal lines. To the left of figure 7 is seen (12) the Pretender, the surreptitious infant of the original, now grown to manhood, whispering in Philip of Spain's ear that though he claims as a Protestant the throne of his father, he is in his heart of the Romish faith. This figure originally represented the midwife, but has been metamorphosed by the addition of a man's hat, wig, and ruffles.

To the extreme left of the foreground of the picture the erstwhile Father Petre is now transformed (13) into a Jesuit confessor, who amorously converses with (14) 'La Courtisane de Bourbon,' Madame de Maintenon. This cruel aspersion on the character of one who was really, though secretly, Louis XIV.'s wife, and whose nobleness of character is now fully established, was characteristic of the times. The Plan de Paix, which was so obnoxious to the author of the satire, would seem to have just fallen from her fingers, and doubtless he is right in recognising that she had a hand in its consummation. Beyond the table sit a monk and a friar (15, 15), as formerly, except that the removal of the cradle has necessitated an extension of their figures. In the background, against the left-hand pillar is (16) the 'Harlequin de France.' In front of him the three figures (17, 18, 19), originally Quakers, are now referred to as 'Esprits Libres.' The man with the telescope (20) is 'The Observer of Foreign Countries.' The other subordinate figures are the same as before, save for the addition, in some cases, of index numbers.

It is interesting to notice that this plate was so successful in its adapted state that it was made the basis of a design engraved for a German broadside of the following year entitled, 'Der Fridens-Hoffzwischen der Rose und der versöhnten Lilie,' with which it has many points in common.

I have treated of this plate at considerable length because it is the most important of the palimpsest plates of this period. I shall close this article by reproducing one other remarkable example designed in its first state to expose the same supposed wicked plot. From the fact that, space permitting, I could have given at least two others dealing with the birth of the Old Pretender, we gain some idea of the extent to which this clever stratagem of the adapted copperplate was made use of in the deliberate days of the seventeenth and eighteenth centuries.

Those that I must pass over for want of space are two elaborate broadsides engraved by Jean Bollard, and entitled respectively 'Aan den Experten Hollandschen Hoofd-Smith' (To the Expert Dutch Head-Smith), and 'Aan den Meester Tonge-Slyper' (To the Master Tongue-Grinder). These, after doing their work against James II. and the Old Pretender, were seized upon many years afterwards by the piratical publisher of a remarkable Jansenist tract, called 'Roma Perturbata, Ofte't Beroerde Romen, &c.,' and adapted to the uses of the anti-Jesuit propagandum, in the same way as 'L'Europe Allarmée pour le fils d'un Meunier,' described above, was adapted after twenty-five years of idleness as a satire upon the Peace of Utrecht.

"Het beest van Babel is aan't vlucsten
Die Godschenst hieft niet meer te duckten"
The plate in its first state

The plate in its second state

F<small>IGURE</small> II

G. S. LAYARD

It was this same piratical tractarian who seized upon the elaborate plate which I am here reproducing, divorced it from its letterpress, cut the plate down to the size of his tract, and appropriated it in its second state to the purposes of 'Roma Perturbata.'

In its first state, which I give here, together with its accompanying letterpress, the line of publication runs : 'Gisling, Geneve, exc.' and the title:

> Het beest van Babel is aan't vluesten
> Die Godschenst hieft niet meer te duckten.
>
> (The beast of Babel is flying,
> Religion has nothing more to fear.)

The design is very elaborate and crowded with figures, those in the foreground being executed with considerable spirit. The Dutch Lion (1) carries a sword in its right front claws, as does that on the Persian flag of to-day. On its back rides William of Orange (7) with lance in rest and bearing a shield upon which St. Michael is represented combating sin in the shape of a dragon. William is supported by mounted soldiers, one of whom bears a flag inscribed with the words 'Prot religion and libe '—(For religion and liberty). Over his head flies a winged Revenge (3) carrying a shield in one hand and the lightnings of God's wrath in the other. Before him flies the seven-headed Beast of Babel (2), shorn of two of his heads, which lie bleeding on the ground beneath the lion. The monster, which 'utters horrible shrieks,' bears upon its back between its wings Father Petre (6), who holds on his lap the infant Pretender (5), to whom his 'brains have so infamously given birth.' The too-old infant carries in his hand the ever-present toy windmill. Blood pours from the decapitated necks of the Beast as he plunges with his accompanying rabble into the 'pool of horrors.' Priests and other Romish officials, some mounted on goats, asses, and wolves, flee (4) or are trampled under foot (8).

In the mid background William of Orange (9), by a poetic licence able to be in two places at once, a fairly common convention even in serious pictures of that and an earlier date,[1] is being greeted by the English nobles as their saviour. To the left, through an archway, James II. (10) is seen fleeing by boat with his wife and infant, though, as a matter of fact, he remained in England some months after the latter were safely abroad. To the right, through another arch, Louis XIV. (11) is seen 'embracing the child and taking pity on his mother,' and putting two of the curious, hearse-like carriages of the period at their disposal. Here we not only find Mary of Modena duplicated, but the infant Pretender triplicated in the same picture ! So much for the plate in its first state.

[1] See, for example, Tintoret's great picture of 'Adam and Eve' in the Accademia at Venice.

183

ROMANCE OF THE COPPERPLATE

In its second and adapted state it takes its place in the armoury of the anti-Jesuits. The Jansenist controversy was at its height in the year of grace 1705, and Jansenism, although nominally subject to Rome, was regarded favourably by the Protestant Dutch as being a reforming movement within the Roman Catholic Church against the theological casuistry of the Jesuits.

This is not the place to go into the anti-Jansenist polemics of the Jesuits since the publication of the 'Augustinus' of 1640, though the interest of the matter is sufficiently tempting. We must content ourselves with remembering that now at the beginning of a new century a supreme effort was being made by the Jesuits in France to destroy completely the pious community of Port Royal; that within four years they were to succeed in dispersing the nuns; within another year the cloister itself was to be pulled down; that in 1711 the very bodies of the departed members of the community were destined to be disinterred from the burial ground with the greatest brutalities and indecencies; and in 1713 the church itself demolished.

But, though Port Royal itself was doomed, Jansenism was finding freedom under the Protestant Government of Holland.

In 1689 Archbishop Codde had been appointed by the Pope Vicar Apostolic in Holland. Soon, however, it was discovered by the Jesuits that he favoured the Jansenists.

By the machinations of the Jesuits he was therefore *invited* to Rome, and treacherously detained there for *three years*, in defiance of all canonical regulations. In the meantime the Pope appointed Theodore de Cock in his place, with the intention of crushing the Jansenists in Holland. Codde thereupon made his escape from Rome, and the well-known struggle of the Jansenists of Utrecht and Haarlem for a legitimate episcopal succession began.

This was the juncture at which our copperplate was to do duty a second time, and for such different ends.

It has been divorced from its letterpress, altered in certain details, and slightly cut away at the top and bottom. Like those dealing with the Headsmith and Tongue Sharpener, it has been appropriated to the uses of 'Roma Perturbata.' It is now entitled on the panel which has been inserted at the spring of the arches 'Door Munnike-Jagt, Word Babel Verkracht' (by chasing monks, Babel is assailed), and the piratical publisher has made many ingenious alterations. The possibly punning publication line runs: 'Benedictus Antisoli-tarius excudit Rom.' Above this appears the chronograph: 'HOS HEROS MonaChos apprenDe bataVe rebeLLes.'

The Lion (1) still represents Holland and hunts the Beast of Babel (2) assisted by the winged Revenge (3), whose lightnings have now been increased to seven to represent the heraldic arrows of the Seven United Provinces. This device also now appears on the shield of Holland's Knight (7) in place of that of St. Michael and the Dragon.

184

G. S. LAYARD

The banner of his followers is now inscribed 'Pro Secularibus.' As champion of the Jansenists the Knight puts to rout 'all the bald heads (4, 4, 4, 4), together with "their protector Kok"' (6), who 'in disguise' rides between the wings of the Beast with an illegitimate child (5) on his lap, from whose right hand the toy windmill of the infant Pretender has been removed. In the background to the left others, in the quaint words of the Dutch letterpress (10), 'escape quickly from the town by water, while they are clothed like gentle men in order not to be known as monks.' In the background to the right others flee 'like great gentlemen in carriages,' a fairly ingenious adaptation of James II.'s flight and Louis' welcome of the fugitives.

The group in the middle background is now made to represent Codde (8.B), who has escaped from Rome and is being welcomed back by the representatives of the State (9, 9).

Although the reproductions of the two sets of plates here given do not exactly tally in size, it must be clearly understood that this is only due to an eccentricity of the photographer, and that the two original prints are impressions from one and the same copperplate.

I hope, at some other time, to be able to enlarge upon this curious romance of the adapted or palimpsest plate, and to reproduce the other extraordinary examples which have come into my hands. For the present I have said enough to introduce the print-collector to a subject which is not unworthy of his attention, and will repay further investigation.

THE ABSURDITY OF THE CRITICISM OF MUSIC. BY GILBERT BURGESS

HILE I was casting about for a title wherewith to head this paper, the Imp of Mischief, who is ever lying in wait to subvert my pen to his wicked uses, tempted me to call it 'The Absurdity of Music.' To do such a thing would have been very immoral; for the pundits of harmony, and the lovers of the art of intermingling the various sound-waves, have of late years claimed Music as a potency for good—they affirm that the Muse is a fit mate for Virtue.

Let me say at once that in writing about the criticism of music I am in a measure justified, seeing that until recently I was for several years a member of the deplorable band of journalists who eat their hearts out in the horrid atmosphere of the concert-halls—who, during the season, are hurried from musical pillar to musical post; who, in the heat of the July evenings, are wont to materialise their critical remarks at the refreshment bar of that extraordinarily uncouth institution which is known as the Covent Garden Opera House.

Nowadays I will have none of the job. As a baby I could play by ear; until recently notable musicians have confessed ungrudgingly that I have more than a passable touch upon the pianoforte. Furthermore, those who knew me to be a professed critic of the art were willing to perform my compositions in public. I studied music in Germany; four times have I sat upon the narrow chairs which are the portion of the audience in the monstrous Festspielhaus at Bayreuth. My gods have been Beethoven, Wagner, and Chopin; Tschaikowsky, too, has had a little offering laid at his shrine by my hands.

And now . . . the Muse has fled from me, feeling, I am sure, that I am surfeited of her charms. They say that a woman is the first to realise, instantly and instinctively, the moment when a man's thoughts turn wistfully from her to another. Thus was it with the Muse: she deserted me suddenly, so that, after the sharp realisation of the parting, I should be able to wend my way elsewhere in comparative peace. Having made all the personal explanation that seems necessary, let me at once to the working out of my initial thesis.

With the exception of M. Alfred Bruneau, a composer of distinction who contributes articles on the subject of music to the Paris *Figaro*, I can find no musical critic (as the accepted phrase runs) who is qualified for the task he undertakes to perform. If the critic were competent he would not be a critic: he would be a composer. If he were capable of sitting in judgment upon the technique of an instrumentalist, he himself would be a performer,

186

for the prizes of performance are much higher than those of comment. Should he nicely appreciate the capabilities of the human voice when employed in song, he would be a singer, or, at least, a teacher of the art.

As a critic you may place your impressions—your personal impressions—of a symphony or a singer upon paper very prettily, or cynically, as did Heine, sometimes. Frequently he was as futile as we moderns: witness his appreciation of Paganini's meretricious fiddle-fireworks. But you must be a musician yourself.

Here steps in Tragedy. Musicians, as a class, when they come to take up the pen with the object of writing words instead of musical signs, are nearly always foredoomed to failure. Wagner himself cannot honestly be exonerated from this charge. The Prelude to 'Tristan und Isolde' is worth all his prose essays.

Before dealing with the critics of the more prominent journals, it is only fair to say that they are generally honest. Only once in my career of five years in their ranks did I come across a case of venality. This was in connection with a certain opera which shall be nameless. It is a modern work, and the composer and his friends made strenuous efforts in order that no dissentient voice should be heard among the chorus of lavish approval with which they themselves were clamorous. I did not like the work, and said so: even now I remember the reproachful, pitying glances which met me the night after my article appeared. I could feel that the little army of critics was grieved with me: the moment after I passed under the portal of the refreshment *foyer* at Covent Garden I knew that I was temporarily a pariah. I take it that to accept a sandwich and a glass of wine from a composer can hardly be classed as venal. It may be convenient; but the 'insult,' as the gentleman said in *The Mikado*, is hardly sufficient to rank as a bribe.

I once reproached a celebrated tenor because he employed a *claque* which was paid to applaud his high notes. ' *Mon ami*,' he replied, ' what else can one do in London? One cannot buy the critics.' Here, at any rate, was first-rate testimony to our honesty. But English critics of music are almost invariably too vague. Many of them surround their subject with set phrases; others are essayists; others describe the various humorous traits which they discover in the audience. They generally have a talent for praise; they rarely possess pluck. I remember the sardonic criticism of an American writer who was called in judgment upon a Glee Club. Said he: ' When eighteen stalwart young men, each with a capacity for pouring forth six hundred cubic feet of air a minute, sing "Hush Thee, my Baby " with such vehemence that the refrain may possibly be heard in Peru, the spirit of the composition somehow is missed, and the sentiment suffers irreparable injury. We may err in proffering advice; but we feel it to be our duty to suggest that this Club will give pleasure in exact ratio with its diminution of lung force. And perhaps it will afford most satisfaction when it learns to sing so that it cannot be heard by anybody without an ear-trumpet.'

Here, at least, is a good sound trouncing.

Parody may be the device of small wits : George Eliot has so described it. But parody is sometimes useful in enforcing one's arguments; if one is so fortunate as to cause a smile to flicker over the face of a possible opponent—lo! at least one company of his battalion of dissent has deserted to your side. Therefore, this fact being admitted, let us proceed to show, by the device of parody, the futility of the methods by which the commentators on musical matters endeavour to satisfy our intellectual needs. A new violinist, let us say, has made his first appearance in England at the St. James's Hall. His name, we will assume, is Herr Tamberlik. Next morning, on unfolding the portly pages of the *Times*, you may expect to read something after the manner of the criticism which follows :

'Yesterday afternoon, at St. James's Hall, Herr Tamberlik, a young Hungarian violinist, made his first appearance in England. He very soon made it evident to his audience that his playing was entirely unconventional. In Bach's " Chaconne " he entirely lacked dignity; his phrasing was eccentric, we had almost said faulty. The exquisite slow movement in Mendelssohn's Violin Concerto he played with an excess of sentimentality for which his youth entitles him to leniency. His rendering of some Paganini studies was certainly brilliant from the technical point of view. We would advise Herr Tamberlik to give another year to study before he again invites the sympathies and suffrage of the British public.'

When Herr Tamberlik's agent brought him the morning papers next day to his hotel the great young man, who was drinking coffee and smoking cigarettes in bed, was, we may assume, depressed on reading the above. But at about half-past nine in the morning the agent reappears with the evening papers.

'Mein lieber Herr,' says that worthy, brandishing in the air the *Pall Mall Gazette*, 'sie haben triomphirt !' (That is the best quality of German that I can muster.) Tamberlik takes the journal and reads :

' " When we sat down to write this criticism, as best we might (ever striving to remember in which wise Mr. Henley would have expressed himself upon the subject), we felt that here, ready to our hands, was a task eminently to our liking. We had heard Herr Tamberlik, and we liked him. A cynic may have been lurking in the stalls in our neighbourhood : we did not care, for, frankly, we liked Tamberlik. One of the gifts vouchsafed to the unwary, from the little gods who tease us, is the power of imbibing enthusiasm. Such a gift, perilous as it may prove, should, we protest, nowise be despised. Yet we regret the possession of it. Why, we do not know. But there is something in the frank expression of pure delight which baffles prudence. We heard Tamberlik—we liked him. This may seem to our readers mere verbiage: as Robert Louis—for yourselves you shall scent the surname of the Master—might have said from under the shade of his cocoa-palms. For his sarcasm was ever sweet, even when it was needfully severe. We repeat, we have heard Tamberlik, and, emphatically, we like him." '

We may assume, once more, that the great Tamberlik was puzzled. He had not much English, nor had he any appreciable amount of acquaintance with the methods of the London Press. He turned to the agent and demanded to know what the article meant. In his own language he cried, ' The fellow likes me—is it not so ? But he says nothing about my playing. And who is this Robert Louis ? Is he musician ? What does it all mean ? He likes me ? It is to me quite equal. But he says nothing about my art.' And he concludes with a very picturesque German oath, which I should blush to place in the permanency of print.

After a day or two, the agent, fearing a bout with his sensitive charge, brings a large quantity of newspapers and reviews, and proceeds to lay them at Herr Tamberlik's feet. The violinist, however, eager to understand the methods of the London critics, demands that every word of the notices devoted to him shall be read at once—filtered, be it at once said, from language to language.

Honesty Herr Tamberlik demanded ; the agent, who had some- times been averse from the sweet and narrow ways of Truth, for once made up his mind to pursue them. By way of preparing the eminent artist for the ordeal which he was presently to suffer, he said, ' Mein lieber, nothing that these people say about you matters at all.' Tamberlik nodded nonchalantly, albeit, like all artists, he was hungry for praise.

' We will first give you,' said the agent, ' the verdict of the *Saturday Review*, an organ which, I am told, has great influence.'

Of course, all these remarks were made in German, and my imagination may have mistranslated them.

But that which follows is the substance of the matter that the accomplished agent read to his victim :

' "Tamberlik and Twaddle. The fellow can play his fiddle. This I grant you. But look at the rot he plays ! The foolish old trivialities of Tartini ; the silly old gymnastics of Vieuxtemps ; I can forgive him these, for they are the sort of thing that the effete idiots who control our national Academies of Music drill into the empty minds of our unmusical dullards. But I cannot forgive

him for playing Mendelssohn's Violin Concerto. At best it is a
rubbishy work ; Mendelssohn, by writing it, did us one great
service ; he taught us how not to write a Violin Concerto. But
why should Tamberlik emphasise the fact ? We all know it.
Mendelssohn was a writer of songs without words simply because he
could not write words without songs." '

Tamberlik interposed.

' Mein lieber,' said he to the faithful agent, ' can you explain
that last sentence ? '

' No, mein lieber,' answered the agent.

' Forwärts,' said Tamberlik. And the agent obeyed.

' " The truth of the matter is that Tamberlik is going on the
wrong track. There are only three great musicians — namely,
Beethoven, Wagner, and Purcell. I forgot for the moment Mr.
Isidore de Lara. He makes four. I am not quite sure that he
doesn't make five. Why doesn't Herr Tamberlik go to them for
his material ? It is true that Beethoven wrote but a small amount
of music exclusively for the violin ; Wagner practically none, and
Purcell less. Still, why does not Tamberlik go to them instead of
to modern and ancient fools who wrote music exclusively for that
absurd instrument ? The whole thing is ridiculous." '

Once more broke in Tamberlik. ' I agree, mein lieber.' And
the agent suggested that a drink would not be a bad idea. Tamberlik
sent for coffee ; the agent, in his capacity as a somewhat lurid
interpreter, felt that a large whisky-and-soda—plenty of whisky,
and the soda-water poured out penuriously—would enable him to
go on reading.

' Now,' he remarked with some seriousness, ' we come to the
Daily Telegraph.' Tamberlik rubbed his eyes, as would one who
wakes from a bad dream with a certain hope of finding that things
are not so blue as they are painted. The agent, stimulated by his
excess of interpretation, perhaps—who knows ?—by his light refreshment, began to worry the prose of the various critics of music who
adorn the pages of that largely-circulated journal.

' " Yesterday afternoon, at St. James's Hall, Herr Tamberlik
made his first appearance in London." '

' Mein lieber,' said Tamberlik, ' I seem to have heard that phrase
before.' (Of course, he said it in German, and I may be a word or
two out).

But from the agent, of whatsoever kind, tact is expected, and
this particular specimen immediately grasped the situation by both
shoulders—the situation, not Tamberlik—and explained to the
musician that the rest of the article was merely a negative series of
statements ; verbose, possibly, but nevertheless non-committal. If
it erred in any way, it could only be impeached on the ground that
it had no yeoman liking for good music.

So the matter passed off happily, and Tamberlik Oliver Twisted for more.

'Here,' said the agent, 'I have journals which you may buy two for one penny. One is called the *Daily Mail*; the other the *Daily Express*.'

At once Tamberlik became aglow with interest. In his own curious although pleasantly guttural language, he expressed impatience to hear the verdict of these quaint expressions of modernity upon his performances with his violin.

The agent was a little bit troubled; but he bore himself bravely. He trembled somewhat, perhaps; but he had to break the truth, and he tried to do it manfully.

'The *Mail* says: "Tamberlik seems to be a boy of extraordinary promise. He has a sure instinct for the instrument which he undoubtedly loves. Among those present——" '

Tamberlik interrupted once again. Said he, 'When I play I see nobody.'

'Why, then,' said the agent, 'should I read you what says the *Express*?'

'Read it,' said the artist with an impatient gesture. The agent felt nervous, but proceeded:

'"Tamberlik is the latest cry of fashion. His magnificent playing has made him the rage of London society. At his first concert, at St. James's Hall, he proved himself to be an artist of enormous potential qualities. Among those present——" '

Up jumped Tamberlik in a rage. '"Among those present—," cried he—'the only one I ever want to see is the person who has not wanted to kiss me, or present me with a new kind of Jew's-harp, or a kettledrum, or a Stradivarius.'

His strange outburst of anger died away. He turned to his agent: there was something almost beautiful in his penitence.

'Forgive me, new friend,' said he: 'have you anything more to read?'

'Well, mien lieber,' said the agent, 'I have fifty-five (and I think fifty-five and a half) papers all praising you.'

Tamberlik beamed facially. 'What,' said he, breaking unconsciously into English, 'is the ghost of their remarks?'

The agent smiled sadly. 'Herr Tamberlik, I fear that you have accidentally hit upon a fact. And one does not expect a fiddler to hit upon a fact. When you said the "ghost" of their remarks instead of the "gist" of their remarks, I saw that you had begun to understand things. Who shall decide when nobody understands? There are other criticisms, in many papers. Why should I read them to you? They all begin: "Yesterday afternoon at St. James's Hall "—you must be tired of that by this time. Others, too, say: " Among those present were Lady Why-ever-do-I-come-here." '

THE CRITICISM OF MUSIC

'That,' says Tamberlik, 'sounds like an Hungarian title.'

'To me,' said the agent, ' it seems a very useful thing for us. Bore them, let them kiss you, give you the hurdy-gurdy, or the accordion; but take the advice of an experienced agent. Work away; work hard; practise with your fiddle. Love music for what it is worth; play the best music. Don't let the thing we call Society hinder you. If the Lady with the name which you think bears an Hungarian sound——'

'Nonsense,' says Tamberlik, in his own sweetly uncouth language, 'you are my agent, and if you lecture me I will get another one. Better than you, *sehen zie?* One who will bribe the English critics——'

'Mein lieber,' said the agent, with his wonted patient smile, 'there are no English critics. You had better leave yourself in my hands. Don't you agree with me?'

'Yes,' said Tamberlik.

HOW AMANDA SERVED THE WRIT
BY LORIN LATHROP

HIRAM J. HICKS, of Hicksville, U.S.A., arrived with his baggage at the Savoy Hotel on a hot July evening. The clink of the ice in the tumbler was welcome to his ears, the sight of green corn on the cob was restful to his eyes, and the subsequent view of a poster of an American company playing 'The Girl from down below,' was refreshing to his heart. Things were not so different after all, and he was not so homesick as he had expected to be. He went to the theatre.

It was not surprising that he met there Mr. Bob Greening, who had been with him at Harvard in the class of 1899 ; but it was surprising and disconcerting to see Miss Vivia Vavasour glowering at him over the footlights from the front rank of the chorus. He had not seen her since his graduation. He had gone home to Hicksville, where his imagination and sympathy had been promptly diverted to Miss Amanda Huntington. Miss Vavasour had objected to this—through a solicitor; hence his annoyance at finding her in the same town with himself. He feigned dissatisfaction with the play, forced Greening to join his retreat, and went away hoping that London was large enough that Vivia and he should not meet.

In the smoking-room of the Savoy he unfolded to his companion the strange reason of his visit to England.

His father, industrious banker, financier, and general adviser of the small town which he had founded, had died two months before, it appeared ; and the son had been astonished and aggrieved to learn that he must divide his patrimony. The old man, under pretence of a two years' innocent holiday in England, had married there, it seemed, had had a son, had quarrelled with his wife, had given her a bag of money, and had sailed away alone for Hicksville, where for twenty years and more he had buried his nefarious secret in his bosom.

'To cut it short,' concluded Hiram, 'the lady's dead, but I have a half-brother, two years younger than myself, and the old man's left him half my four hundred thousand dollars.'

Bob Greening was deeply shocked. With the imposing command of language which had gained him fame in his senior year he summed up the situation.

'A man,' he said gravely, ' of supposed local patriotism, believed to be of exemplary character, who secretly marries abroad and leaves half his fortune to foreigners, would crumble the foundations of confidence in any town.'

'It would—it did,' cried the injured heir, ' you express the general feeling. The faith of Hicksville in all men is shaken.'

HOW AMANDA SERVED THE WRIT

He rang the bell for the waiter, and proceeded with his tale.

To prove the will, it appeared, it was necessary to have the formal assent of the two people who benefited by its provisions ; hence before Hiram J. could be absolute master of his share, his half-brother must be found and served with a friendly citation to appear by counsel before the Orphan's Court on the day fixed for the probate.

'And that's the trail I'm on,' said Hiram J., producing from his pocket a large legal looking paper. 'I said I'd come myself ; Henry J. is not to blame. I dare say he's a white man. I shall just walk to him and say, "you are my long lost brother, I bring you half my hard-earned fortune" — good situation, heigh ? '

Bob laughed, and asked slyly if that Miss Huntington that Hiram had mentioned casually in his letters was still in Europe.

Hiram burst into a vivid and lengthy description of her charms and admitted that she was the real magnet. 'When I heard that Henry J. was an artist living in Cornwall I looked on the map and saw that it was next to Devonshire. Miss Huntington and her mother are staying in Devonshire ; see ? '

Bob saw and grinned.

'Her mother,' continued Hiram J., 'is a very narrow prejudiced woman ; she has been very unjust to me. Amanda has a great deal of character, but she just wilts when her mother looks her way. I am sure that that heartless woman dragged her unwilling daughter over here to put the Atlantic between her and me. I think she heard about Miss Vavasour. She does not understand that every fellow at Harvard catches the disease, and that my attack was very light.'

'Vivia's thirty,' remarked Bob.

'She looked forty to-night,' said Hiram J., who was in a prejudiced mood. 'Who would have expected to see her here ? '

'My dear boy,' cried Bob, 'they're *all* over here. Did you ever get your letters back ? '

'No ; I suppose she burnt 'em long ago. She threatened suit for breach of promise ; but her lawyer dropped it when he found I hadn't a cent of my own.'

'The boys would have liked to read 'em in print,' grinned Bob.

'Heaven forbid,' cried Hiram J., 'they're the usual sort.'

And then the two fell to discussing things with which this chronicle need not concern itself.

At four o'clock the next afternoon Hiram J., was putting the final touches on his afternoon toilet—he generally changed at that hour from a cut-away to a Prince Albert coat—when his friend burst in, clapped a hat on his head, and dragged him to the top of a staircase.

LORIN LATHROP

'Go to the Union Hotel, Penzance,' cried the breathless Bob, 'and I'll send on your belongings. There's a ferret in the office asking for you. I spotted him. He's got a writ from Vivia, I'm dead certain. The elevator's coming up. Fly!'

The fugitive found himself on the Embankment. He told a cabman to drive him to the depôt for Penzance; and of course was given a chance to see a generous slice of London, before his driver thought fit to drop him on the Paddington platform. He found that he could not get farther than Exeter that night, unless he waited for some hours; so at the Rougemont Hotel in that cathedral city, warm and dishevelled, he appeared about midnight. Having answered as best he could a bewildering query as to whether he was coffee-room or commercial, and made the usual deposit 'in lieu of luggage,' he was assigned to a room. He tossed restlessly through the night, dreaming with perturbed mutterings that Miss Vivia Vavasour and Mrs. Huntington were alternately stamping on his prostrate form. The thought that he was sleeping in the same county with his Amanda was only partial solace.

At Penzance no word and no luggage awaited the anxious man. His costume was strikingly unsuitable for weather and seaside. The least hideous thing he could find in local shops was a bicycle costume. It did not fit very well, but it was very cheap. The disguise was as complete as though it were intentional. He looked a 'Arry.

At Newlyn he quickly got news of Henry J. Hicks. That promising and improvident young artist had been married a week before in Plymouth, and the couple had bicycled away on a wedding tour. There were no reasons for concealments in Newlyn. The ingenuous fisherman's daughter, who was in charge of the cottage which was to be the home of the newly-wedded pair, stated that 'traps' had that day been forwarded to Badminton in Gloucestershire, and that the couple would remain for several days in that picturesque village.

Hiram J. refused to fish for pollack on the return journey to Penzance. He had cast a line in coming at the suggestion of the guileless boatman, and would pay extra therefor. But now he was thinking. He was 'enthused' over the romantic situation. Henry J. was as poor as a rat. That was quite clear from the home he was coming back to—picturesque—oh, undoubtedly, inside and out—but miles away from having hot-water heating, electric bells or lights, or other necessities of life. Hiram J. even gravely doubted whether there was a bath-room. What happiness to this couple to learn of the stupendous wedding gift. He must go himself and tell them. 'Here, my cherubs,' he would cry, 'are forty thousand pounds. Heaven bless you!'

Tears of joy would almost certainly suffuse the shy gentle eyes of the bride; and perhaps in the excitement she would fling

195

impulsive arms round his neck and kiss him. Then he would slip quietly away from the scene of bliss, leaving sunshine behind, and go and find his Amanda. How Amanda's alert hazel eyes would soften when he told her about it ; and perhaps she would praise him for the generous way in which he accepted the loss of half of his fortune. How she—but there was a sudden bump ; and dreams of his Amanda were banished by astonishment at the boatman's charges.

He found a letter at the hotel. The foiled ferret, wrote Bob, had burst into the deserted room, and used horrid imprecations at the escape of his victim. Since then Bob had been shadowed, and the luggage had been watched. It was only now that a chance had come to smuggle a bag and hat-box out of the hotel. The rest of the things were stored away, the room surrendered ; and Hiram was safe so long as he kept out of London.

This good news relieved Hiram J. of the last shadow of care.

Alas ! How could he know that the sleuth hound of the law had lain in ambush, had emerged at the proper moment, had seen the label on the bag in the receiving office of the railway, and was now on his way to Penzance, carrying a brief-bag, which contained a clean collar, and a large blue writ. If Hiram J. had suspected the possibility of such a blow from inconstant fortune, he certainly would not have directed that when the bag arrived it should be sent after him to Badminton, nor would he have mentioned incidentally that he was stopping the night in Bristol.

In the train a companionable stranger, who knew the county of Gloucester, told him how inaccessible Badminton was.

' But you're cycling,' said his fellow traveller, looking at his costume with some interest. It was not the usual dress of a cyclist who travelled first class.

' Yes, I am,' responded Hiram J., catching at the idea ; ' how far is it from Bristol ? '

' Some twenty miles, good roads, lots of hills at the fag end,' was the answer ; and that answer explains the arrival before the door of the inn at Badminton, about one o'clock the next day, of a perspiring cyclist, coated with thick layers of dust from the crown of his head to the rim of his wheels, his eyes protected by blue goggles, his mouth parched, his legs trembling. For the machine which he had purchased that morning in Bristol, being new, was as stiff as the hills it had wearily been made to climb.

The arrival of Hiram J. Hicks attracted little attention at the quaint and charming hostelry. He was clearly a passing customer who would patronise the tap-room for a mug of beer or a lemonade ; but his first inquiry removed him entirely from the commonplace. He asked for some ice cream.

The startled but respectful little maid saw that he was in

absolute earnest, and explained that he might get such things in Bristol, but certainly not nearer, whereupon Hiram J. left the matter entirely in her hands, and presently emerged with a large can of bitter, which he carried to a shaded seat.

As he raised the can to his lips his eye fell on a figure sitting some twenty feet away under a spreading tree. It sat motionless in its summer silk covering, except for the lazy waving of a fan, and it seemed intent on a book. But the gasping Hiram J. had no doubt as to what or who it was. There was only one head in the world poised as was that one, only one coil of lustrous dark hair of precisely that shade, only one profile with that short upper lip, that redeeming hint of a tilt at the end of the nose, that soft pencil shading which he knew was the tip of a curling lash. Hiram J. sat dazed, with pewter mug poised in air, as he looked through blue spectacles at the astounding sight. He recognised the fan too. It was a flimsy thing, but he had given it to her at a church sociable.

He cried out in his astonishment, but his Amanda made no movement. Then he realised that his dry throat had gone on strike. He drank the liquid, and as he bent back his head to swallow he saw his shoe at the end of his crossed leg. He laid down the can deliberately and surveyed himself. He remembered that the few things he had forwarded from Bristol were crawling along the road by carrier and that the bag from Penzance would probably never reach that out-of-the-way place at all. He saw that if he spoke to his Amanda, she would probably give him a ten-cent piece, and advise him with kindly charity to try and get work. In the dreadful situation there was however one redeeming feature. His disguise was complete. He pressed his hand firmly against his breast lest she should hear the beating of his heart and feasted his eyes on her fresh beauty. The stifling air seemed to get cooler as he looked. Amanda always dominated the thermometer, and radiated ozone on the hottest summer day.

She moved. Hiram started but controlled himself. She turned her head round, quite away from him until he could see the other side of her face. He thought she smiled as her eyes fell on the ground. The eyes of her eager watcher followed her glance. They lighted on the figure of a man.

Hiram J. uttered a hoarse cry and overset his can of beer. Amanda flashed a casual glance at him and resumed her reading.

Devonshire—Amanda had been staying there. Henry J. Hicks had married in Plymouth—Plymouth was in Devonshire. The bridal couple were at Badminton! The conclusion was almost irresistible. Hiram J. was about to attack the sleeping man and force the truth from his craven lips, when a dog-cart drove up to the door, and a wiry little man, carrying a brief-bag, stepped lightly to the ground.

197

HOW AMANDA SERVED THE WRIT

'Don't take the harness off, driver,' he said, 'I must get back to Yate for the three o'clock train.'

The stranger stepped into the hall and asked for Mr. Hicks.

Hiram J. started, but remembered that there was now another Mr. Hicks in the world.

'Mr. 'Icks is cycling,' said the little maid.

'No,' corrected the waiter, ''Im and 'is wife's come back. I saw 'em sitting under the tree.'

'His wife—I didn't know he was married.'

'Likely not, sir, they're 'oneymoonin'.'

'Oh ho!' cried the man with the brief-bag as he stepped outside.

Mr. Webb was a merry little lawyer's clerk, in great request for comic songs at smoking concerts, and of repute in his circle as a raconteur. It was delightful to step in on a wedding tour with a writ for breach of promise. He understood now why the lady in London was so keen on prompt service.

He went over to the tree, and gazed with deep interest on the sleeper, then with deep sympathy on Amanda. He raised his hat politely, and remarked that it was very warm.

Amanda pleasantly agreed with him. Hiram J. had always considered that Amanda was too affable to strangers. He remembered that when she had started for Europe she had announced her intention of talking with everybody, that she might get to understand the people.

'Excuse me,' said the stranger, 'but is that Mr. Hicks who is slumbering so sweetly?'

'It is Mr. Hicks,' answered Amanda with a smile.

'It seems a pity to disturb him,' he remarked compassionately.

'You speak as if you were going to do it anyhow,' she responded; 'I wouldn't.'

Mr. Webb looked at her with admiration and pity. He thought it a case for the exercise of tact. He would break the news to her as gently as he could.

'My business is very important,' he said solemnly.

'Business—to-day—have you noticed what the thermometer registers?'

'I have registered the heat myself, ma'am,' he said respectfully, as he removed his hat, and wiped his forehead, 'but the fact is, the law takes no account of climate.'

Mr. Webb drew from his brief-bag a long blue envelope.

'The law,' cried Amanda severely, 'should leave a man in peace during his wedding journey.'

'The law might, ma'am,' was the answer, delivered with pathos, that she might be prepared, 'but,' he continued, 'the lady won't.'

'The lady?'

' Yes, ma'am, I grieve to say that this is a case of breach of promise of marriage.'

Amanda's little scream drowned the hollow groan which proceeded from Hiram J.

' Oh,' she said, ' you cannot have the heart. Let me persuade you. You must go soon, I heard you say so as you rode up. You must have something to eat before you go. Come and have some lunch with me, and let me persuade you not to do it. No, don't wake him, please ; afterwards, if you must. See, you can sit in the coffee-room by the window. It looks out here. Come.'

She rose and walked into the house. To lunch with a bride—and such a bride—at such a crisis—was too tempting. He looked about in uncertainty ; then suddenly wheeled a dusty bicycle from the sleeper's vicinity.

Meanwhile the perfidious Hiram J. sat silent.

He heard Amanda, alas ! no longer his Amanda, enter the coffee-room behind him.

' H-s-t.' He jumped as he heard her voice in his ear. ' Warn him,' she whispered.

He rose mechanically, ordered a can of beer, and carried it out to the seat which Amanda had so lately ornamented. He felt that the eyes of the minion of the law were boring through his back, as he looked from the corner of his eye at the loathed and detestable half-brother who had stolen his Amanda.

' He does not know her as I do,' he murmured bitterly, ' or he could not sleep like that.'

With his finger he flipped beer into the sleeper's face, as he gazed gloomily ahead at the little waves in the air which made the heat visible. The sleeper moved.

' H-s-t,' whispered Hiram J.

Henry J. opened lazy eyes and directed them along the ground as though idly looking for a snake.

' It's me,' whispered Hiram J., ' I'm doing it to wake you up.'

Henry J. looked at him, and then said with a yawn, ' You should rub it well with St. Jacob's oil.'

' Beware, we are observed,' whispered Hiram J., ' and my neck is not stiff, thank you. Your bride is eating cold beef with a stranger.'

' She does not touch beef this weather,' said Henry J. mildly. He thought it well to conciliate this obvious lunatic.

' You have learned her tastes quickly,' answered Hiram J. with spiteful emphasis, ' but to-day she is making an exception. She is humoring the man while you make your escape.'

' I am to fly, am I ? ' said the other affably. ' It is deuced hot for that.'

' The man has a writ.'

199

HOW AMANDA SERVED THE WRIT

The lazy man sat up suddenly. Hiram J. chuckled hoarsely.

'It's that Plymouth tailor,' muttered the unhappy bridegroom ; 'it's an outrage. A chap owes me for two pictures. I explained it all. I can't pay till he pays.'

'You better slope,' said Hiram J.

'Slope ?'

'Vamoose—fly. She advises it.'

'She is right,' groaned Henry J. 'If he gets judgment before I get paid, the bailiffs 'll be among the wedding presents.'

'Wriggle along to that clump,' said Hiram J. 'You must keep the tree between you and the coffee-room window. If I see you getting out of line I'll whistle. "Yankee doodle," twist to left ; "God save the King," to the right. If the man stays on, can I give your wife any last messages, where she could meet you in a week's time, say ?'

'No,' said the bridegroom firmly, 'if he stays I must surrender.'

'Come back quietly,' advised the good Samaritan, 'you might hide in that clump and hoot like an owl. Then she will come to you.'

'I never heard an owl in Newlyn, but——.'

'Hark !' interrupted Hiram J. starting, 'I thought I heard them getting up from the table. You better go—quick. Farewell !'

The beaten rival sat and watched his half-brother writhing along the ground, jerking abruptly to the right and left, according to the recessional obligingly whistled for him ; and at last he disappeared in the cover

'He's got my Amanda, and half my fortune,' said Hiram J. as he rose abruptly, 'and he can have my breach of promise too.'

He heard the solicitor's clerk and Amanda laughing heartily in the coffee-room. Amanda could be very amusing when she chose. He gritted his teeth at her light-hearted duplicity. She could laugh like that when her husband was probably prostrate from sunstroke in that clump of bushes.

It seemed to him a good time to disappear, so he mounted his bicycle and rode out into the heat. He had gone nearly ten miles ere he remembered that if he did not serve the citation there would be a delay of months perhaps before he could obtain his own share of the estate. He turned hastily round.

If the man with the writ had gone, he would tear the blue glasses from his eyes, snatch the cap from his head, let the perfidious girl see in the stranger that Hicks of Hicksville whose affections she had betrayed, and fling the paper which represented an ill-got fortune at her husband's feet.

All was quiet when he got back. Not a soul was about, and the trap which had brought the man with the brief-bag had gone. The weary cyclist lay down under the tree, pulled his cap over his face, and proceeded to think.

He was awakened by a persistent fly. He brushed it away several times but it refused to go. Wide awake at last, his attention was attracted by a strange booming noise. It was the distant cry of an owl, apparently in great anger. He sat up, and was greeted by a shriek of terror.

A little golden-haired, blue-eyed lady, all in white except for the blue sash about her left shoulder, was standing abashed before him.

'I—I—thought,' she cried tearfully, 'that—you were my husband; I am very sorry.'

She held the tip of an ostrich feather tied to the end of a stick, and she had evidently been reaching round the tree trunk and tickling his neck.

'I'm sorry I'm not,' answered Hiram J. politely; and the little lady blushed the more.

'Ah' she cried in a tone which seemed to say that everything would be all right now, 'there he comes.'

Henry J. Hicks was bounding along over the field.

'I fear,' said Hiram J. feebly, 'that he has been hooting at you. Did you hear an owl?'

Suddenly he set up a shout, and pointed eagerly towards a rapidly approaching dog-cart; but the angry husband came on regardless of consequences.

The triumphant Mr. Webb and his victim arrived together.
'Aha, Mr. Hicks,' cried Mr. Webb, 'I thought you hadn't got far.'

He leaped from the cart, waving the familiar blue envelope. Striking an imposing and merciless attitude, he drew from it a neatly folded wine-card of the little hostelry.

He looked at it dazed.

'I'll have the law on her,' he cried. 'Your wife has stolen the writ.'

'Sir,' cried Mrs. Henry J., indignantly, placing a hand on her husband's arm.

'You—are you Mrs. Hicks?' cried the dumbfoundered Mr. Webb.

'Cynthia,' interrupted her husband, 'have you ever seen this person before?'

'Never.'

'Nor this one?' pointing to Hiram J.

'Never.'

They stood gazing at one another in perplexity and distrust.

The suave landlord appeared on the scene.

'Do you see that cloud of dust?' he asked. He addressed Mr. Webb in particular, and he smiled pleasantly.

HOW AMANDA SERVED THE WRIT

All looked at the cloud of dust.

'That's a motor car,' he explained. 'It has just gone out of the yard. It contains a lady and her mother who are touring this country. They have left for ever. There's a message for you. The young lady thought you might come back. Will you step this way?'

Hiram J. rushed to his bicycle.

Amanda was still his Amanda, and was flying. Ere he had gone twenty yards his hind tire exploded with a loud report. As he wheeled back the wreck, the landlord remarked casually that he should not have left the machine standing on the cold stone of the archway. It brought a sudden contraction of the air that often resulted in explosions, he explained. Then he resumed his talk with Mr. Webb.

'The young lady,' he said, 'has taken a great fancy to the bride, and thought it a shame that this writ should be served. Here is the bridegroom's permanent address at Newlyn. Let it rest till he gets home. And here's a tenner she left for expenses.'

And Mr. Webb accordingly made the best of things, pocketed the money, and disappeared with a polite bow to Mrs. Henry J. Reprieved miraculously from this danger, Henry J. wished to quarrel with Hiram J., but ere he had found an excuse the little maid approached him with the news that a bag and a hat-box had come for him.

'They are mine,' said Hiram J., and he disappeared into the inn with much dignity, leaving the young couple to explanations about tailor's bills, and the oddity of there being other Mr. Hickses living.

When Hiram J. reappeared an hour later the contrast was such that the bride exclaimed audibly ; and so profound was the effect of a top-hat amid these rural scenes that she and her husband accepted without demur the stranger's invitation to take tea with him under the tree which had already that day stood silent witness of strange happenings.

His story was a long one ; and there was suspicious shying at the citation ; but everything came out at last just as Hiram J. had foreseen. His brother clasped him affectionately by the hand, and when it was quite clear to the bride about the forty thousand pounds, she clasped him about the neck and kissed him. As he felt her soft lips against his cheek, he heard the dolorous cry of the motor car, sounding apparently about two feet from his ear.

He sprang up. Amanda and her mother, not three yards away were sitting stonily gazing at the picture.

'Oh, Mrs. Huntington,' cried Cynthia, 'my husband has found a brother—and he is American, like you.'

'Then you are his sister-in-law ?' said Amanda, softening.

LORIN LATHROP

'Yes, yes—do come and hear about it—it is too wonderful.'

Mrs. Huntington shook hands with the new-comer, rather amiably, he dared to think. Amanda's return of the gentle pressure on which he presumed was distinct and reassuring. They joined his tea-party quite sociably. He retold the tale with remarkable brilliance under the influence of Amanda's smiling eyes. He did not know whether it was a good sign or a bad sign that she gave little heed to the partial loss of fortune. She might regard it as a matter which could never affect her personally. Then again she might be thinking so much of him, that she had no time to think of his money. He hoped it was the latter when she invited him into the motor car that she might show him how completely she was mistress of its peculiarities.

'Only a half mile, mamma,' she cried; 'I must show him my new toy.'

Hiram J. looked timidly at the old lady and was thunderstruck to see her smile acquiescence.

No sooner were they out of sight of the people under the tree than Amanda snatched a sudden hand from the wheel and handed Hiram J. an envelope.

He incautiously grasped it.

'Hide that horrid paper,' she cried, 'it's been burning my pocket. A dreadful man came here after the bridegroom, and I stole it. He might come back.'

Hiram J. turned white to the lips, and uttered a low cry of horror.

The startled Amanda involuntarily twisted the steering wheel and only by the exercise of great presence of mind prevented the car from succeeding in its eager attempt to enter the door of a wayside cottage.

'Never show emotion in a motor car,' she said calmly when the danger was over, 'it is the first rule.'

'Amanda,' he cried hoarsely, 'I will do my best. Do you know what you have done? Alas! all is over between us.'

At these words the car made a sudden swoop for a steep bank by the roadside, but was arrested ere it essayed the leap. It stopped dead.

'I think,' she said, 'that we will rest here. I can listen better.'

She turned an anxious face towards him.

He spoke with such firmness as he could command.

'Amanda,' he said, withdrawing the fatal blue paper, 'you have legally served me with Vivia Vavasour's writ for breach of promise of marriage.'

She gave a little moan.

'Yes,' he continued brokenly, 'she is in London, and she has begun an action there. She has some boyish letters, written by a boy——'

HOW AMANDA SERVED THE WRIT

'It was only two years ago,' interrupted Amanda, coldly.

'I was a boy then,' he said sadly, mourning over his lost youth ; 'sorrow has made me a man. I could not bear to have those letters read in court. I must divide what is left of my fortune with her—or marry her.'

'And I saved the wrong man,' said Amanda in a tearful voice ; 'and does this happen because I gave you that paper ?'

'I cannot deny,' he answered, 'that if I had not been handed this paper, I might have stolen away unharmed from these inhospitable shores. Not that I blame you, Amanda,' he cried, 'it was only a tragic accident. I see only poverty or shame before me. Take me to the nearest railroad depôt, Amanda. I came to Europe for you, Amanda—only for you ; but I must go back alone. It was not your fault that you turned sheriff's officer—it was Fate.'

Amanda's answer was to snatch the paper from his hand, tear it into fragments, fling them into the hedge, touch a lever, and fly with him along the road.

'I am still a sheriff's officer,' she said firmly, 'and you are my prisoner in this black maria. I shall take you back with me to momma ; and you shall go the rest of our tour with us.'

'But she—— ?'

'Was long ago reconciled to the inevitable. Now, don't contradict me or the machine will go over the bank.'

'But I am a law-abiding man,' he protested.

'Yes, and I am the sheriff.'

'Then,' he answered, 'I will submit. If you will give me your heart, I will place myself in your hands.'

'Done,' she cried.

Careless of danger he clasped the little hand that held the lever. The sympathetic machine started so madly for home, that in three minutes, they were once again under the now deserted tree.

Amanda was the second who that day kissed him under its branches.

'THE VISIT': A PAINTING BY GEORGE MORLAND, IN THE HERTFORD HOUSE COLLECTION. BY MAX BEERBOHM

NEVER, I suppose, was a painter less *maladif* in his work than Morland, that lover of simple and sunbright English scenes. Probably, this picture of his is all cheerful in intention. Yet the effect of it is saddening.

Superficially, the scene is cheerful enough. Our first impression is of a happy English home, of childish high-spirits and pretty manners. We note how genial a lady is the visitor, and how eager the children are to please. One of them trips respectfully forward—a wave of yellow curls fresh and crisp from the brush, a rustle of white muslin fresh and crisp from the wash. She is supported on one side by her grown-up sister, on the other by her little brother, who displays the nectarine already given to him by the kind lady. Splendid in far-reaching furbelows, that kind lady holds out both her hands, beaming encouragement. On her ample lap is a little open basket with other ripe nectarines in it —one for every child. Modest, demure, the girl trips forward as though she were dancing a quadrille. In the garden, just beyond the threshold, stand two smaller sisters, shyly awaiting their turn. They, too, are in their Sunday-best, and on the tip-toe of excitement—infant *coryphées*, in whom, as they stand at the wings, stage-fright is overborne by the desire to be seen and approved. I fancy they are rehearsing under their breath the 'Yes, ma'am,' and the 'No, ma'am,' and the 'I thank you, ma'am, very much,' which their grown-up sister has been drilling into them during the hurried toilet they have just been put through in honour of this sudden call. How anxious their mother is during the ceremony of introduction! How keenly, as she sits there, she keeps her eyes fixed on the visitor's face! Maternal anxiety, in that gaze, seems to be intensified by social humility. For this is no ordinary visitor. It is some great lady of the county, very rich, of high fashion, come from a great mansion in a great park, bringing fruit from one of her own many hot-houses. That she has come at all is an act of no slight condescension, and the mother feels it. Even so did homely Mrs. Fairchild look up to Lady Noble. Indeed, I suspect that this visitor is Lady Noble herself, and that the Fairchilds themselves are neighbours of this family. These children have been coached to say 'Yes, my lady' and 'No, my lady' and 'I thank you, my lady, very much'; and their mother has already been hoping that Mrs. Fairchild will haply pass through the lane and see the emblazoned yellow chariot at the wicket. But just now she

is all maternal—'These be my jewels.' See with what pride she
fingers the sampler embroidered by one of her girls, knowing well
that 'spoilt' Miss Augusta Noble could not do such embroidery to
save her life—that life which, through her Promethean naughtiness
in playing with fire, she was so soon to lose.

Other exemplary samplers hang on the wall yonder. On the
mantel-shelf stands a slate, with an ink-pot, and a row of tattered
books, and other tokens of industry. The school-room, beyond a
doubt. Lady Noble has expressed a wish to see the children here,
in their own haunt, and her hostess has led the way hither,
somewhat flustered, gasping many apologies for the plainness of the
apartment. A plain apartment it is: dark, bare-boarded, dingy-
walled. And not merely a material gloom pervades it. There is
a spiritual gloom, also—the subtly oppressive atmosphere of a
room where life has not been lived happily.

You know how, sometimes, when you enter a strange room,
you feel yourself gladdened or saddened for no palpable reason.
A light and well-proportioned room may sadden you, a poky
garret gladden you. Why is this? It is because your nerves are
affected by just that spirit which has been exhaled by the occu-
pants of the room, and which lingers within its walls. According as
whether happy or unhappy lives have been lived there, your vitality
is braced or relaxed. Often, of course, you have no means of
tracing the effect that a room has on you to the kind of life that it
has enclosed. But whenever you can ascertain what that life was
you will find invariably that your sensation accorded to it. You
are never depressed where happiness has been; where misery, never
exhilarated. How this spirit is exhaled and lingers, how it is
received, I know not; Science, which is just beginning to touch the
fringe of psychic mysteries, will perhaps penetrate this mystery
some day. All I know is that all persons of sensitive constitution
are indeed affected in this manner. The 'haunted room' is no
monopoly of old families; all rooms are haunted. Even the house
on whose walls the plaster is not yet dry is haunted by the workmen who have built it. Their hods and their trowels they carry
away with them at last; but their spirits are left in possession, to
mingle with those of the first tenants. A brand-new house is
notoriously depressing to live in; and this is because the British
workman is usually depressed; would he but rejoice in the dignity
of manual labour one would be happy from the outset in the work
of his hands.

Though these children are happy now, it is borne in on us by
the atmosphere (as preserved for us by Morland's master-hand)
that their life is a life of appalling dreariness. Even if we had
nothing else to go on, this evidence of our senses were enough.
But we have other things to go on. We know well the way in

which children of this period were upbrought. We remember
the life of 'The Fairchild Family,' those putative neighbours
of this family—in any case, its obvious contemporaries; and we
know that the life of those hapless little prigs was typical of
child-life in the dawn of the nineteenth century. Depend on it,
this family (whatever its name may be : the Thompsons, I conjec-
ture) is no exception to the dismal rule. In this school-room every
day is a day of oppression, of forced endeavour to conform with an
impossible standard of piety and good conduct—a day of tears and
texts, of texts quoted and tears shed, incessantly, from morning
unto evening prayers. After morning prayers (read by Papa), breakfast. The bread-and-butter, of which, for them, the meal consists,
must be eaten (slowly) in a silence by them unbroken except with
prompt answers to such scriptural questions as their parents (who
have ham-and-eggs) may, now and again, address to them. After
breakfast, the Catechism (heard by Mamma). After the Catechism,
a hymn to be learnt. After the repetition of this hymn, arith-
metic, caligraphy, the use of the globes. At noon, a decorous walk
with Papa, who for their benefit discourses on the General Depravity
of Mankind in all Countries after the Fall, occasionally pausing by
the way to point for them some moral of Nature. After a silent
dinner, the little girls sew, under the supervision of Mamma, or of
the grown-up sister, or of both those authorities, till the hour in
which (if they have sewn well) they reap permission to play (quietly)
with their doll. A silent supper, after which they work samplers.
Another hymn to be learnt and repeated. Evening prayers. Bed
time : ' Good-night, dear Papa ; good-night, dear Mamma.' Such,
depend on it, is the Thompsons' curriculum. What a painful
sequence of pictures a genre-painter might have made of it ! Let
us be thankful that we see the Thompsons only in this brief inter-
lude of their life, tearless and unpinafored, in this hour of strange
excitement, glorying in that Sunday-best which on Sundays is to
them but a symbol of intenser gloom.

But their very joy is in itself tragic. It reveals to us, in a flash, the
tragedy of their whole existence. That so much joy should result
from mere suspension of the usual *régime*, the sight of Lady Noble,
the anticipation of a nectarine ! For us there is no comfort in the
knowledge that their present degree of joy is proportionate to their
usual degree of gloom, that for them the Law of Compensation
drops into the scale of these few moments an exact counter-weight
of joy to the misery accumulated in the scale of all their other
moments. We, who do not live their life, who regard Lady Noble
as a mere Hecuba, and who would accept one of her nectarines only
in sheer politeness, cannot rejoice with them that rejoice thus, can
but pity them for all that has led up to their joy. We may reflect
that the harsh system on which they are reared will enable them to

enjoy life with infinite gusto when they are grown up, and that it is, therefore, a better system than the indulgent modern one. We may reflect, further, that it produces a finer type of man or woman, less selfish, better-mannered, more capable and useful. The pretty grown-up daughter here, leading her little sister by the hand, so gracious and modest in her mien, so sunny and affectionate, so obviously wholesome and high-principled—is she not a walking testimonial to the system? Yet to us the system is not the less repulsive in itself. Its results may be what you please, but its practice were impossible. We are too tender, too sentimental. We have not the nerve to do our duty to children, nor can we bear to think of any one else doing it. To children we can do nothing but 'spoil' them, nothing but bless their hearts and coddle their souls, taking no thought for their future welfare. And we are justified, maybe, in our flight to this opposite extreme. Nobody can read one line ahead in the book of fate. No child is guaranteed to become an adult. Any child may die to-morrow. How much greater for us the sting of its death if its life shall not have been made as pleasant as possible! What if its short life shall have been made as unpleasant as possible? Conceive the remorse of Mrs. Thompson here if one of her children were to die untimely—if one of them were stricken down now, before her eyes, by this surfeit of too sudden joy!

However, we do not fancy that Mrs. Thompson is going to be thus afflicted. We believe that there is a saving antidote in the cup of her children's joy. There is something, we feel, that even now prevents them from utter ecstasy. Some shadow, even now, hovers over them. What shadow is it? It is not that mere atmosphere of the room, so oppressive to us. It is something more definite than that, and even more sinister. It looms aloft, monstrously, like one of those grotesque actual shadows which a candle may cast athwart walls and ceiling. Whose shadow is it? we wonder, and, wondering, become sure that it is Mr. Thompson's—Papa's. The papa of Georgian children! We know him well, that awfully massive and mysterious personage, who seemed ever to his offspring so remote when they were in his presence, so frighteningly near when they were out of it. In 'Mrs. Turner's Cautionary Stories in Verse' he occurs again and again. Mr. Fairchild was a perfect type of him. Mr. Bennet, when the Misses Lizzie, Jane and Lydia were in pinafores, must have been another perfect type: we can reconstruct him as he was then from the many fragments of his awfulness which still clung to him when the girls had grown up. John Ruskin's father, too, if we read between the lines of 'Praeterita,' seems to have had much of the authentic monster about him. He, however, is disqualified as a type by the fact that he was 'a wholly honest merchant.' For one of the most salient peculiarities in the true Georgian Papa was to have apparently no occupation whatever—to be simply and solely a Papa. Even in social life he bore no part: we never hear of him calling on a neighbour or being called on. Even in his own household he was seldom visible. Except at their meals, and when he took them for their walk, and when they were sent to him to be reprimanded, his children never beheld him in the flesh. Mamma, poor lady, careful of many other things, superintended her children unremittingly, to keep them in the thorny way they should go. Hers the burden and heat of every day, hers to double the *rôles* of Martha and Cornelia, that her husband might be left ever calmly aloof in that darkened room, the study. There, in a high arm-chair, with one stout calf crossed over the other, immobile throughout the long hours sate he, propping a marble brow on a dexter finger of the same material. On the table beside him was a vase of flowers, daily replenished by the children, and a closed volume. It is remarkable that in none of the many woodcuts in which he has been handed down to us do we see him reading: he is always meditating on something he has just read. Occasionally, he is fingering a portfolio of engravings, or leaning aside to examine severely a globe of the world. That is the nearest he ever gets to physical activity. In him we see the static embodiment of perfect wisdom and perfect righteousness. We take him at his own valuation, humbly. Yet we have a queer instinct that there was a time when he did not diffuse all this cold radiance of good example. Something tells us that he has been a sinner in his day—a rattler of the ivories at Almack's and an ogler of wenches in the gardens of Vauxhall, a sanguine backer of the Negro against the Suffolk Bantam, and a devil of a fellow at boxing the watch and wrenching the knockers when Bow Bells were chiming the small hours. Nor do we feel that he is a penitent. He is too Olympian for that. He has merely put these things behind him —has calmly, as a matter of business, transferred his account from the worldly bank to the heavenly. He has seen fit to become 'Papa.' As such, strong in the consciousness of his own perfection, he has acquired, gradually, quasi-divine powers over his children. Himself invisible, we know that he can always see them. Himself remote, we know that he is always with them, and that always they feel his presence. He prevents them in all their ways. The Mormon Eye is not more direly inevitable than he. Whenever they offend in word or deed, he knows telepathically, and gives their punishment, long before they are arraigned at his judgment-seat.

At this moment, as at all others, Mr. Thompson has his inevitable eye on his children, and they know that it is on them. He is well enough pleased with them at this moment. But alas! we feel that ere the sun sets they will have incurred his wrath. Presently

'THE VISIT'

Lady Noble will have finished her genial inspection, and have sailed back, under convoy of the mother and the grown-up daughter, to the parlour, there to partake of that special dish of tea which is even now being brewed for her. When the children are left alone, their pent excitement will overflow and wash them into disgrace. Belike, they will quarrel over the nectarines. There will be bitter words, and a pinch, and a scratch, and a blow, screams, a scrimmage. The rout will be heard afar in the parlour. The grown-up sister will hasten back and be beheld suddenly, a quelling figure, on the threshold: 'For shame, Clara! Mary, I wonder at you! Henry, how dare you, sir? Silence, Ethel! Papa shall hear of this.' Flushed and rumpled, the guilty four will hang their heads, cowed by authority and by it perversely reconciled one with another. Authority will bid them go upstairs 'this instant,' there to shed their finery and resume the drab garb of every day. From the bed-room-windows they will see Lady Noble step into her yellow chariot and drive away. Envy—an inarticulate, impotent envy— will possess their hearts: why cannot *they* be rich, and grown-up, and bowed to by every one? When the chariot is out of sight, envy will be superseded by the play-instinct. Silently, in their hearts, the children will play at being Lady Noble. . . . Mamma's voice will be heard on the stairs, rasping them back to the realities. Sullenly they will go down to the school-room, and resume their tasks. But they will not be able to concentrate their unsettled minds. The girls will make false stitches in the pillow-slips which they had been hemming so neatly when the yellow chariot drove up to the front-door; and master Harry will be merely dazed by that page of the delectus which he had almost got by heart. Their discontent will be inspissated by the knowledge that they are now worse off than ever—are in dire disgrace, and that even now the grown-up sister is 'telling Papa' (who knows already, and has but awaited the formal complaint). Presently the grown-up sister will come into the school-room, looking very grave: 'Children, Papa has something to say to you.' In the study, to which, quaking, they will proceed, an endless sermon awaits them. The sin of Covetousness will be expatiated on, and the sins of Discord and Hatred, and the eternal torment in store for every child who is guilty of them. All four culprits will be in tears soon after the exordium. Before the peroration (a graphic description of the Lake of Fire) they will have become hysterical. They will be sent supperless to bed. On the morrow they will have to learn and repeat the chapter about Cain and Abel. A week, at least, will have elapsed before they are out of disgrace. Such are the inevitable consequences of joy in a joyless life. It were well for these children had 'The Visit' never been paid.

Morland, I suppose, discerned naught of all this tragedy in his picture. To him, probably, the picture was an untainted idyll, was but one of those placid homely scenes which he loved as dearly as could none but the brawler and vagabond that he was. And yet . . . and yet . . . perhaps he did intend something of what we discern here. He may have been thinking, bitterly, of his own childhood, and of the home he ran away from.

THE KING'S DECLARATION
BY THE REV. CANON MAC COLL

HE person chiefly affected by the Declaration imposed on the Sovereign of this realm at the opening of his first Parliament is the Sovereign himself. Yet in all the discussions of the subject in Parliament and in the press the Sovereign is the only interested party whose views and feelings have never once been consulted or considered. The feelings of the Roman Catholics have been considered, though with small skill and tact. The feelings and even prejudices of the most intolerant section of that amorphous abstraction called Protestantism have been more than considered : the Government has endeavoured in vain to placate them by concessions which satisfy no one. No thought has been given to the feelings, dignity, self-respect of our Sovereigns, present and future. The present Declaration is resented by Roman Catholics as an insult. But an insult to a multitude is less intolerable—at least, when it is not intended to have a personal application —than an insult directed to a particular individual. Now I hold that the King's Declaration, alike in its present and in its amended form, is an insult to the Sovereign. Let us look at it in its amended form :

I, A. B., by the grace of God, King (or Queen) of Great Britain and Ireland, Defender of the Faith, do solemnly and sincerely, in the presence of God, profess, testify, and declare that I do believe that in the Sacrament of the Lord's Supper there is not any transubstantiation of the elements of bread and wine into the Body and Blood of Christ at or after the consecration thereof by any person whatsoever. And I do believe that the invocation of the Virgin Mary, or any other saint, and the Sacrifice of the Mass, as they are now used in the Church of Rome, are contrary to the Protestant religion in which I believe. And I do solemnly, in the presence of God, profess, testify, and declare that I do make this Declaration, and every part thereof, unreservedly.

I call this Declaration insulting to the Sovereign because a Roman Catholic is already excluded from the throne by statute. For the Act of Settlement provides ' that any person who is reconciled to the See of Rome, or shall profess the Papal religion, or shall marry a Papist, shall be excluded, and be for ever incapable to inherit, possess, or enjoy the Crown and Government of this realm.' It follows that no Roman Catholic can occupy the throne except by the grossest hypocrisy and deceit, to which he must at his coronation add the guilt of sacrilege, for reception of the Eucharist according to the Anglican rite is part of the Coronation Service. The Declaration, therefore, in its amended as well as in its existing form, assumes that every one of our Sovereigns for the last two centuries has probably been a sacrilegious hypocrite, and that all our future Sovereigns are likely to be so. Apart from that assumption the words have no meaning. No avowed Roman

Catholic can inherit the crown or retain it. Consequently, the Declaration is of necessity aimed at a crypto-Papist. Is it fitting that the nation should cast this imputation on all our Sovereigns in succession as each begins to reign? What good purpose can it serve? For if the King is a Papist at heart, and yet is ready to occupy a throne from which a Papist is excluded by statute, it is evident that he will not be restrained by the Declaration. In other words, the Declaration is not needed against an honest man, and is futile against a dishonest one. In either case it is useless. But a useless Declaration is mischievous in addition. Is it not an outrage on one's feelings of reverence and propriety that a girl of eighteen like our late gracious Queen, when she came to the throne, should have been compelled, 'solemnly and sincerely, in the presence of God,' to 'profess, testify, and declare that' she 'believed that in the Sacrament of the Lord's Supper there is not any transubstantiation of the elements of bread and wine into the Body and Blood of Christ at or after the consecration thereof by any person whatsoever'? To begin with, the English of the sentence is nonsense, for 'thereof' belongs grammatically to 'the Body and Blood of Christ.' So that the Declaration is one which any Roman Catholic might make without any violent wrench to his conscience.

But I may be told that a straightforward honest man would be guided by the evident intention of the framers of the Declaration. It is, I believe, good law that a subscriber is not bound by the *animus imponentis,* but only by the grammatical meaning of what he signs. However that may be, the King's Declaration is not intended for a straightforward honest man: for him no declaration is necessary. It is intended for a dishonest man, for a man who, being a Papist at heart, desires to occupy a throne from which Papists are excluded by statute. Such a man would take advantage of any loophole which grammar and casuistry could give him, and would, without scruple, make the proposed declaration. The Declaration is, therefore, absolutely futile. It does not bind the hypocrite, for whom it is intended, and is a gratuitous affront to the honest man, for whom it is not intended.

Nor is the second limb of the Declaration more defensible :

> And I do believe that the invocation of the Virgin Mary, or any other saint, and the Sacrifice of the Mass, as they are now used in the Church of Rome, are contrary to the Protestant religion in which I believe.

That sentence is a marvel of ingenious fatuity. It leaves our future Sovereigns free to believe in such invocation of saints and in such Sacrifice of the Mass as vary from the present practice of the Church of Rome. So that if the Church of Rome were to alter its use—a conceivable contingency—the Declaration would become obsolete. Moreover, the declarator expresses no disapproval of the invocation of saints and the Sacrifice of the Mass : he only says that the present Roman use of them is contrary to ' the Protestant religion in which I believe.' What does that mean ? Does it mean the particular species of Protestantism in which the Sovereign for the time being believes ? Lord Tweedmouth strongly objects to any declaration which would pledge our Sovereigns to belief in the doctrines of the Church of England in particular. He is anxious to leave them at liberty to choose the specific form of Protestantism to which they may feel inclined. That is indeed a comprehensive choice. For the various denominations of Protestantism are reckoned by hundreds, ranging from believers in the Trinity and Incarnation, through Unitarianism, down to Agnosticism. The late Professor Huxley called himself a Protestant, and he gloried in the appellation of Agnostic, of which indeed he claimed the paternity. If this is the meaning of the phrase, each of our Sovereigns in future may, as far as the Declaration binds him, select his own form of Protestantism. In that case the Declaration makes him affirm that the present usage of the Roman Church as to invocation of saints and the Sacrifice of the Mass is contrary to *that* form of Protestantism, leaving all other forms untouched.

But if by ' the Protestant religion ' we are to understand Protestantism in general, how can any intelligent human being believe in such a conglomeration of contradictories ? Some forms of Protestantism are more opposed to each other than any of them is opposed to the Church of Rome. How can a man believe in a bundle of contradictories ? The human mind is not capable of such a feat of intellectual legerdemain ! The Bishop of Worcester—an Evangelical of the Evangelicals—has declared in a letter to the *Times* that he does not know what ' the Protestant religion ' means. All sensible men must share his ignorance. The phrase is incapable of definition. You might as well talk of ' the Protestant fever ' or of ' the Protestant medicine.'

Is it wise, is it dignified, is it fair to force upon all our future Sovereigns a Declaration which is self-contradictory and meaningless, and compel them to add : ' And I do solemnly, in the presence of God, profess, testify, and declare that I make this Declaration, and every part thereof, unreservedly ' ? No honest man can pledge himself ' unreservedly' to a Declaration to which it is impossible to affix an intelligible meaning. Surely, if there is such a sin as taking God's name in vain, we have a painful example of it here.

It is to be observed, further, that the Declaration is one of present belief only. Suppose the declarator changes his mind : what then ? Is he bound to publish his new belief ? There is nothing in the Declaration which obliges him to do so ; and the question of honour does not come in, for the Declaration assumes him to be a man whom honour does not bind. A man of honour who accepted the doctrines and claims of the Roman Church would decline the throne. A Roman Catholic who was not a man of honour would not be precluded by this Declaration. Let it be clearly understood that all our future heirs to the Crown are assumed by this Declaration to be persons without honour, and it will be seen at once that the Declaration, as it stands, does not bind the declarator a day after he makes it. To be effective, it ought to be renewed, if not daily, at least frequently ; or it ought to pledge the person who makes it never to change his mind ; and that would be a promise incapable of fulfilment, which, therefore, no honest man would make.

So much as to the particular form of Declaration imposed upon our Sovereigns, amended or unamended. It is indefensible on every ground. It is entirely useless. It is insulting to the Sovereign. It makes him pledge his belief to what is seen on analysis to be nonsense, and it compels him to call God to witness that he makes this public profession of superfluous nonsense ' unreservedly.'

Let us now look at the question from a more general point of view. Any one who considers the matter without passion or prejudice must admit that the whole system of official and judicial oaths needs revision. Waiving for the moment the question whether oaths are at all expedient—whether they do not, on the whole, do more harm than good—there can be no question that the multiplication of oaths —and the King's Declaration is a form of oath—is a very serious evil. No oath is justifiable which cannot be proved to be absolutely necessary. It was the practice, and may be still, to oblige the Primate of all England, as President of the Society for the Propagation of the Gospel in Foreign Parts, and the other bishops as vice-presidents, to take an oath to discharge faithfully the duties of their office. Does any one suppose that there ever was any necessity for this oath? But if not absolutely necessary, it must be condemned as an insult to the Episcopal Bench, and a violation of the spirit at least, if not of the letter, of the Gospel. I believe that morality in general, and veracity in particular, would gain by the abolition of all oaths of office. Let us glance at some of them.

It is not so long since undergraduates at our Universities were obliged to swear that within the colleges they would speak no language but Latin while, in matter of fact, they spoke English daily. They were made to swear that they would employ a certain number of hours out of every twenty-four in disputations ; but the oath was treated as an empty form alike by those who exacted and by those who took it. The demoralising effect of such oaths was increased rather than lessened by the various interpretations sanctioned by the authorities, such as that there is no perjury if the man who takes the oath submit to the penalty, or if there be no gross and obstinate negligence. The young man was left to decide for himself where permissible negligence ended and gross negligence began, with the natural result that gross negligence became the rule. And these useless oaths to keep the statutes were exacted not only from boys on their matriculation, but also when they took their bachelor's degree and every other degree.

And can anything be imagined better calculated to blunt the conscience than the practice of the cardinals during the vacancy of the Holy See? Each signs and swears to observe, in case of election, a document prescribing certain reforms in the Papal Government. Not only is this solemn engagement habitually violated, but also each new Pope finds reasons for its violation which are considered valid—for example, that the august dignity and spiritual endowments which the election confers releases the Pope from a promise made in a position of less responsibility and discernment. It is easy to cast ridicule on this practice. But is it much more ridiculous than some of the practices still prevalent among ourselves? Take the oath against simony, of which the gist is: 'I do swear that I have made no simoniacal payment for obtaining this ecclesiastical office: so help me God through Jesus Christ.' In practice this is held only to forbid the direct payment for an ecclesiastical office by the man who is to enjoy it. But a father may, with the consent of his son, invest the son's patrimony in the purchase of a living for him. Or a relation or friend may, with the knowledge of a clergyman, buy a living for him, to which the clergyman may legally present himself. Or a clergyman may act as 'a warming-pan' for a minor—that is, enjoy the possession of a living for years on promise to vacate it as soon as the patron's nominee is ready to take it.

Formerly every man who voted for the election of a member of Parliament was obliged to take the following oath: 'I do swear I have not received, or had, by myself or any person whatsoever in trust for me, or for my use and benefit, directly or indirectly, any sum or sums of money; office, place, or employment; gift or reward; or any promise or security for any money, office, employment, or gift, in order to give my vote at this election." Bribery is unfortunately still far too common at Parliamentary elections; but it is notorious that it is far less common than it was while the oath against it was imposed on all electors. What is the inference? That the oath, so far from acting as a deterrent, was a nursery for perjury. And why has bribery diminished? For two reasons: first, because of the growth of a healthier public opinion; secondly, because the penalty for bribery has been made more stringent and comprehensive, both against the elector and the candidate.

Take, again, the oath of allegiance: 'I do sincerely promise and swear that I will be faithful and bear true allegiance to His Majesty King Edward.' What does that oath mean ? Is there any difference between being ' faithful ' and ' bearing true allegiance'? If there is, what is it ? And to what do those who take the oath bind themselves ? In Germany allegiance is interpreted so strictly that a careless remark by a washerwoman on the street may expose her to the penalty of *lèse majesté*. The oath is taken but by a small fraction of King Edward's subjects. Does any one believe that these are more faithful and loyal to his Majesty than the mass of his subjects who do not take the oath ? No one will say so. Then, what is the use of the oath ? And if it is useless, it is mischievous. No wonder authorities stumble and flounder when they attempt to interpret the oath. Paley says that ' the oath excludes all design, at the time, of attempting to depose the reigning sovereign.'[1] ' At the time ' ! Does that mean on the day on which the oath is taken ? or a month, or six months, later ? Strictly interpreted, the oath excludes Paley's qualification, for it binds the swearer to the future, not the present ; not against any design cherished at the moment, but against any design attempted at any future time and amid all circumstances. Not only the opponents of Charles I., but also the adherents of William of Orange, forswore their allegiance, and the Non-jurors alone were thus the only true and loyal subjects. Paley proceeds to qualify the oath in such a way as makes it entirely nugatory. ' It permits,' he says, ' resistance to the king when his ill behaviour or imbecility is such as to make resistance beneficial to the community.' If this interpretation of the oath had been adopted by the British Government of the day, the United States of America would now be a British possession, and Ireland would probably have been pacified. Did any oath of allegiance ever avert a revolution anywhere ? It is a futile formula, a political superstition, which offers no sort of safeguard for his Majesty's throne or dynasty. His dynasty is, in fact, founded—like every dynasty in Europe— on a violation of the oath of allegiance, and is none the less secure for that. The true rampart of his gracious Majesty's throne, like that of his mother, rests on a firmer and more stable foundation. It is ' broad-based upon a people's will ' : a safer bulwark than the artificial barrier of a fragile oath which experience proves to be no protection in the hour of need.

And as the logic of events obliges us to interpret the oath of allegiance in accordance with reason and common sense, so we are bound to give the Sovereign the benefit of the principles on which his subjects act. In the fierce controversy on the disestablishment of the Irish Church the Coronation oath was quoted by Lord Derby and others as a barrier which could not be passed without perjury on the part of her late Majesty. Not only was this interpretation of

[1] 'Moral and Political Philosophy,' book iii. c. xviii.

the oath repudiated by the Liberal Government, which included some of the ablest and most conscientious men of the day : it was repudiated also by the present Premier, who rightly argued that the nation, through its Parliament, had as much power to release the Soveriegn from the bonds of the Coronation oath as it had to bind him, and that the oath was therefore binding only so long and so far as the nation chose to make it so. When his present Majesty shall swear to maintain the existing relations between Church and State, every one will understand that the oath does not bind him to veto a Bill for the dissolution of the connection between Church and State in England or Scotland should both Houses of Parliament pass such a Bill. Thus the utility of the Coronation oath is not apparent.

There is another aspect of the reciprocal duties between Sovereign and subjects and between Parliament and portions of the nation which may soon become a burning question. Mr. Chamberlain, in his recent speech at Blenheim, has been understood to foreshadow a scheme of redistribution which shall diminish the Parliamentary representation of Ireland. But that means the repeal of a fundamental article of the Act of Union. At the time of the Union the population of Ireland entitled it to 220 Members of Parliament, and the Irish complained bitterly that the Act gave them a smaller representation than they were fairly entitled to. The justice of their complaint was admitted, and they were promised, by way of solatium, that it should be a fundamental article of the Act of Union that, in the event of the population of Ireland decreasing below the line of fair representation, the number of their representatives should, nevertheless, remain the same. A reduction of the Irish representation would thus be an infringement of the Act of Union, and would undoubtedly weaken the force of the argument against Home Rule. But it is not in that connection that I refer to the matter. I appeal to it as an illustration of the futility of all these illusory safeguards, whether on the part of Sovereign or subjects.

The practice of our Constitution is singularly inconsistent in the matter of oaths. When peers sit in judgment on one of their own body, even in capital cases, they are not sworn. They give their judgment of guilty or not guilty 'upon my honour.' Yet no one imagines that their judgment or evidence on such rare occasions is less conscientious than when they are sworn on ordinary occasions. The Society of Friends and Moravians, and now every one who claims exemption, are at liberty to make a declaration instead of an oath both in courts of justice and on taking their seats in Parliament. Does that prove that the word of one who merely declares is less trustworthy than the word of one who swears? Or would any one object to the evidence of a witness or the verdict of a juror who chose to declare rather than swear? I have never heard or read of any such objection. Does not that prove that oaths are altogether superfluous, adding nothing to the force of a mere declaration ?

I am inclined to think that oaths in evidence are, of all oaths, the most mischievous and demoralising. The witness swears to 'speak the truth, the whole truth, and nothing but the truth.' Is the requirement of this oath satisfied when the witness answers truthfully every question that counsel asks him ? The law says that it is. Yet the witness may have knowledge vital to the issue, which, nevertheless, he is understood not to be bound to reveal unless a question germane to his secret is put to him. If, on the other hand, any one should argue that a witness is bound to state every detail within his knowledge bearing on the case, then hardly a trial could ever take place without perjury on the part of witnesses.

One inevitable effect of the oath system is to depreciate the sacredness of truth by erecting two standards of veracity—one standard when the man is on his oath and another when he is not. Counsel asks a question, and receiving an answer which does not help him to prove his case, he asks sternly : 'On your oath, sir, do you mean to say ?' &c. What is that but a plain intimation that falsehood becomes sin only when it is backed by an oath ? The witness retires from the witness-box with his reverence for veracity undermined ; and we have thus artificially diminished the public reprobation for lying by imposing oaths. The whole system tends inevitably to propagate the belief that there is a difference in the degree of obligation not to lie and not to swear falsely. Now, as the business of life and the well-being of society depend largely on the virtue of veracity, while oaths are imposed rarely and on the few, it is manifest that any depreciation of the obligation of veracity, apart from an oath, is a serious injury to the commonwealth. And for this injury the system of oaths provides no compensation. It may be seriously questioned whether oaths ever, of themselves, supply an additional motive to veracity. It is possible that a man on his oath is sometimes more likely to speak the truth than he would be if he only made a simple affirmation. But the restraining motive in such a case is the fear of penalty and the force of public opinion, not the religious sanction of the oath. The facts in support of this view are so many and so various that it hardly admits of doubt. Where capital punishment was inflicted for petty offences, the moral sense of the multitude was so outraged that juries systematically refused to convict. They were on oath to give their verdicts according to the evidence, and they deliberately returned verdicts plainly and openly against the evidence. And the reason was that there was no legal penalty for their perjury, and no public opinion to restrain them. We have thus the strange spectacle of the professional and propertied classes and the *élite* of society supporting a code of laws

so barbarous and so contrary to natural justice as to be worthy only
of savages, while their repeal was secured by the outraged consciences,
operating through perjury, of the comparatively uneducated and
humble classes of which juries are composed. A monster petition
against the repeal of a law which sent men, women, and children to
the gallows for the theft of anything above the value of five shillings
was sent to Parliament, and the signatories claimed to represent the
whole legal profession, from solicitors to judges, and the whole
banking and commercial and landed interest. And when the Bill
for the repeal of that inhuman law reached the House of Lords it
was thrown out by a large majority, which included all the law peers
and seven bishops. The result was the revolt of the juries, so that
in London alone, according to the declaration of the Chief Justice
of the Common Pleas, ' five hundred perjured verdicts ' were given
by juries in the course of three years. Those verdicts were so mani-
festly perjured that there could be no question about them. For
instance, a woman was caught in the act of stealing a ten-pound
Bank of England note. The facts were undisputed ; but the jury,
determined to save the woman's life and to express their abhorrence
of so monstrous a law, found that the note did not exceed five
shillings in value. The result all over the country was that no
conviction at all against theft could be obtained, and the very
classes who had petitioned against the repeal of a law which they
regarded as the only secure safeguard of property, now petitioned
for its repeal because juries perjured themselves rather than
enforce it.

Does not this one fact alone prove that an oath by itself has very
little effect on consciences when it is not backed by penalty or
public opinion ? The inevitable inference is that if falsehood be
exposed to the same legal penalty and public reprobation which are
now attached to perjury, the same result will be obtained, with the
additional gain that the standard of simple veracity will be immeasurably enhanced. Abolish oaths, and the public reprobation of
falsehood will immediately increase in power, and cause at the same
time an increase in the efficiency of the religious sanction. The
present relative estimate of lying and perjury is a very inaccurate
test of the efficiency of oaths. Having artificially reduced the
abhorrence of lying, we argue illogically that this debilitated abhorrence is not strong enough to bind men to the truth. In brief, then,
the case stands thus. Oaths are designed to enforce a strong religious sanction. But they do not enforce it unless they are seconded
by the apprehension of penalties or the fear of disgrace. This apprehension and fear may be attached to falsehood pure and simple. It
follows that all those motives which bind men to veracity may be
applied to falsehood as well as to perjury. In other words, oaths
are needless for their purpose, and they do incalculable harm in all

directions. The persons influenced by them from a purely religious motive are just the persons who do not need them, for they would speak the truth without them.

I have already observed that our sanction of an affirmation in lieu of an oath, without any detriment to the public service or the cause of justice, is proof positive not only of the inutility of oaths, but also of our conviction that they are useless. And this is only one proof out of many. In some of the most important affairs of public life an oath is never required. The Houses of Parliament dispense with oaths in their examination of witnesses : a clear proof that they consider an oath unnecessary. But if it be unnecessary in matters which come before Parliament, in some of which large private as well as public interests are involved, can it be seriously maintained that an oath is necessary in the petty affairs of ordinary life ? Strange inconsistency ! The very Legislature which declares by its own practice that oaths are unnecessary insists on imposing them on its own members, as if these were less trustworthy than chance witnesses that appear before it on a railway or sewage Bill. The Parliament which thinks that the word of a costermonger may be trusted without oath declares that the Constitution will be in peril unless the Sovereign of the realm is bound by a solemn oath to pledge his belief ' unreservedly ' to certain recondite theological propositions. Indeed the absurdity goes farther. For the legislators, who bind themselves by oaths to fulfil faithfully the duties of their office, proceed forthwith to the discharge of those duties upon the mere word of persons of whose character, in most cases, they know nothing.

Again, evidence on oath is not required by military courts of inquiry. In the name of reason and common sense, why should it be assumed that a man can be trusted to speak the truth on affirmation before military officers, but not before a judge in a civil court of justice ? Arbitrators, too, commonly proceed on mere affirmation, and nobody seeks on that account to discredit the evidence thus given.

Perhaps a more striking example of the inutility, and consequently of the folly and mischief of oaths, is supplied by the practice of the American Courts, which exact no oaths. No one will suggest that failure of justice is characteristic of American tribunals. But if they secure justice without the administration of oaths, we are forced to the conclusion that oaths are needless, unless, indeed, we are prepared to admit that the American people are so far in advance of ourselves in the virtue of veracity that they can afford to dispense with a safeguard which we consider necessary on this side of the Atlantic.

Another important consideration is the difficulty of conviction for perjury owing to the elastic definition of the offence. Perjury is defined by Coke as ' a crime committed when a lawful oath is ministered, by any that hath lawful authority, to any person in any judicial proceeding, who sweareth absolutely and falsely in a matter material to the issue or cause in question, by their own act, or by subornation of others.' [1] Blackstone, commenting on this definition, says that the law ' takes no notice of any perjury but such as is committed in some court of justice having power to administer an oath, or before some magistrate, or proper officer invested with a similar authority in some proceedings relative to a civil suit or a criminal prosecution : for it esteems all other oaths unnecessary at least, and therefore will not punish the breach of them.' [2]

These quotations from two of our greatest authorities on the subject are alone sufficient to condemn the whole system of oaths. To constitute perjury there must be a violation, wilful, absolute and false, in a matter material to the issue, of a lawful oath administered in a judicial proceeding. Violation of all oaths not within the four corners of this definition, however gross and open, does not constitute legal perjury. The judges, in a case reserved, ruled unanimously that conviction for perjury could not be obtained for the violation, however deliberate and gross, of an oath taken before a surrogate for the purpose of obtaining a marriage licence. Yet not only the oath, but the very terms of it, are required by statute. Can anything be imagined more demoralising than the imperative exaction by the Legislature of a multitude of oaths which the law regards as ' unnecessary at least,' while it refuses to recognise the violation of them as perjury? All oaths of office are thus condemned in the lump, and all Parliamentary oaths, and even all oaths of evidence which do not conform to Coke's narrow definition.

And what are we to say of subscription to Articles of Religion—the Thirty-nine, for example? The form of subscription till about a generation ago required an assent *ex animo* to every proposition in the Articles. Yet it is notorious that hardly one of the multitude of subscribers gave this assent in the literal sense, and Paley justifies as follows this mental reservation :

> They who contend that nothing less can justify subscription to the Thirty-nine Articles than the actual belief of each and every separate proposition contained in them must suppose that the Legislature expected the consent of ten thousand men, and that in perpetual succession, not to one controverted proposition, but to many hundreds. It is difficult to conceive how this could be expected by any who observed the incurable diversity of human opinion upon other subjects of demonstration.[3]

'It is difficult to conceive,' forsooth, 'how this could be expected'! Then, in the name of immutable and eternal truth, why exact a

---

[1] Inst. iii. 164.   [2] Book iv. c. 10.
[3] 'Moral and Political Philosophy,' book iii. c. xxii.

promise of which it is difficult to conceive the fulfilment ? But the point was decided judicially against Paley by anticipation :

One Smyth subscribed to the Thirty-nine Articles of Religion with this addition—*so far as the same was agreeable to the Word of God;* and it was resolved by Wray, Chief Justice in the King's Bench, and all the judges of England, that this subscription was not according to the statute of 13 Eliz., because the statute required an absolute subscription, and this subscription made it conditional ; and that this Act was made for avoiding diversity of opinions ; and by this addition the party might, by his own private opinion, take some of them to be against the Word of God, and by this means diversity of opinions should not be avoided, which was the scope of the statute ; and the very Act made, touching subscription, of none effect.[1]

It is hardly an exaggeration to say that on this interpretation the innumerable host of subscribers to the Thirty-nine Articles, lay and clerical, down to the recent change in the terms of subscription, were perjurers. The form of subscription is now so vague that one wonders why it should be imposed on any one. Is it not evident that the effect of all this trifling with solemn engagements is to diminish the influence of religion altogether, and to induce a habit of indifference towards religious sanctions and sacred things? Hence the whole moral character becomes deteriorated through the corrosion caused by the carelessness and lightness with which the oath system has infected men's thoughts as to the sacred obligation of veracity, which remains as binding without as with an oath.

Let us, in conclusion, glance at the oath system in the light of the Gospel :

Ye have heard that it hath been said by them of old time, Thou shalt not forswear thyself, but shalt perform unto the Lord thine oaths : but I say unto you, Swear not at all ; neither by heaven, for it is God's throne ; nor by the earth, for it is His footstool ; neither by Jerusalem, for it is the city of the Great King. Neither shalt thou swear by thy head, because thou canst not make one hair white or black. But let your communication be Yea, yea ; nay, nay. For whatsoever is more than these cometh of evil.

I venture to say that these words would infallibly leave on the mind of one who heard or read them for the first time the impression that the Speaker intended to forbid all oaths under all circumstances. Let us consider their plain meaning. 'It hath been said by them of old time, Thou shalt not forswear thyself.' Why refer to the precept 'of old time'? Clearly to differentiate it from the new precept which He was about to lay down. The old precept said, 'Swear not falsely,' 'do not commit perjury.' The new precept says, 'Swear not at all, truly or falsely.' The contradistinction between the old precept and the new is meaningless unless it means this.

Those who wish to avoid this inevitable inference argue that our

[1] Inst. v. c. 74.

223

Lord intended only to forbid swearing by certain objects, but did not intend to forbid lawful appeals to God on oath. That interpretation, however, has been precluded by anticipation. St. James, who was not only one of Christ's disciples, but was in addition a near relation who had frequent opportunities of learning his Master's mind in the privacy of domestic life, says : 'Swear not ; neither by heaven, neither by the earth, neither by any other oath.' We may take this as an authoritative commentary on our Lord's words by one who had the best right to make it. Nor is this interpretation invalidated by our Lord's answer to the adjuration of the High Priest, or by St. Paul's calling God to witness the truth of a certain statement. Schlensner, in explaining the High Priest's adjuration and our Lord's answer, says that the High Priest did not mean, 'I make to swear, or put upon oath,' but 'I solemnly and in the name of God exhort and enjoin' ; and, moreover, whatever the High Priest meant, our Lord was in no sense upon oath. It might just as well be argued that His answer to the evil spirit who said, 'I adjure thee by the living God that thou torment me not,' was upon oath. The appeal to St. Paul's example is still less to the point : 'God is my witness that without ceasing I make mention of you always in my prayers.' There is nothing here of the nature of an oath. The Apostle says, in effect : 'God knows, though ye may not, how ceaseless are my prayers for you.' An oath, according to Milton, involves 'a curse upon ourselves' in case of its infraction ; or, according to Paley, 'an invocation of God's vengeance.' To no expression in the New Testament is this definition applicable. The great authorities of the early Church took our Lord's words literally. 'Christ forbids all swearing,' says Tertullian. 'I say nothing of perjury, since swearing itself is unlawful.'[1] Chrysostom says : 'Do not say to me, I swear for a good purpose : it is no longer lawful for thee to swear either justly or unjustly.'[2] Gregory of Nysse is equally emphatic : 'He who has precluded murder by taking away anger, and who has driven away the pollution of adultery by subduing lust, has expelled the curse of perjury from our life by forbidding us to swear ; for where there is no oath there can be no infringement of it.'[3] Gregory Nanzianzen, in poetry and prose, forbids oaths absolutely. He compares the whole system to a stone set rolling down a steep with increasing velocity, till at last it reaches the brow of a precipice, when with one bound it plunges into the gulf below, which gulf is perjury. 'Fly from every oath,' he says. 'What is worse than an oath ? Nothing, as I maintain.' 'How then shall we be believed ? By our word, and by a life which makes our word worthy of credit.' St. Augustine, as usual, tries to be

[1] 'De Idol.' c. x. 11, 17, 23.
[2] In Gen. ii. Hom. xv.
[3] In Cant. Hom. xiii.

moderate and to regard the question from all sides. ' Avoid,' he says, ' an oath as much as possible. It is better not to swear even to the truth. By the practice of swearing perjury is often incurred, and is always approached.' He sums up the case in a pregnant sentence : ' False swearing is fatal ; true swearing is dangerous ; swearing not at all is safe.' He allows that an oath is permissible to a Christian when his evidence in an important cause is not otherwise believed. This concession he makes with the reservation that even in that case the oath springs from evil, but the evil is in him who imposes, not in him who makes the oath.[1]

This may suffice for the teaching of Christ, of His apostles, and of the Church of the first four centuries. Add to this the demoralising effect of oaths as evidenced by experience, and surely the case against the whole oath system is irresistible when examined in the dry light of dispassionate reason. But the difficulty is to evoke the play of dispassionate reason against an inveterate prejudice. It is so difficult for people in general to place themselves in the position of independent inquirers. One of the most powerful causes of the slow reform of public institutions and old customs is the tendency in most minds to justify what is, rather than to consider whether it ought to be amended or even to exist at all. It may be admitted that age is not necessarily an argument against existing institutions or customs—nay, that it may be a strong argument in their favour— without going to the opposite extreme of maintaining that ' whatever is is right.'

But if the oath system in general is indefensible on grounds of reason and expediency, the form of it which is imposed in the King's Declaration on his accession combines every objection to the system without a single compensating benefit. Not a man in the House of Lords defended it on its simple merits. It was defended on both sides of the House on the ground that public opinion insisted on it, in proof of which the Lord Chancellor appealed to his letter-bag. As if that were any evidence at all ! It was this sort of evidence that retained so long in the Statute Book the atrocious penal laws which were a disgrace to human nature. But those who then appealed to public opinion misunderstood it egregiously, as the event proved. And so it is now. What is mistaken for public opinion is but the fanatical clamour of prejudice and unreasoning religious passion, and is confined to a few. Statesmen and electioneering wire-pullers may safely, on the lowest grounds, pay no heed to it. But shall we ever again have statesmen who will dare to enlighten and lead public opinion instead of dancing attendance on its whims and prejudices ? Our leading public men, with but few exceptions, have come to realise Plato's picture of the

---

[1] Si non a malo jurantis, a malo est non credentis. A malo est quod facis, sed illius qui exiget (' In Jac.' v.).

THE KING'S DECLARATION

political society of his day : on the one hand the democracy, a fierce wild beast; on the other the rulers who vied with each other in caressing, cajoling, pampering, never resisting, the beast, for fear it should bite them. It is this decay of virility and political courage in our public men that must seem to a reflecting mind the most ominous sign of our era. Nations may survive and surmount disaster, but not the dry rot of habitual pusillanimity.

SHERIDAN: SOME UNPUBLISHED LETTERS. BY WILFRED SHERIDAN

Y Lord Rochester, in the epigram which he wrote on his Sovereign's bedchamber door, pronounced a verdict on Charles II. that might well fit many another prominent man, 'who never said a foolish thing and never did a wise one,' but perhaps none so well as Richard Brinsley Sheridan.

Biographers have vied with one another in attempting to portray a character so many-sided. In many cases, were it not for the name, one would imagine that it was not the same person each was attempting to describe. In the opinion of people most capable of deciding, no memoir yet written has depicted Sheridan as he really was, the reason being that no one yet has approached his subject with a sufficiently broad mind. Sheridan's nature presented many characteristics, some stronger than others; and the majority of people, seizing on these leading points and ignoring the remainder, have pointed a moral and adorned a tale much to their own satisfaction and the complete misrepresentation of a life as brilliantly unique as it was pathetically splendid.

The purpose of this article is to present to the readers of the ANGLO-SAXON REVIEW a few hitherto unpublished letters, which, if they form no connecting link in Sheridan's life, throw occasional gleams on him and the age in which he lived.

Not the least interesting episode of Sheridan's career was his elopement and subsequent marriage with Miss Linley, the daughter of Mr. Thomas Linley, a doctor of music, whose charming melodies did much to make the 'Duenna' the success it eventually became. Miss Linley was very lovely—how lovely only those who have seen Sir Joshua Reynolds' picture of her as 'St. Cecilia' best can say. Two years before his death, when hearing and sight were alike failing him, Sir Joshua addressed this letter to Sheridan:

'*January 20th*, 1790.

'DEAR SIR,

'I have according to your orders bespoke a very rich frame to be made for Mrs. Sheridan's picture. You will easily believe I have been often sollicited to part with that picture and to fix a price on it, but to those sollicitations I have always turned my deafest ear, well knowing that you would never give your consent and without it I certainly should never part with it. I really value that picture at five hundred guineas. In the common course of business, exclusive of its being Mrs. Sheridan's Picture, the price of a whole length with two children would be three hundred; if, therefore, from the consideration of your exclusive right to the Picture, I charge one hundred and fifty guineas, I should hope you will think me a reasonable man.

227

SHERIDAN

'It is with great regret I part with the best picture I ever painted, for tho' I have every year hoped to paint better and better and may truly say "nil actum reputans dum quid superesset agendum" it has not allways been the case. However there is now an end of the pursuit; the race is over whether it is won or lost.

'I beg my respectfull compliments to Mrs. Sheridan.

'I am with the greatest respect,

'Your most humble and obedient servant,

'JOSHUA REYNOLDS.'

It would be interesting to know the value of this hundred and fifty guineas worth to-day. When Mrs. Sheridan died much that was good in Sheridan died with her. While she was alive he sounded the highest note of the lyre of fame. With her death came failure after failure, neglect, disappointment, and the miserable close, which has been so vividly and eloquently described by various authors.

The motto which the first Lord Holland gave to his son, 'Never do to-day what you can put off till to-morrow, and never do yourself what you can induce some one else to do for you,' was the one which Sheridan, in all his dealings, political and theatrical, seemed to have adopted as peculiarly his own. We have several lights on this subject. The following letter from Edmund Burke, himself the most conscientious and painstaking man, is curious evidence of this :

'MY DEAR SIR,

'Excuse the anxiety I feel that the Irish deputies should not be delay'd and that Fox and you may make something of the rough materials I have left you, which rude as they are are still better than those he has. For God's sake don't leave the matter to be wrought on the Copy he has. Do not be surprised that I am somewhat apprehensive of the only fault you have and which is redeemed by an hundred virtues. 'Yours ever,

'EDM. BURKE.'

A further illustration of Sheridan's dilatory method may be found in the ensuing letter. Who Shaw was it is hard to say; but it may have been Sir James Shaw, who was Lord Mayor of London about that time.

'CHANCERY LANE, NR. HOLLOWAY'S,
'Wednesday.

'DEAR SHAW,

'I wish extremely you could call on me at the Albany before ten this evening, if not I will meet you here punctually at twelve.

'Yours truly,

'R. B. SHERIDAN.'

WILFRED SHERIDAN

This note was endorsed :

'Sheridan. He did not attend at either place herein mentioned. Mem. sent me to Mr. Moore, who, he said, had some money for me from him (Sheridan). I met Mr. Moore and mentioned this. His answer was that he had none etc.'

Mr. Moore, mentioned in the dry, business-like endorsement, was Mr. Peter Moore, member of Parliament for Coventry, and one of Sheridan's life-long and most devoted friends. It is noticeable that the faults which a person possesses in himself most markedly are, as a rule, those which he contemns and objects to most in other people. Sheridan had very little idea of keeping an appointment ; but that he should make an attempt, however belated, to keep one, and that then should find that the person for whom this effort, alike so unusual and praiseworthy, had taken a leaf out of his own book and gone elsewhere, was too much to be borne. Such seems to have been the case in the following letter. The author is George Tierney, one of whose chief claims to be remembered is that he fought a duel with William Pitt.

'HERTFORD STREET,
'*March 20th*, 1800.

'DEAR SIR,
'Your favour of the second was brought to me late on Sunday night.
'A letter which from what passed when I met you on Friday se'nnight I understood I was to find upon my table on my return home I now learn has been destroyed by you. It seems you wrote it under the impression that there was something little short of intentional incivility to you when you called at my house, and I presume I am to collect that it was worded in a style which it would have been unpleasant for me to peruse.
'To all this I can only say that your appointment made on the 15th of last month was to be with me the next day Sunday at one o'clock, and that so far from any incivility being shown I stayed at home for you till two, when I went out, desiring my servant if you called to tell you it was not in my power to wait any longer. At four o'clock I found you had been at my door and had left a message announcing your intention to call again about five. It did not suit me to make any more engagements for that day, and therefore on my again going out I directed the servant to say that the time of my return would be very uncertain. In all this I can perceive no mark of incivility on my part, and if my man's manner gave it any such appearance he must have expressed himself improperly and in a way not authorised by his instructions.

229

SHERIDAN

'You allude to an accidental conversation in the street the week before last which you trust was satisfactory to me. If the statement you then made was with a view to convince me that the suggestion of the D. of Bedford being indisposed towards me did not originate with you, that distinct fact I cannot hesitate upon your assertion to believe. I understood from you it was Mr. Fox who mentioned to the Prince at Carlton House the Duke's supposed objection to me and that you explained to him how much he was (and I am convinced he was very much indeed) mistaken. I cannot guess on what Mr. Fox grounded his opinion, but it is impossible to suspect him of any wish to represent the Duke of Bedford as the cause of my not being appointed Secretary, because, with a degree of candour for which I feel obliged to him, he himself told me he had always been desirous that Mr. Elliott should have that appointment. I beg to be distinctly understood as not complaining of what passed on the part of Mr. Fox, for if he conceived, however erroneously, that there was a disinclination towards me on the side of the Duke, I know no reason why for the Prince's information at a select and confidential meeting he should have forborne to mention it. What I do complain of is that I was represented out of doors as one to whom the Duke had personal objections, and I should have been wanting in proper respect to him, from whom I have under all political circumstances experienced uniform kindness, not to have felt on such an imputation as I did and do feel. Why could not Mr. Elliott's nomination to the Irish secretaryship be stated in the manly way pursued by Mr Fox—namely, as an avowed preference given to him with which I could have no right or pretence to find fault? To those parts of your letter which refer to the Prince of Wales I do not feel myself called on to make any answer unless I am given to understand that they are written by his order or with his Privity. It is my intention to ask of H.R.H. the honor of an audience, that I may have an opportunity to secure myself if possible against misrepresentation! If I have omitted to notice some passages in what you have favoured me with I hope it will not be attributed to any want of civility. I am desirous to avoid what would only lead to a description extremely unpleasant to myself and which could be attended with no advantage to either of us.

'I am dear Sir,

'Your obdt. servt.,

'GEORGE TIERNEY.

Much that is in this letter remains hidden history; but Tierney was among those whom Byron had in his mind when he gave Moore the advice, 'In writing the life of Sheridan never mind the lies of the humbug Whigs.' The great bane of Sheridan's life was his intimacy with the Prince of Wales. The glamour of untruthfulness that hung over Carlton House enveloped him in its folds, and severed him from men like Grey and Grenville. Had their jealousy of his supposed influence with the Prince been in proportion to the amount he actually possessed, Sheridan would have had little to fear.

From this disagreeable letter, hinting of intentional misrepresentation and calumny, it is a relief to turn to the next. It was written in 1800. Parliament met on November 11—it was a time of great distress. The price of provisions was very high. Napoleon was rapidly crumpling up all Europe before him. Pitt was beginning to realise that as a Minister for War he could not compare with his father, and was soon to be succeeded by that hopeless mediocrity, Addington. There are sentences in the letter that follows which the most enthusiastic supporters of the present Government's policy in South Africa may well feel only too appropriate for the present occasion. It is pleasant to read in this letter of the trust which his correspondent places in Sheridan and in his powers as a formidable member of an Opposition which included in its ranks some of the greatest orators the world has ever known.

'DEAR SHERIDAN,

'If I remind you it was in the course of the present autumn that you faithfully promised we should have the pleasure of seeing you and Mrs. Sheridan, I confess it is not with very sanguine hopes of that promise being fulfilled at this advanced season of the year, but more with a view of recalling to your memory that there is such a place as Oakley, where at all times any days, however few you may borrow from scenes of more gaiety and amusement to bestow on its inhabitants, will be gratefully acknowledged by Lady John and myself. I conclude, and I must add I flatter myself, you mean to attend the meeting of Parliament ; it is essential at such a moment as this to speak a bold and unequivocal language. The people are suffering every horror of accumulated distress, and it is fit they should not be lured by false hopes into a dangerous security nor deceived as to the indicial cause of the miserable state of the country. The war must be sounded in their ears till they feel the dreadful grievances it has heaped upon us are owing to that and almost to that alone. Wasteful, ruinous and absolutely destructive as it is, what hopes of returning plenty while it is suffered to be carried on with so much vigorous improvidence ?

'Canting hypocrites who are daily supporting the profligate system by which this war was engendered, and by which it is still nourished and supported, should not be suffered to play upon the feelings of a deceived and deluded people by a senseless cry against mistaken [illegible], or by a plea of shameful assertion that a partial scarcity produces Distress and Famine independent of other and more fatal causes ; but above all the country should be impressed with the important and undeniable truth that no peace can reasonably be expected from the hands of the men who now rule them. They may again negociate and Mr Pitt may again rejoice in the ill success of the negociation.——Grenville may possibly go to [illegible], and if he conducts the negociations as ably as Lord Malmesbury did, may possibly be rewarded by a Peerage, Pension or Ribbon on his return, as I see Lord Malmesbury is just created an Earl as a recompense for his twice successful failure—let the Minister smart under the powers of your eloquence and let the nation perceive some light from that penetrating genius which you so well know how to direct with Energy and Truth. We are miserably in the dark, or, what is worse, we are lost in apathy. Expeditions which our indignation alone ought to prevent us from mating with the utmost contempt of ridicule are heard of by the public with the most perfect indifference. Failure follows failure and yet all is as it should be—Good God how long is this to be endured ? As for me if the presence of a silent member could be of use I should certainly attend ; as it is, I shall remain quietly at home and hope to hear that you have not been idle, and I think I may venture to predict your exertions at such a moment will not be without effect.

' Excuse my writing at so much length on this subject ; you probably will not take the trouble of reading it, but whether you do or not I flatter myself you will always believe me

' Sincerely yours,

' JOHN RUSSELL.'

The next letter, written in much the same spirit, is from the eminent Scotsman Sir James Mackintosh, who, though more of a philosopher than a politician, was even then engaged in writing political pamphlets, though he did not enter Parliament till twenty years later :

' LITTLE EALING,
' *December 1st,* 1791.

' DEAR SIR,
' Not having been so fortunate as to find you at home on Monday I use this mode of stating what I wish personally to have communicated. It had been supposed that the mock armaments which have made the Cabinet a bye word over Europe and the diastrous issue of that war of rapine in India which was ushered in with so much parade and triumph marked the opening of the session as the moment for striking a decisive blow against the character of Mr Pitt as a statesman. Fortune in the former part of his administration had in some measure hidden his blunders from the

WILFRED SHERIDAN

vulgar eye, but during the last two years she seems to have abandoned them to their own undisguised and naked absurdity. The varnish of Success has been wanting. The interesting episodes of Excise, the Test Act, the Press, the Birmingham riots etc. would harmonise the justice of the interior government with the wisdom of the foreign policy. A review of the last two years of Mr. Pitt's administration was proposed to me and though the mode was circuitous and unavowed the proposition seemed to me to have originated with some gentlemen of the Party. I saw that such a publication could not fail of producing an impression: My own Sentiments were entirely congenial with the ideas that would guide it and though nothing could be more foreign to my occupations and views than the composition of political pamphlets I was willing to bestow some time on this subject. I wished the honour of a conversation on it with you in which I principally meant to solicit your advice with respect to it and to know whether a communication and revision both confidential by the Gentlemen of the Party were to be expected. Without both it might be deficient in the correctness and must want the importance the hope of which could alone induce me to undertake it. I should be particularly happy to be indulged with an interview, or to hear from you your opinion on the subject, and I have the honour to be,

'Dear Sir,

'Most respectfully yours,

'JAMES MACKINTOSH.'

The dramatic part of Sheridan's life was chequered with a series of brilliant successes and disastrous failures. A complete want of method marked his management of both Drury Lane and Covent Garden. Actresses without salaries and playwrights with unacted tragedies filled the air with their cries.

A letter from Miss Farren, the celebrated actress, lies before me as I write. It is written in a villainous hand, and bears the obvious marks of ill-temper coupled with haste.

'Miss Farrens compliments to Mr Sheridan and begs to inform him that she cannot think of playing tonight till he has given an order for the return of her salary which she has had so unjustly stopped from her. She comes out tonight at the danger of her life has been extremely ill the whole week and accustomed as she always is to serve the Manager in every way in her power she cannot but look on this as the greatest instance of cruelty and contempt she has ever known.

'DRURY LANE THEATRE,
'Saturday Evening.'

233

SHERIDAN

Sheridan, as the following letter indicates, had suggested to Coleridge, through a mutual friend, that he should write a tragedy to be produced in due course at Drury Lane. He had also suggested that W. L. Bowles, the author of a volume of sonnets warmly praised by Charles Lamb, should try his hand. The history of these attempts is as follows : Each wrote a play : the fate of Bowles' is unknown. Coleridge sent his to Sheridan, who took no notice of it. It was published in 1813 under the name of ' Remorse.'

' February 6th, 1797.

' DEAR SIR,

'I received a letter last Saturday from a friend of the Rev. W. L. Bowles importing that you wished me "to write a tragedy on some popular subject." I need not say that I was gratified and somewhat elated by the proposal and whatever hours I can wile from the associations by which I earn my immediate subsistence shall be sacred to the attempt. The attempt I shall make more readily as I have reason to believe that I can hope without expecting and of course meet rejection without suffering disappointment. Indeed I have conceived so high an idea of what a tragedy ought to be that I am certain that I shall find myself dissatisfied with my production : and I can therefore safely promise that I will neither be surprised or wounded if I should find you of the same opinion. I should consider myself well paid for my trouble by the improvement which my mind would have received from it as an exercise and by the honour conferred on me by your having proposed it. The phrase "popular subject" has a little puzzled me. Mr. Bowles will perhaps be able to inform me whether you meant by it to recommend a fictitious and domestic subject or one founded on well-known history. The four most popular tragedies of Shakespeare—Lear, Othello, Hamlet and Romeo and Juliet—are either fictitious or drawn from Histories and part of History unknown to the many ; and the impression from Schillers "Fresco" is weak compared to that produced by his "Robbers." There are however great advantages in the other scale. The Spectators come with a prepared interest. I shall not cease to remember this your kind attention to me and am pleased that I have to add the feeling of individual obligation to the deeper and more lofty gratitude which I owe you in common with all Europe.

'S. J. COLERIDGE.

' STOWEY, NEAR BRIDGEWATER.'

The final defeat at Stafford, the death of his wife and infant daughter, the burning of Drury Lane theatre, were successive blows to Sheridan. Reckless extravagance, coupled with a habit of

WILFRED SHERIDAN

intemperance, played havoc alike with life and the means of livelihood.

The following letter, piteous in its expression of the state to which he had sunk, tells its own tale. It is without date, but from the handwriting I should judge it to be quite in his last years.

'Denbigh's.

'MY DEAR PEAKE,

'If you gave me £8 on Monday night I have lost a £5 or gave it by mistake to the coachman I find Mrs S. here without a shilling to pay even washing and I have not a farthing left. I conjure you to send me £10 and by G—d this shall be the last advance you shall make.

'Yours ever.

'I shall return early on Friday quite reconciled by three days quiet and fresh air.

'Yours ever,

'R. B. S.'

No article about Sheridan would be complete without a letter from Thomas Moore, his biographer. It is written in answer to one from Charles Brinsley Sheridan, second son of Richard Brinsley. The touch of conceit in the last few lines is eminently characteristic.

'MY DEAR SHERIDAN,

'Having but a few minutes to catch the Post I can only say that your letter has given me the most real and heartfelt pleasure. I assure you I was more anxious about your opinion than that of the public, and that you should be pleased with what I have done is to me the sincerest delight. My wish was to leave the same impression on my readers as your father did on those who knew him—namely, a feeling of love towards him in spite of all his irregularities and faults—and this I most anxiously hope I have effected. I had two female hearers crying over the last pages today as if it were a novel. I hardly know what I write but as this is the last post day till Saturday I did not like to defer so long acknowledging the great gratification you have given me.

'Yours my dear Sheridan,

'Very truly,

'THOMAS MOORE.'

With this letter my task comes to an end. Most people in writing about Sheridan try to whitewash him. To my mind he

SHERIDAN

requires no apologist. Since the death of Shakespeare, who wrote for unborn ages, there has been no dramatist to compare with Sheridan.

Harrow sent forth within a short space of time two distinguished men. I will quote the last four lines of Byron's monody to prove that, despite the great poet's rancour and bitterness, his heart was capable of the warmest praise where it was deserved :

Long shall we seek his likeness, long in vain,
And turn to all of him which may remain,
Sighing that nature formed but one such man,
And broke the die in moulding Sheridan.

LIBERALISM
BY W. EARL HODGSON

It is absurd in such a period as this to expect to find the Liberal Party in its full strength. Liberalism is, after all, the party of discontent; and the irregular social movements, such as Chartism, Socialism, and Irish Nationalism, are necessarily the fuel of its strength.

H. W. MASSINGHAM.

*O wud some power the giftie gi'e us
To see oursels as ithers see us!*

ROBERT BURNS.

Could you believe that the human race had been thus long abused without ever discovering the cheat?—SOCRATES.

I loathe all Liberalism as I loathe Beelzebub.—JOHN RUSKIN.

N the serene pages of the ANGLO-SAXON REVIEW 'the wordy trucklings of the transient hour' are carefully eschewed. The REVIEW is permanent; the wordy trucklers change their attitudes almost week by week. Therefore, the REVIEW is not a proper theatre for the discussion of contemporary party politics. Take an example. Not long ago Lord Rosebery wrote a letter, which was published in all the newspapers, intimating to the City Liberal Club that he could not accept the Club's invitation to go to dinner and make a speech, and that never again would he voluntarily take an active part in public affairs. Forty-eight hours afterwards, without a word of explanation, Lord Rosebery made the very speech which he had avowed he would never voluntarily make. In doing so he proclaimed defiance towards all those in the Liberal Party who were not at one with him in reverence for the Empire and in resolution to maintain and to extend it. As regards the affairs of Liberalism and the Empire, Lord Rosebery would 'plough his own furrow alone.' That illustrates the kind of wordy truckling which cannot be discussed in this REVIEW. If an article on it had been written just after the speech was made, the REVIEW could have had no assurance that it would not look extremely foolish when it presented itself to the world in September. Liberalism and Liberals are chameleonic. They have one hue and one tendency one day; two hues and two tendencies next week; Heaven only knows what will be their hues and tendencies a month after any particular moment.

Meanwhile, however, writing at the beginning of September, one perceives that there will probably be a temporary cessation of

LIBERALISM

chameleonising. We have entered upon a time of holiday. No one wishes to hear what Liberalism has become, or what any Liberal thinks. Nor could any one have his wish appeased if he did entertain a wish; for Sir Henry Campbell-Bannerman has abandoned his seat on the fence in favour of a more graceful position behind a butt on a grouse moor, Lord Rosebery is probably yachting, and as to where the other Liberal Leaders are their own lack of followers does not care. This, therefore, is a timely season in which to consider, from the point of view of the student of natural history, what Liberalism really is, and what Liberals really are. That is a serene subject which the REVIEW can properly entertain. It is not likely to be abolished before the September Number is issued. Liberalism and Liberals are given to dissension; but they are not given to suicide. Let us, therefore, consider them scientifically: as Darwin considered the earth-worms, as Doctor Koch is considering tuberculosis. And let there be no moaning at the bar. Liberalism calls its opponents 'the stupid party' without hesitation, and with equal alacrity says that the Prime Minister is a 'nepotist.' It has no right, then, to moan, or groan, or otherwise complain, if we put it under an experiment in vivisection. Liberalism and Liberals are not unworthy of this treatment. It is generally assumed that they must have some part to play in the economy of nature.

What is that part? It seems to be vital. Perhaps the most conspicuous domestic incident of the Session which closed in August was the inordinate interest which the Liberal Party took in itself and the anxiety with which certain Ministerialists yearned for the welfare of the Liberal Party. The Party entered upon the new Parliament with grave internal dissensions. During the General Election it was not united, and the differences of attitude towards public affairs which then divided it were much emphasised when the Party had to face in the House of Commons a Government of Anti-Radicals which was unprecedentedly strong. The Session was still in progress when the Opposition had to meet in the Reform Club to discuss the possibility of uniting. This Conference was looked upon with solicitude by the Conservatives in Parliament and throughout the country as well as by the Liberals themselves. It ended in a formal peace between the sections of the Liberal Party which are led respectively by Sir Henry Campbell-Bannerman, Mr. Asquith, and Sir Edward Grey; but the formal peace was shown to be merely formal when Lord Rosebery, as mentioned above, made his speech within two rounds of the clock afterwards. However, the break-up of the Liberal Party is not at this moment the thing to be considered. That, Lord Rosebery said, 'has been inevitable from 1885.' What is important in this consideration of Liberalism, from an abstract and natural-history point of view, is the singular

238

earnestness with which both the Liberals themselves and many Ministerialists regarded it as necessary that there should be a strong Opposition of Liberals. One hears this from both sides of politics as often as one hears the remark that cigarettes are ' the worst form of tobacco.' The persons who tell you that cigarettes are ' the worst form of tobacco ' are echoing a statement which sounds impressive because it is paradoxical. I rather think that the statement, common to both sides of politics, that a strong Liberal Opposition is necessary, is in the same category of cheap wisdom. Still, as it is so frequently heard, it deserves consideration as expressing the general belief that England has need for the Liberal Party.

Let us look into this belief. What is the Liberal party ? The first thought that strikes one on a microscopical examination is that the Liberal Party is a dual entity. Throughout the constituencies there are thousands of persons who vote for Liberal candidates. In the House of Commons there are a good many persons who sit on the Liberal benches. These sets of persons consider themselves as being a Party, one and indivisible ; but what are the facts ? How does this assumption square with the theory of Liberalism ? In order to answer this question, we must discover what the theory of Liberalism is. What is it ? In order to arrive at a true answer to this further question, we must perceive that the Liberal Party as represented by the Liberal Parliamentarians is not by any means the same thing as the Liberal Party in the country. When you meet any Liberal Parliamentarian in London you behold a person quite different from the same gentleman addressing his constituents. To all appearance he might as well be a Tory as a Liberal. In the country he is overflowing with high moral emotions and eloquence about the need for Government of the People by the People for the Benefit of the People ; in the Club smoking-room in London, or in the House of Commons, you hear from him none of these stirring sentiments. In London the gentleman who in the country was a fervent apostle of some vague but exalted ethical principle is just as other men are. Of this let me give an illustration. Not long ago I chanced to meet after dinner a Liberal Member of Parliament who represents a constituency in Scotland which is half-Highland. This was at the time of the Conference in the Reform Club. Ingenuously I remarked that I did not see any reason why the Liberal Party should be making such a fuss about itself. I could not perceive what function it had to fulfil in the life of the Empire. Beyond that, I saw many signs that the methods of Liberalism were equivocal. ' Give me an instance,' said my friend. ' Well,' I answered, ' take the Access-to-Mountains Bill. You, as an owner of an estate in Scotland on which there are many mountains, must know that, excepting when the

239

grouse are nesting, no one who wishes to go up a mountain is refused leave if he asks it. Is that so?' 'Yes,' said the Liberal statesman: 'that is so.' 'Now, don't you think,' I said, 'that the owners of mountains are much more hospitable than, for example, the owners of London clubs? If some one not a member of this Club walked in here and ordered dinner, what would you think of him? Should you think that there ought to be an Access-to-Clubs Bill? I acknowledge that this is an extreme instance. I only want to direct your attention to the rights of property, any infringement of which in London you would resent, whilst you are prepared to allow much infringement in the Highlands.' The distinguished Liberal's answer was a hearty laugh, and then the remark: 'I know that any one in Scotland can get leave at almost any time to go up any mountain if he asks it. I know also that very few people do ask it. But I myself have been backing this Bill for fifteen years, and you have no idea how popular it is with my constituents!' This, coming from a highly respected member of the Party which proclaims itself to be the ethical party in politics, a gentleman who is also an elder in the Church of Scotland, struck me as being so strange that a few leisure hours, if they were to be found, might well be devoted to considering the question already stated. What is the Liberal Party? What are its members? What are its methods? Has it any morals?

Here, again, we must go back to our original distinction: that is to say, the distinction between the Liberal Party in Parliament and the Liberal Party in the country. This is a distinction with a difference. Practically the apostles of Liberalism are the Liberals who are in Parliament; the disciples are very many persons in the country who support the Liberal candidates. In order to see how far from being united these two bodies are, we have to recall some of the catchwords which were much in vogue when Liberalism 'swept the country.' I will give a few of these. One, derived from Rousseau, was that all men were born free and equal, and that as regards the government of the State the peasant was as good as the peer. This principle used to be emphatically asserted from every Liberal platform in the provinces. What happened when, after this appeal to the megalomaniacal imagination of the people, the Liberal Parliamentarians were sent into power? Liberalism, which had affirmed that every man was as good as any other, invariably proceeded to show that many men were better than most: it did this by creating peerages, baronetcies, and knighthoods to an extent which only Whitaker can recount. It is a fact that within the last fifty years twice as many titular distinctions have been bestowed by Liberal Prime Ministers as were bestowed by the stupid and aristocratic Party which the Liberals pretend to despise. This indicates that the attitude of the Liberal Parliamentarians towards themselves is not in unity with the attitude in which they hold themselves to the simple-minded voters from whose favour they derive their power. I have often wondered what would be the feelings of a Liberal Parliamentarian to whom should come the Chairman of his Association, saying: 'Look here. The right principle in politics is Government of the People by the People for the Benefit of the People: I am the People: let me take your seat in the House of Commons for a Session.' If such a speech were made to Mr. Asquith or to Sir Edward Grey by the Chairman of the Liberal Association through which either of these gentlemen is returned to Parliament, what would Mr. Asquith or Sir Edward Grey think? I am afraid that the Chairman of the Liberal Association would return to the country crestfallen. It is quite certain that neither Mr. Asquith nor Sir Edward Grey would give an affirmative response to such an unpractical appeal in behalf of a fundamental principle of Liberalism.

This, however, directs us to a still more serious point in our examination of the ethical assumption which governs the minds of the many thousands of people in our land to whom Liberalism is a fetish, and the minds of the many other thousands who, either supporting or opposing the fetish in the polling booths, have not philosophically considered the claim of Liberalism to the respect of thinking men.

Three propositions emerge:

(1) In the period which closed about fifteen years ago every Liberal candidate in the land used to say, in addressing his constituents, that the Voice of the People was the Voice of God. In most cases he said this in these very words; in other cases he gave it to be understood in some way or another. That was when the Liberal Party was normally in the majority in the House of Commons. What I cannot understand is why the Voice of the People, which was the Voice of the God fifteen years ago, is regarded by latter-day Liberal Thinkers as the Voice of the Devil now. The only explanation I can offer is that the Voice of the People is the Voice of God when by its clamour the Liberal Party is enabled to achieve its ideal, that the chief end of man is for the Liberal Leaders to be squat on the Treasury Bench. This leads to the perception of a philosophical disturbance for the settlement of which I would appeal to Lord Rosebery or to Mr. Augustine Birrell, the only two humorists of the Liberal Party, both of whom, probably because they have the gift of humour and therefore the gift of thinking, are what Mr. Disraeli called 'exhausted volcanoes.' Liberalism can stand neither wit nor humour, either of which is only a mode of clean and accurate reflection. If the Voice of the People is understood by the Liberal Party to be the Voice of God, or even only the Voice of Reason, clearly, as the People support England in the war

with the late lamented Dutch Republics, Liberalism should approve and support the war.

(2) Liberalism conceives itself to be the means by which the immature tendencies of society are developed and the wrongs of classes are redressed. It believes that these good ends are achieved by the Liberal Party, which Mr. Chamberlain, before conforming conscience obliged him to join the Tories, described as 'that great instrument of progress.' What are we to say to this? Is the great instrument of progress that part of the people which is in the majority and shouts most loudly; or is it that varying moiety of the House of Commons which directs the shouting? I think that it is neither the one nor the other. It is quite true that until about fifty years ago the people of Great Britain and Ireland were in a state which could not be called economically correct. The great landowners, the great manufacturers, and the great traders were in a position, given to them by their wealth, which rendered the position of what Mr. Gladstone called the masses subservient and unnatural. Until about that time, it cannot be denied, the humbler people, who were in a great majority, were practically serfs to the feudal landlords and to the plutocrats. Who were then, however, responsible for this wrong? Liberalism, which was on the side of the plutocrats, would affirm that the injustice was done by the Feudal System. That is to say, Liberalism would attribute all the wrongs of the masses, of the working men, to the selfishness of what is ungrammatically known as 'the landed aristocracy.' There are several fallacies in this conception of the evolution of our society. In the first place, the society of Great Britain and Ireland had necessarily, in the course of nature, to be evolved towards liberty, political economy, and effectiveness; and any doctrinaire of Liberalism who arraigns a particular class for the imperfection of society at large is, when we reason the matter out, simply saying that he himself could have done better than God Almighty, or nature, if he had had the process of evolution at his own direction. In short, every Liberal Thinker implicitly affirms that all would have been well with the world if he himself, or Mr. Gladstone, or some other ethical hero with a passion for platforms, had been born five hundred years before the actual nativity. The trouble is that God Almighty, or nature, seems to take insufficient notice of the Liberal Thinker. This gentleman forgets that he himself is a product of evolution. He forgets, also, that he is a product of evolution which has no right to regard itself with pride. What did the Progressive gentleman do? There are a few actions with which he can be credited in the persons of Mr. Cobden and Mr. Villiers, who raised an agitation which resulted in the repeal of the Corn Laws, a reform which, although this has not been conclusively proved, seems to have been to the advantage of the State as a whole. However, the doctrinaire of Liberalism

took other steps. He was always divided in his instincts. He hated the landed aristocracy, and he pretended that all his affections were for the masses who toil and spin. What did he do to serve the masses? He opposed every attempt on the part of Tory Prime Ministers to ameliorate the condition of the humbler classes by measures such as the Factories Act. He was always ostensibly on the side of the humbler classes; but he never really was so. Mr. John Bright and other eminent Liberals who opposed the efforts of Mr. Disraeli to improve the condition of the working classes may have been economically not without some justification. Whether they were so or not the evolution of our society, contrasted with that of other European societies, may ultimately show. The point for immediate consideration is this. To all intents and purposes, the Liberal Party has from all time been, as it is now, a class of plutocrats, more or less hereditary, occupying seats in the House of Commons, who have been animated by spite against their betters, the territorial classes, and by distrust of their inferiors, the working classes. Liberalism has hitherto been represented by nothing more nor less than a band of men who, through their wealth and their gift of exciting popular passions, have won positions in the House of Commons, which they have used in order to curb the imperial instincts of the nation, and at the same time have gained their power to achieve this purpose by deceiving the humbler classes from whom their ambiguous authority was derived. If any proof of this is wanted, let us consider what at any time of emergency the Liberals in past years have always considered their trump card. As Lord Salisbury recently remarked, when the Liberal moralists could get steam up in no other way, they invariably played the Franchise. They played it in 1864; but played it in such a dishonest jerrymandering manner that the Reform they suggested, which was in principle right, had actually to be brought about by the Tory Leader, Mr. Disraeli. They played it early in the 'eighties, exactly in the same way, and again the Reform had to be sanctioned by the Tory Party. They will play it again, or try to do so, over the matter of inequality of the representation of Ireland as compared with the representation of the rest of the kingdom. Ireland has thirty-one seats more than her population, considered arithmetically, entitles her to have. When the present Ministry introduce their Bill to redress this inequality the Liberal Party, we may be quite sure, will support the Irish-Nationalist contention that the 103 seats which Irish Members at present occupy in the House of Commons were settled for all time by the Act of Union. What will this mean? It will mean only that Liberalism is a system neither of truth-telling nor of truth-seeking: that it is a system of opportunism merely. States under constitutional government must periodically change their methods of representation according to the fluctuations of the populace. In having thirty one seats more than the Rule of Three entitles her to, Ireland is exactly in the position of that body of landlords and 'tenpounders' in England and in Scotland against whom in the 'sixties and the 'eighties Liberalism demonstrated throughout the length and breadth of the land with all the garish accessories of a Liberal loaf weighing 4 lbs. and a Tory loaf weighing 1 lb., and with that cunning appeal to the emotions of the ignorant of which Liberalism, although when buying the *Daily News* it ostensibly purposes to 'spread the ethical teaching of Jesus Christ,' is a past master not inferior to the most lachrymose Sorrower for Satan.

(3) Liberalism conceives itself to be a philosophy based on ethical principles. Is it indeed? Let us quote a passage from an article which Mr. Massingham, most candid of Liberals, contributed to the June Number of the ANGLO-SAXON REVIEW. 'It is absurd,' says Mr. Massingham, ' in such a period as this to expect to find the Liberal Party in its full strength. Liberalism is, after all, the party of discontent ; and the irregular social movements, such as Chartism, Socialism, and Irish Nationalism, are necessarily the fuel of its strength.' This is an opportune utterance. What is its real significance? Surely it is this : that when there are no irregular social movements in the country, there is no use for the Liberal Party. Mr. Massingham himself would not deny this; neither, if he thought the matter over, would Lord Rosebery, or Mr. Asquith, or Sir Edward Grey, or Sir Henry Campbell-Bannerman. These gentlemen, who have occasional lapses into humour and the light, can surely perceive the incongruity of the Liberal Party as defined, quite accurately, by Mr. Massingham. Liberalism 'is the party of discontent.' Its furnaces are stoked by irregular social-movement-mongers. It takes to its chaste and capacious bosom Chartists, Socialists, Fenians, Believers in Small-pox, Atheists, Ritualists, Dissenters, and even, notwithstanding that wine made summer in the veins of the statesmen who conferred at the Reform Club, Superior Persons who tell other men to be total abstainers from alcohol. Unfortunately, however, come times when there are not in the constituencies many irregular-movement voters, and then Liberalism, which 'is, after all, the party of discontent,' is in straits. It and its ' glorious traditions' depend entirely upon emergencies, and thus the Liberal Party is in the remarkable position of claiming applause and place and power because of its lugubrious sympathy with the wrongs and the fads of classes in generations still unborn. If in our State there be no wrong to redress, surely there is no need for redressers of wrongs. If redressers of wrongs do spring up, or continue in their ancient occupation, one must look at them, as we proposed to consider Liberalism at the beginning of this article, exactly as Darwin considered the earth-worms, and as Dr. Koch is

considering tuberculosis. In Great Britain and Ireland at this moment, if we except London, whose multitudes are trampled on by the Irish oligarchy, which Liberalism is certain to support, there is no class which has any wrong to be redressed. What use, then, have we for his Majesty's Opposition as at present constituted? One may survey the whole distraught commando and find no use for any of the champions of Liberty, Equality, and Fraternity. One can see no use for any prominent man in the Opposition as an exponent of Liberalism. However, Liberalism, by stinging the Tory Party into action, has continually, through the Tory Party, which is the national party, brought about all those institutions of freedom which a great race could desire. It has done this in some strange way which we have not yet the capacity to understand. It is very difficult indeed to realise how the evolution of the greatest empire in the world has come about largely through the pin-pricks of a political party which never had, and has not now, any principle which it could affirm in Codger's Hall without having it destroyed within a quarter of an hour. Liberalism, in relation to the people, has been continually 'keeping the word of promise to the ear and breaking it to the hope.' It has derived its power from the humbler classes, whom Mr. Gladstone, with histrionic ingenuity, called 'the masses.' By the decree of those very classes in a time of great national stress, the Liberal Party is now constrained to devote all its energies to dining and speech-making, one faction against another, in the wan hope that the antiphonal symposium may prevent Freedom of Opinion from developing into the right of one faction to drum another out of the Party and the Fraternity of Liberalism from thus becoming the fratricidal brotherhood of Cain.

Liberalism, as the passage from the article by Mr. Massingham which I have quoted indicates, is for the present devoted not to the promulgation of principle but to an effort in empirical criticism. It thinks, among a few other things, that the million and a half a week which we have been spending on the war in South Africa might have been more profitably used if it had been spent on extending the great railways of the United Kingdom. This is the most instructive of Mr. Massingham's announcements. Even if we should regard the Empire as a matter of great railways, we see no sign of the need for Liberalism. Surely Lord Salisbury himself, who is, or recently was, a director of a great railway company, is as good an adviser on railways as Sir Edward Grey, who knows railways mainly as a means of going to fish in Hampshire or in the Highlands of Scotland; or as Sir Henry Campbell-Bannerman, who would probably criticise a Westinghouse brake no better than he manages a party; or as Mr. Asquith, who knows nothing about any trade at all. As a matter of fact, however, in this war in South Africa we have been fighting

LIBERALISM

not for our rights or our claims there alone. We have been fighting
for the British Empire. As the Indian servant of Mr. Rudyard
Kipling remarked to that very great man, 'Sahib, this war in
South Africa is not for South Africa only: it is for all you
have.' Any Liberal statesman who is incapable of seeing this is
incapable of seeing anything; and for any statesman who is incapable of seeing anything, England has no use. The collapse of
Liberalism is not surprising. Liberalism never was, and is not now,
a philosophy. It is the negation of principle, and without a principle
there can be no philosophy. Liberalism is not, and never has been,
Government of the People by the People for the Benefit of the
People. It is, and has always been, an attempt to govern the people
by an oligarchy of plutocrats through the help of the cupid emotions of the ignorant for the benefit of the ill-informed, socially
jealous, and therefore ineffectual plutocracy. Liberalism, in short,
has always taken the names of the People and of God in vain. It
has no principle within itself; it has no principle in relation to the
people; it has no principle in relation to the Empire. The bubble
of the blatant and long-lived hypocrisy is burst. Liberalism is
comically achieving its own inevitable doom. Next Session it will
be too frail even to sit upon the fence.

Printed by BALLANTYNE, HANSON & CO.
London & Edinburgh